Ministerial Survival During Political and Cabinet Change

Political leaders need ministers to help them rule and so conventional wisdom suggests that leaders appoint competent ministers to their cabinet.

This book shows this is not necessarily the case. It examines the conditions that facilitate survival in ministerial office and how they are linked to ministerial competence, the political survival of heads of government and the nature of political institutions. Presenting a formal theory of political survival in the cabinet, it systematically analyses the tenure in office of more than 7,300 ministers of foreign affairs covering more than 180 countries spanning the years 1696–2004. In doing so, it sheds light not only on studies of ministerial change but also on diplomacy, the occurrence of war, and the democratic peace in international relations.

This text will be of key interest to students of comparative executive government, comparative foreign policy, political elites, and more broadly to comparative politics, political economy, political history and international relations.

Alejandro Quiroz Flores is Senior Lecturer in the Department of Government at the University of Essex, UK. His work has appeared at *Political Science Research and Methods*, the *British Journal of Political Science*, and *International Studies Quarterly*, among others. He is also the manager of the Comparative Political Economics Division at the Department of Government.

Routledge Research on Social and Political Elites
Edited by Keith Dowding
Australian National University
and
Patrick Dumont
University of Luxembourg

Who are the elites that run the world? This series of books analyses who the elites are, how they rise and fall, the networks in which they operate and the effects they have on our lives.

1 **Coalition Government and Party Mandate**
   How coalition agreements constrain ministerial action
   Catherine Moury

2 **The Selection of Ministers in Europe**
   Hiring and firing
   Edited by Keith Dowding and Patrick Dumont

3 **Parliamentary Elites in Central and Eastern Europe**
   Recruitment and representation
   Edited by Elena Semenova, Michael Edinger and Heinrich Best

4 **The Selection of Political Party Leaders in Contemporary Parliamentary Democracies**
   A comparative study
   Edited by Jean-Benoit Pilet and William P. Cross

5 **The Selection of Ministers around the World**
   Edited by Keith Dowding and Patrick Dumont

6 **Party Members and Activists**
   Edited by Emilie van Haute and Anika Gauja

7 **Political Representation**
   Roles, representatives and the represented
   Edited by Marc Bühlmann and Jan Fivaz

8 **Ministerial Survival During Political and Cabinet Change**
   Foreign affairs, diplomacy and war
   Alejandro Quiroz Flores

Ministerial Survival During Political and Cabinet Change
Foreign affairs, diplomacy and war

Alejandro Quiroz Flores

LONDON AND NEW YORK

First published 2017
by Routledge
2 Park Square, Milton Park, Abingdon, Oxon OX14 4RN

and by Routledge
711 Third Avenue, New York, NY 10017

Routledge is an imprint of the Taylor & Francis Group,
an informa business

© 2017 Alejandro Quiroz Flores

The right of Alejandro Quiroz Flores to be identified as author of this work has been asserted by him in accordance with sections 77 and 78 of the Copyright, Designs and Patents Act 1988.

All rights reserved. No part of this book may be reprinted or reproduced or utilised in any form or by any electronic, mechanical, or other means, now known or hereafter invented, including photocopying and recording, or in any information storage or retrieval system, without permission in writing from the publishers.

Trademark notice: Product or corporate names may be trademarks or registered trademarks, and are used only for identification and explanation without intent to infringe.

British Library Cataloguing in Publication Data
A catalogue record for this book is available from the British Library

Library of Congress Cataloging-in-Publication Data
A catalog record for this book has been requested

ISBN: 978-1-138-19364-2 (hbk)
ISBN: 978-1-315-63924-6 (ebk)

Typeset in Times New Roman
by Apex CoVantage, LLC

Contents

List of figures vi
List of tables vii
Preface viii
Acknowledgments ix

1 Introduction 1

2 The study of cabinet change 19

3 Political survival and cabinet change 38

4 Data on foreign ministers 60

5 Foreign affairs, diplomacy, and war 77

6 Evidence in autocracies 95

7 Global evidence 114

8 Conclusions 132

References 141
Index 149

Figures

3.1	A leader's probability of reelection	47
3.2	A leader's probability of party retention: no private goods	48
3.3	A leader's probability of party retention: private goods	48
3.4	Probability of cabinet change: no private goods	50
3.5	Probability of cabinet change: private goods	51
4.1	Number of cabinet positions, February 2009	61
4.2	Survivor function of foreign ministers, 1696–2004	71
4.3	Hazard rate of foreign ministers, 1696–2004	73
4.4	Hazard rate of foreign ministers by W	75
6.1	Hazard rate of leaders, 1840–2004	97
6.2	Data organization	98
6.3	Model 2: probability of minister deposition in autocracies and $W = 0$	107
6.4	Model 1: probability of minister deposition in civilian autocracies and $W = 0$	109
6.5	Model 2: probability of minister deposition in military autocracies and $W = 0$	109
7.1	Model 2: probability of minister change and leader continuation in parliamentary systems and $W = 1$	122

Tables

4.1	Number of cabinet positions for selected countries, February 2009	62
4.2	Number of cabinet positions per 100,000 people, February 2009	62
4.3	The Hall of Fame of foreign ministers	73
6.1	Summary statistics	101
6.2	Coalition size and system	102
6.3	Instrumental variable probit	105
6.4	Instrumental variable probit	108
6.5	Instrumental variable probit	111
7.1	Bivariate probit	120
7.2	Bivariate probit	124
7.3	Bivariate probit	127
7.4	Bivariate probit	129

Preface

This book is founded on my doctoral work at New York University. The idea first emerged during a PhD seminar led by Bruce Bueno de Mesquita and Alastair Smith, who would later become my PhD supervisors. At that particular time, it occurred to me that the argument in *The Logic of Political Survival* (Bueno de Mesquita et al. 2003) could and should be extended to cabinet ministers. Over the years, I worked closely with Bruce and Alastair in order to develop the theory and collect the relevant data to test my hypotheses.

As I made progress and collected data, I published an article in *Foreign Policy Analysis* in 2009 that presents an empirical analysis that served as a stepping stone to the more sophisticated econometric analysis of this book. In addition, Alastair and I published a game theory model of cabinet change and political survival in *Economics and Politics* in 2011. Chapter 3 is an extended version of this article, although the text here differs significantly from the article version, as it elaborates on a number of issues and presents more examples that illustrate the intuition of the model.

As I completed the dissertation and became an assistant professor at the University of Essex, I started to collaborate with a network of researchers interested in political elites – the Selection and Deselection of Political Elites (SEDEPE) network – and particularly with Keith Dowding and Patrick Dumont. Keith and Patrick first invited me to write a chapter about the cabinet in the US for their recent edited book *The Selection of Ministers Around the World* (2015), which complements their edited volume on *The Selection of Ministers in Europe. Hiring and Firing* (2009). Together, these two volumes have put together the largest set of recent work on ministerial politics. A significant proportion of the research presented in this book is informed by the studies developed by the SEDEPE network and my interaction with them.

Alejandro Quiroz Flores
March 2016
Colchester, United Kingdom

Acknowledgments

The first set of acknowledgments goes to my former supervisors Bruce Bueno de Mesquita and Alastair Smith. Bruce and Alastair inspired me to explore new questions on political survival that continue to drive my current research agenda as a senior lecturer. I am very grateful to Bruce and Alastair for their guidance, unparalleled support, and friendship throughout these years.

I am also thankful to the other members of my research committee at NYU. Neal Beck provided great suggestions on the empirical sections of the project as well as unique training during my years in New York. I am also thankful to the late George Downs, as well as Mike Gilligan, who also trained me during my PhD and served as members of the committee.

This book could not have been written without the encouragement and patience of Keith Dowding and Patrick Dumont. Keith and Patrick read my dissertation and invited me to turn it into a book. They provided guidance and many detailed comments and suggestions over the last few years that strengthened the overall project and made it more relevant and easier to read.

I also want to thank several anonymous reviewers who gave me very useful feedback and suggested how to improve the book. Any weaknesses found in the pages that follow are my responsibility.

Over the years, many friends and colleagues in universities in the United States and Europe provided encouragement in multiple ways, both professional and personal. I have also presented my work in conferences, workshops, and universities that are too many to list here. I am grateful for all the invitations and feedback that I have received over these years.

On a personal note, my brothers have been a constant source of motivation and humor, and for that I am very thankful. My new niece Renata has given me much happiness.

My wife Barbara Czarnecka is often curious about my research and always patient about the long hours I devote to my work. I could not have completed this manuscript without her support. This book is dedicated to her and to our new baby, Alex.

1 Introduction

On April 30, 2015, Hyon Yong-chol, North Korea's minister of defense, was executed by anti-aircraft guns. This execution was part of Kim Jong-un's systematic policy of elimination of elites at the very heart of North Korean politics; as reported by Barbara Demick of *The New Yorker*: "Of the seven elder statesmen who carried Kim Jong-il's coffin down the snowy streets of Pyongyang in December 2011, five have been fired, retired, demoted, or killed."[1] In 2015 alone, at least fifteen high-ranking officers have been executed. A cabinet position offers a unique opportunity to advise a head of government and determine the direction of public policy. Nevertheless, as illustrated by the execution of Hyon Yong-chol, cabinet positions also carry risk. He was not the first, and he will not be last, minister to lose his life while holding office.

Consider Lakshman Kadirgamar, Sri Lanka's foreign minister, who was assassinated in Colombo in 2005. The Oxford-trained lawyer and former president of the Oxford Union, a powerful enemy of Sri Lanka's Tamil Tigers, was shot by a sniper in his private residence. Shahbaz Bhatti, Pakistan's minorities minister and the only Christian cabinet member at the time, was shot dead in 2011 in an ambush in a residential neighborhood of Islamabad. Walter Rathenau, German minister of foreign affairs during the Weimar Republic, was assassinated in 1922 by right-wing groups just a few months after taking office. In some cases, not even exile can protect former cabinet ministers. Orlando Letelier, Chilean minister of foreign affairs and defense during the government of Salvador Allende, was killed in 1976 in Washington DC, three years after the Allende government came to an end in a military-led coup. Recently declassified documents indicate that General Augusto Pinochet ordered the assassination of the former cabinet minister and that he was also planning the murder of his own head of intelligence.[2]

The assassination of cabinet ministers is a relatively rare event. More often than not, cabinet ministers quietly retire after serving their countries and their parties and enjoy peaceful lives as private citizens, businessmen, or academics. Egas Moniz, Portugal's former minister of foreign affairs, was a trained doctor who went on to win a Nobel Prize in Medicine for his contribution to the treatment of psychoses in 1949. Cabinet secretaries with financial portfolios have often moved on to positions in the banking and finance industry. Robert Rubin, US secretary of the treasury during the Clinton administration, went on to work for Citigroup with a compensation of approximately $7 million in 2007. More recently, Timothy Geithner, secretary of the treasury in the first Obama administration, joined a private-equity firm in 2014. Jobs in private finance are so lucrative that even deputy ministers do not wait to be promoted; Jean Boivin, former Canadian associate deputy minister of finance in 2012, left office to join BlackRock, the world's largest money manager, as managing director and investment strategist.

Other ministers have left the cabinet for positions in international organizations. Robert S. McNamara became president of the World Bank after his resignation as US secretary of defense. McNamara led the Department of Defense under Presidents Kennedy and Johnson and was one of the architects of the Vietnam War. McNamara, a statistician and former president of Ford, led the World Bank from 1968 to 1981. Paul Wolfowitz, former US deputy secretary of defense, and Robert Zoellick, former US deputy secretary of state, were also presidents of the World Bank. Like the World Bank, the United Nations has been led by former cabinet ministers. In fact, almost all UN secretaries-general have had cabinet positions in their own countries. Boutros Boutros-Ghali was Egypt's deputy prime minister for foreign affairs, while current UN secretary-general Ban Ki-moon was South Korea's minister of foreign affairs and trade from 2004 to 2006. The first secretary-general of the UN, Trygve Halvdan Lie, had been Norway's foreign minister since 1941.

Perhaps the most fascinating cabinet ministers are those who became heads of government. United States presidents Thomas Jefferson, James Madison, James Monroe, John Q. Adams, and Martin Van Buren were former secretaries of state. Although US cabinet positions did not lead to the presidency in the twentieth century at the same rate as in the past, Hilary Rodham Clinton might bring this trend to an end. Clinton, the highly energetic secretary of state during the first Obama administration and wife of former president Bill Clinton, is the leading Democratic presidential candidate in 2016. Like Hilary, other talented women have occupied cabinet positions before becoming heads of government: Golda Meir, Angela Merkel, and Michelle Bachelet had key cabinet positions in Israel, Germany, and Chile, respectively, before they took the helm of their countries. Angela Merkel has led Germany since 2005, while Bachelet was reelected to office for a second term as president in 2014. Taro Aso, prime minister of Japan, was first minister of internal affairs and communications from 2003 to 2005, and minister for foreign affairs from 2005 to 2007. Thabo Mbeki, the controversial president of South Africa from 1999 to 2008, was first deputy president – a cabinet position – from 1996 to 1999. In Mexico, all presidents from 1940 to 1994 were members of the cabinet before they were selected as presidential candidates.

These stories indicate that cabinet positions can end in different ways. A few members of the cabinet have died in office, sometimes violently, and occasionally due to medical conditions. Other cabinet members retire from politics never to return to the public arena. A few others remain in the public domain as heads of international organizations, academics, public speakers, or captains of industry.

Some cabinet members become their countries' leaders. Understanding how ministers lose office is important because they reflect a country's political, economic, social, and even cultural characteristics. In a healthy liberal democracy where human rights are well protected and corruption is largely absent, ministers would be more willing to implement necessary but drastic policy changes. In contrast, few cabinet members would execute the same political changes if by doing so they risk assassination, exile, or imprisonment. Likewise, cabinet secretaries would be less exposed to rent-seeking forces if there were institutions that prevent them from working for private firms once they leave office.

If an understanding of how cabinet ministers lose office is important, explaining why ministers stay in office for as long as they do is even more crucial. At the end of the day, there is no loss of office without tenure in it. More importantly, tenure in office might determine how ministers lose their position in the cabinet. Indeed, time in office provides space for the accumulation of influence, for the implementation of policy, for the creation of new political networks of support – both domestic and international – and the formation of strong links to industry, among other activities. Governments and their ministers need time to negotiate bills with legislators. Negotiations with other executive departments and agencies, both at home and abroad, are equally important and time consuming. Time in office also buys the opportunity to meet future employers or visit other countries in order to build alliances and secure votes that might be necessary to win a position at an international organization. Tenure in office provides space to demonstrate competence and show loyalty and allegiance to a leader, a party, or a political coalition. More importantly, time in office is closely connected to accountability and democracy (Fischer, Dowding, and Dumont 2012) and overall to the health of a political system and the strength of institutions during political change.

If there is variation in the form in which ministers lose office, there is more variation in ministers' tenure in office. Angela Merkel had been in the cabinet for seven years before she became chancellor in 2005, while Michelle Bachelet had accumulated four years of ministerial experience before becoming president of Chile. In typical American tradition, Robert Rubin, Lawrence H. Summers, and Tim Geithner led the US Treasury Department for only four years; this coincides with the four-year presidential period in the US. Nevertheless, Robert S. McNamara was US secretary of defense from 1961 to 1968 under two different presidents. Lakshman Kadirgamar, Shahbaz Bhatti, and Walter Rathenau had been in the cabinet for less than three years when they were assassinated, but so had Egas Moniz, who lived until the age of 81 and won a Nobel Prize years after he left the Portuguese Ministry of Foreign Affairs in the late 1910s. In other countries, ministers held on to office for decades, only to retire in relative obscurity: Andrei Gromyko, for instance, was foreign minister of the Soviet Union for almost thirty years before he resigned to take a ceremonial position and write his memoirs. The current emir of Kuwait, Sheikh Sabah Al Ahmad, was Kuwait's foreign minister for twenty-nine years. Arnold Green, an Estonian politician, led Estonia's Ministry of Foreign Affairs also for twenty-nine years when the country was part of the Soviet Union.

4 *Introduction*

Is it a coincidence that these cabinet ministers with long tenure in office served in nondemocratic countries, while cabinet members with short times in office worked in largely democratic countries? As I will argue in this book, this is not a coincidence: cabinet members in nondemocratic countries stay in office longer than their counterparts in democratic ones. What is most striking about the argument I will develop here is that ministers in nondemocratic nations hold on to office for extended periods of time in spite of their poor performance there. In other countries, such as presidential democracies, this trend is reversed. Of course, the examples presented above are not random and do not constitute scientific evidence in favor of my argument. It is precisely for this reason, however, that I embarked on a quest to build a rigorous theory of cabinet change and collect the largest database available on the tenure in office in one of the oldest and most influential and prestigious cabinet positions: the Ministry of Foreign Affairs. This database not only facilitates our understanding of specific historical episodes across dozens of countries, but most importantly, and for the purposes of this book, it allows me to carry out the empirical tests necessary to validate my theoretical argument and draw out generalizations about ministerial careers.

The theoretical argument in this book is based on one inescapable fact about cabinet politics: permanence in the cabinet is determined, to a huge extent, by a leader's incentives to stay in office. Ministers use their time in office to show competence and loyalty to the leader in anticipation of a tradeoff that is essential in a leader's strategy to maximize tenure in office: ministerial competence buys votes and facilitates policy implementation, but it might also improve the political standing of a cabinet minister who can then challenge a leader. Of course, the extent and seriousness of this threat depends on political institutions, which ultimately shape the ease of leader and cabinet change. To explain why this is so, I need to elaborate on political survival.

The logic of political survival

This is a book that approaches politics from a positive perspective, that is, it is concerned with the understanding of politics as it is practiced and not as it should be executed. In other words, my focus is not on whether politicians should represent constituents, promote justice and reduce inequality, or avoid wars. Instead, I am interested in explaining why politicians implement these policies in the first place and how that helps them to survive in political office. More specifically, I am interested in a puzzle first articulated by Bruce Bueno de Mesquita et al. (2003: xi): "leaders who produce peace and prosperity [were] turned out of office after only a short period of time, while those who produce corruption, war, and misery endure in office." This puzzle motivated these authors to write *The Logic of Political Survival* (2003), perhaps the most influential study of leaders' tenure in office, and the theoretical foundation of this book. As it is, my study of cabinet change is a contribution to the numerous extensions of *The Logic of Political Survival*, which include the imposition of international sanctions (McGillivray and Smith 2008), foreign aid (Smith 2008; Bueno de Mesquita and Smith 2009), revolutions and institutional change (Bueno de Mesquita and Smith 2010), cabinet change (Quiroz Flores and Smith 2011), leader change and war termination (Quiroz Flores 2012), and natural disasters (Quiroz Flores and Smith 2013; Quiroz Flores 2016), among many others.

The logic of political survival as developed by Bueno de Mesquita et al. (2003, 2004) relies on advanced game theory and is therefore highly mathematical. Yet their argument is quite intuitive and can be easily articulated in the form of a narrative. In this story, leaders aim at holding office for as long as they can. Holding office provides unique benefits, from significant salaries and incredible perks in some countries to the opportunity to steal large quantities of money in others. In order to keep office and its rewards, leaders need supporters. This applies to absolutely all leaders, regardless of the exclusiveness of a political system. The difference between political regimes resides on the number of political supporters needed in order to stay in office. North Korea's Kim Jon-il and his son Kim Jong-un rely on a small number of supporters who, some argue, are no larger than three thousand individuals. In contrast, Justin Trudeau, Canada's new prime minister, and his Liberal Party, require the political support of hundreds of thousands of voters. Bueno de Mesquita et al. call this set of supporters the "winning coalition." By obtaining and keeping the support of this winning coalition, a leader secures political power over the rest of society. Countries with small coalitions resemble autocracies, while countries with large coalitions resemble democracies.

In politics, most things are relative. So is the winning coalition. The members of the winning coalition are drawn from a larger group of people, the selectorate. Technically, the selectorate is a subset of a country's population whose institutional role is to choose the national political leadership. The winning coalition is a subset of the selectorate. In order to capture the concept of the selectorate, consider the US, where millions of illegal immigrants live and work. Many of these immigrants leave their countries for the better working and life conditions in the US. It is well known that the US economy depends on the labor of these immigrants. Moreover, social and cultural life in the US would not be the same without them. In spite of the importance of immigration, these individuals are in the country illegally and therefore they cannot vote for, say, members of Congress or president of the United States. Illegal immigrants are not part of the selectorate in the US because they do not have the institutional prerogatives to cast a legal vote. In general, all adult citizens in the US have the right to vote and are therefore members of the selectorate. In the UK, a person who is 18 years or over who is a British citizen and is not subject to any legal incapacity to vote is a member of the selectorate. Convicted persons detained in pursuance of their sentences cannot vote in general elections and are therefore not members of the selectorate.

Leaders keep the support of members of the winning coalition by providing goods. The type and mix of goods provided depend on the number of members of the winning coalition. When leaders need the support of a small number of people, they can provide them with private goods, as they are known in economics – these are items that can only be consumed by an identifiable group of people and cannot be shared once they are used. Typical examples of these private goods are luxury cars, mobile phones, bank accounts, and residences. In a country such as North Korea, where people die of starvation by the millions, being a member of the ruling elite and having access to private goods is essential. The purpose of the 2006 UN Security Council Resolution 1718, which banned the supply of luxury goods to North Korea, was to diminish Kim Jon-il's ability to provide these items for his supporters and therefore to weaken his hold on power. This type of small-coalition politics allows authoritarian leaders to rule for long periods of time despite their poor record of economic growth, food security, and human rights, among other generally beneficial policies.

In contrast, Justin Trudeau and his Liberal Party cannot feasibly provide private goods to the hundreds of thousands of voters whose support is essential for ruling Canada. Instead, when leaders need the allegiance of hundreds of thousands, or even millions, of people, they provide them with public goods, which are non-excludable and non-rival in consumption. There are no real examples of pure public goods, but a good approximation is perhaps sunlight or the beauty of a mountain range – in most normal situations, a person's consumption of the scenery cannot be reduced by a second person, and the first person's use of beauty will not reduce the second's rate of consumption. In countries with large winning coalitions, leaders provide a larger mix of public goods, which include economic growth, prosperity, and national security. An excellent example of a public good in politics is the 2016 lifting of the sanctions on Iran. As the International Atomic Energy Agency certified in January 2016 that Iran had placed significant restrictions on its nuclear activities, many sanctions imposed by the UN, the US, and the EU were lifted. On the one hand, the entire international community would benefit from a reduced risk of nuclear proliferation. As stated by President Obama in a press conference, "Under the nuclear deal that we [the US], our allies and partners, reached with Iran last year: Iran will not get a chance at a nuclear bomb. The region, the United States, and the world will be more secure." This is certainly a public good that will be enjoyed not only by American citizens, but also by all countries on the planet. On the other hand, a large proportion of the population in Iran will also benefit from the lifting of sanctions, as they will be able to restart economic growth, which was stalled by this pack of sanctions that imposed losses of approximately US$160 billion since 2012.[3]

The logic of political survival as developed by Bueno de Mesquita et al. (2003) has helped us understand why leaders in some countries provide more public goods, such as the economic growth that Japan experienced during the postwar years, while others provide more private goods, such as personalized protection against natural disasters, as exemplified by Burma's relatively new capital Naypyidaw, where members of the ruling coalition are protected from the cyclones that often hit the country. How does this theory help us understand leader survival in office and particularly the pattern whereby democratic leaders providing public goods stay in office for a short period of time while autocrats delivering benefits to a small number of supporters keep office for decades? It is only fair to think that leaders who implement 'good policy' should stay in office longer while those who do not should be fired quickly.

Having established the causes of public and private goods provision across regimes, the second part of my argument is related to the likelihood of obtaining these goods. This is a crucial part of Bueno de Mesquita et al.'s (2003) argument and will be central to the logic of cabinet change presented in this book. Consider the following hypothetical case where there are 1,000 voters; this is the selectorate. I will assume that an incumbent leader stays in office if she obtains 50 percent of the votes plus one. In other words, the leader needs only 501 votes to be elected. Hence, the size of the winning coalition is 501. According to the theory, the leader will promise goods to any 501 voters in order to secure their support and remain in office. Clearly, the probability that any voter is part of this winning coalition is 501/1000, or more formally, W/S. This number itself is only relevant when it is compared with a different political system where the selectorate is also made up of 1,000 voters but where the winning coalition is made up of any 51 individuals. In this case, the probability that any voter will be in the winning coalition in this alternative political system is 51/1000. Evidently, a voter's likelihood of obtaining goods provided by the leader is higher in the first political system than in the second. This will make a huge difference in the probability of leader change across these two political regimes

One key part of the argument is related to loyalty. The logic of political survival assumes that there is an incumbent leader. Incumbent leaders already have a set of well-known supporters who receive a stream of public and private goods. Hence, incumbent leaders do not have to promise goods to other potential supporters; they just need to credibly continue providing benefits to their current allies. In political science this is known as 'incumbency advantage.' A challenger, on the other hand, can only promise goods to potential supporters, who could be any members of the winning coalition. In other words, we as observers of political processes have a very good idea of who the members of the winning coalition are for incumbent leaders but we are less certain of who will be included in the winning coalition of a challenger if she is to replace the incumbent. In terms of my previous discussion, this means that everyone knows who the 501 members of the existing winning coalition are in the first political system and the 51 members in the second system. Nevertheless, nobody knows who will be coalition members under a new political leadership.

Members of the winning coalition, as any other rational, strategic actors, are very well aware of this and make careful calculations on whether to support an incumbent or a challenger. Consider a member of the winning coalition in the first political system, where the size of the coalition is 501. This member is already receiving goods, and if she is to shift her allegiance and support a challenger, the probability of being included in the challenger's coalition and receiving goods under that new government is 501/1000. Membership in the new coalition is probabilistic because, as credible as the challenger might be, she cannot really assure others that they will be in her coalition. Therefore, current members of the winning coalition trade off a secure stream of goods with the incumbent leader against joining a new coalition and obtaining goods with a probability of 501/1000. Clearly, once leaders and their supporters have committed to an exchange of goods for political support, members of the winning coalition have few incentives to support a challenger and replace their leader. These incentives are minimal in the second type of political system, where the winning coalition has only 51 members. Indeed, if a member of the winning coalition decides to support a new leader, her probability of being included in the new ruling coalition is 51/1000, which is ten times smaller than in the more inclusive political system.

This discussion suggests that in countries where the ratio of *W/S* is very small, members of the winning coalition are very loyal and therefore have few incentives to replace their leader. Relative to countries where the ratio of *W/S* is small, nations with larger *W/S* ratios experience more changes in leadership because members of the winning coalition are less loyal. Notice that this is a statement that requires comparative analysis. In each system, members of the winning coalition lack motivation to replace a leader; doing so only gives them probabilistic access to goods under a new leader. However, coalition members in countries with large coalitions have more incentives to replace a leader relative to members in countries with smaller coalitions. In other words, a coalition member's comparative risk for replacing a leader – due to the probabilistic access to goods under new leadership – is smaller in countries with large *W/S* ratios than in countries with small *W/S* ratios. Clearly, in the former, coalition members are more likely to be members of a new coalition than in the latter. For this reason, they are less loyal in countries with large ratios of *W/S* but much more loyal in nations with a small *W/S* ratio. Hence, the ratio *W/S* determines what Bueno de Mesquita et al. (2003) define as the loyalty norm. The smaller the ratio of *W/S* is, the more powerful the loyalty norm is. This norm will play a very important role in my argument of cabinet change.

It follows that as the loyalty norm decreases – because the ratio of *W/S* increases (for instance, when the size of the selectorate stays constant and the size of the winning coalition increases, making the political system more inclusive and democratic) – the rate of leader change increases. This is why there is more leader change, and consequently shorter time in office, in countries with large-coalition systems. Notice, however, that although there is more leader change in these democratic systems, the citizens of the country receive relatively the same amount of public goods. Indeed, all leaders in large-coalition systems will be providing more or less the same level of public goods. This maximizes their time in office. At the same time, this drives leader change because members of the winning coalition know that they will receive approximately the same level of public goods with *any* leader. Moreover, due to the nature of public goods, members of the winning coalition and the selectorate, and even the disenfranchised – such as illegal immigrants – will benefit from these policies. In contrast, in countries with small coalitions – for instance, where the size of the selectorate stays constant and the size of the winning coalition decreases – we do not observe either leader change or new winning coalitions, as both are very loyal to each other and have very strong incentives to maintain the status quo. At the same time, these countries are characterized by a larger provision of private goods, which benefit only members of the winning coalition. The wealth of members of the selectorate and the disenfranchised is unchanged and relatively minimal compared with the wealth of coalition members. It is therefore not a surprise that revolutions occur at a higher rate in these types of nondemocratic systems, such as Syria and Libya.

Selectorate theory as developed by Bueno de Mesquita et al. (2003) has drawn some criticism, mostly in terms of its empirical validity. The theory relies heavily on the effects of the size of the selectorate and the winning coalition, and empirical analyses use several measurements of the openness of a political system to produce them. Some authors argue that the effects claimed by Bueno de Mesquita et al. (2003) are spurious because their measurement of the winning coalition omits important variables (Clarke and Stone 2008). This problem seems to be caused by the fact that Bueno de Mesquita et al. (2003) only capture the presence or absence of political institutions (Kennedy 2009). Other authors argue that the measurement of the winning coalition in autocracies is particularly flawed because institutions in these political systems are in fact irrelevant (Gallagher and Hanson 2015).

As argued by Morrow et al. (2008), and originally by Bueno de Mesquita et al. (2003), the measurement of the political institutions at the heart of selectorate theory could be improved. This imperfect operationalization, however, does not invalidate the cogency of the theory, and in fact the criticisms mentioned above largely result from an inadequate understanding of the theory. As mentioned before, political institutions shape the incentives of leaders to provide public and private goods – in small-coalition systems leaders provide relatively more private goods, while in larger coalitions politicians provide relatively more public goods. It is the provision of goods that determines a leader's tenure in office and not the size of the winning coalition. Morrow et al. (2008) thus show that the size of the winning coalition does an excellent job at predicting the provision of public and private goods, exactly as predicted by their original theory. In fact, new laboratory experiments of the arguments developed in selectorate theory find that democratic leaders provide more public goods than their autocratic counterparts and that citizens are better off under democratic rules (Bausch 2014). In this light, this book makes the correct connection between political institutions and leader and cabinet change – indeed, my emphasis is on the relationship between ministerial competence and the provision of goods as determined by the political incentives shaped by institutions such as the winning coalition. In addition, the empirical analyses presented here take into consideration alternative and more nuanced measurements of political institutions, such as those of presidential and parliamentary regimes, as well as other aspects of political life, such as the existence of veto players, coalition governments, and executive constraints. The results not only confirm my expectations, but are also in line with the literature on cabinet politics that I will describe in Chapter 2.

Ministerial survival during political and cabinet change

Selectorate theory is the theoretical foundation of this book. I too assume that leaders maximize tenure in office but argue that cabinet ministers also try to maximize their time in office. In order to do so, they rely on the fact that leaders cannot rule alone and therefore need to delegate authority to their cabinet ministers. This delegation is crucial both practically and for the purposes of this book because it drives the relationship between leaders and their cabinet ministers, and provides space for both good and bad policy and politics. Ministers also rely on the opportunity to demonstrate competence and loyalty, although in some cases ministers will display only one or the other based on the leader's incentives to stay in office and how these incentives are shaped by political institutions such as the winning coalition and the selectorate. Specifically, I will argue that whether a minister stays in office depends on a leader's tradeoff between external and internal political threats. In some cases, leaders will remove ministers to eliminate internal challenges to their rule. In other cases, they will keep them in office to fend off the electoral threat presented by potential challengers. In other words, this is a book about how leaders manipulate their cabinets in order to fend off internal and external threats and consequently extend their tenure in office.

As I explained above, the provision of public and private goods is essential to our story of political survival. Providing these goods requires a measure of competence. The spending policies implemented in the United States and Europe during the financial crisis that started in 2008 were incredibly complex and could only be executed by an able group of policymakers and politicians. Negotiations with Iran over its nuclear weapons program required the labor of skillful diplomats over the course of many years. The redistribution of millions of hectares of land that took place in the aftermath of the Mexican Revolution also needed talented leadership and massive bureaucratic efforts. In this sense, competent cabinet ministers play a key role in politics because they contribute to the efficient provision of goods, whether they are private or public.

Conventional wisdom suggests that leaders carefully choose their high-level colleagues to administer strategic functions of government, including defense, diplomatic representation, market regulation, and the administration of justice. David Halberstam in his book *The Best and the Brightest* (1972) famously described how President-elect John F. Kennedy spent a considerable amount of time and effort to 'assemble a cabinet that was composed of the best America had to offer.' Consequently, it is reasonable to expect that when ministers underperform, they should be replaced. In this book I qualify this statement and argue that ministerial incompetence might lead to ministerial replacement only in certain political environments. In other political settings, lack of ability enhances ministerial survival. Quite shockingly, I will show that in some circumstances, a minister can find herself replaced if she is actually good at her job. This is ironic and yet is a rule of ministerial survival in countries associated with authoritarian practices.

In North Korea, Zimbabwe, Imperial Ethiopia, and other small-coalition systems, leaders do not depend on winning the support of the masses. Robert Mugabe, president of Zimbabwe since 1987, has presided over a failing economy with an astronomical rate of inflation that has turned the national currency into worthless paper. Leaders like Mugabe are not preoccupied with the provision of public goods such as health or economic growth. Instead, they are more concerned about internal threats to their leadership, which is why they spend considerable resources keeping their few supporters loyal to them. Of course, the masses can and do depose autocrats, often through revolutionary means, but the costs are high and probably marked by violence. In a context of a small coalition, internal threats are much more salient. They also tend to originate within a party or among the ranks of trusted officers. Captain Moussa Dadis Camara, Guinea's military leader, experienced a 2009 assassination attempt by a military aide. Dadis Camara survived, but the event effectively ended his rule in Guinea. Other leaders are not as lucky. In early-twentieth-century Mexico, newly elected president Francisco Madero appointed Francisco Leon de la Barra as minister of foreign affairs. A couple of years after Madero took office, Leon de la Barra and General Victoriano Huerta, a member of the old regime, succeeded in deposing Madero and his vice president. Huerta became the new president of Mexico and Madero, his brother, and his vice president had been murdered.

Leaders in small-coalition countries have incentives to clear their political landscape of potential challengers – outstanding ministers are quickly replaced in order to prevent them from deposing the leader. In turn, incompetent cabinet members are retained in office, as they have few prospects of retaining ministerial power under alternative leadership, and so are loyal to the leader. As Alastair Smith and I argued (2011: 363), "autocratic governments are led by paranoid leaders and their incompetent, but loyal, ministers." For instance, military positions in autocratic systems often go to family members, as in Jordan and Morocco, or to loyal associates who may not have a military background at all, as in Saddam Hussein's Iraq in 2003 (Bausch 2014). This dynamic produces mediocre cabinets that strengthen the corruption and lack of growth that characterize countries with small-coalition systems. This trend is quite evident in Putin's Russia, where conspicuously incompetent cabinet ministers have kept office for significant periods of time. According to Semenova (2015), Mikhail Zurabov, Alexey Gordeev, and Andrey Fursenko, ministers of social affairs, agriculture, and education, respectively, had been rated the 'worst' ministers in government and yet they kept their office for years. Zurabov was ranked 'worst' minister in 2005 and only left office two years later. In the case of Fursenko, in spite of being considered the 'third worst' minister, he held office from 2004 to 2012.

The previous discussion suggests that competence is not essential for holding a cabinet position in autocratic countries. In contrast, recent research indicates that democracies are 20 percent more likely to select highly educated leaders (Besley and Reynal-Querol 2011) than autocracies. This notwithstanding, I am not arguing that cabinet secretaries are not competent. Instead, I suggest that rational, strategic cabinet members in autocracies maximize time in office by not showing competence and by assuring their boss that they do not constitute a threat to her leadership. As I will explain later in Chapter 5, ministers in small-coalition systems might even follow a strategy of inaction, so as not to show competence or the lack of it. How do ministers' strategies change in large-coalition systems? The answer has to do, again, with how the particular political institutions of democratic presidential and parliamentary systems shape ministerial ambition and competence, as well as a leader's incentives to stay in office. Let me start with presidential democracies.

In presidential democracies, a president is both the head of state and the head of government. This position often coexists with legislative and judicial branches of government in a republican context. In most presidential systems, the legislative branch is composed of a lower and an upper chamber; members of the former tend to represent constituents across the country, while members of the latter represent provinces or states. The chief executive and members of the legislative branches are elected by popular vote, and they face fixed terms in office that are not subject to mutual confidence (Carey 2008). Members of the judicial branch, the highest court in a country, are often appointed by the executive power and confirmed by the legislature. Although all presidential systems feature some form of separation of powers between branches of government, this separation varies across countries. In the United States, widely considered the archetype of democratic, presidential systems, the constitution has provided for strong checks and balances between branches, and particularly between the executive and legislative ones (Quiroz Flores 2015). This strong separation of powers is further complemented by the role of the Supreme Court, which rules on constitutional interpretation and has the power to settle disputes among the other branches of government. This type of political system has been widely adopted by other countries, particularly across Latin America. Yet, other presidential systems such as South Korea do not feature this strong separation of powers (Kang 2015), particularly at the cabinet level.

In terms of the discussion on cabinet change, the most relevant aspect of presidential systems is that voters elect presidents to office, and the latter mostly lose office by term limits or elections. This gives presidents a measure of protection against the powers of other branches of government. This does not mean that presidents are immune to replacement during office. However, presidential impeachment is relatively rare and presidents do enjoy a more stable office, at least relative to prime ministers. Perhaps accidentally, this feature of democratic, presidential systems solves the potential problem of competent cabinet secretaries as internal threats to a leader. In these regimes, cabinet secretaries do not have nor desire elected political positions, and even if they did, they do not ordinarily threaten the president. Therefore, democratic presidents do not have to trade off external and internal threats, as the latter are negligible. This allows them to recruit ministers who will contribute to the distribution of public goods and help them secure political support and, often, the possibility of reelection. Democratic, presidential systems thus allow cabinet ministers to hold on to office for significant periods of time, or at least until the leader's term of office expires. As mentioned in the examples above, many cabinet members become leaders themselves after serving in the cabinet.

The most perplexing cases of ministerial deposition take place in parliamentary democracies. This is related to the complexities of political life in these systems and particularly to the fact that prime ministers, unlike presidents, are selected to office by the legislature. Perhaps more important for the purposes of my argument is that a prime minister's term in office is subject to legislative confidence (Carey 2008). Just as the US is the archetype of democratic, presidential systems, the UK is the prime example of a parliamentary one. In the UK, Parliament has three components: the House of Commons, the House of Lords, and the monarchy. UK voters elect members of parliament to represent them in the House of Commons. The House of Lords, as the second legislative chamber, is independent of the House of Commons, and most of its members are appointed by the queen on the advice of the prime minister. Members of parliament in the House of Commons may form a government, and its ministers are chosen from both the House of Commons and the House of Lords. The government essentially functions as the executive power as long as it retains the confidence of a majority in the House of Commons. When governments lose the confidence of the Commons, a new general election is called so that a new government may be formed.

What is crucial for the argument on cabinet change presented in this book is that leaders in democratic, parliamentary systems can be deposed by a popular vote but also by their party members, often led by senior cabinet ministers. This is nicely illustrated by a 'coup' against Gordon Brown carried out by two former cabinet members who called on a secret ballot to elect a new party leader in January 2010. Although the ballot did not materialize, allowing Brown to keep 10 Downing Street, other prime ministers have been removed by their own party peers, such as Margaret Thatcher. This shows that prime ministers in large-coalition systems do need to fend off internal as well as external threats of deposition. Ministerial politics in Australia presents more recent illustrations of such dynamics. For instance, Labor leader and prime minister Kevin Rudd was replaced by his deputy Julia Gillard in 2010, who in turn was deposed by Rudd in 2013 – he had been appointed minister of foreign affairs by Gillard in 2010. The Labor Party lost the 2013 general election to a coalition led by Tony Abbott, the Liberal Party leader. Two years later, Abbott was also forced out of office by his own party in 2015. This was not the first time this had happened in Australia. According to Dowding and Lewis (2015), three Australian prime ministers were forced out of office by their own party between 1949 and 2010.

Furthermore, in democratic parliamentary regimes, the internal threat of deposition is strongly influenced by the perks received by party members. Affiliation with a political party is sometimes accompanied by certain material benefits. However, the number of perks received by party members is inversely proportional to the size of the party. This has important implications for a leader's survival in parliamentary systems. When party members do not receive substantial perks, they can easily replace their leader because this does not change the low stream of benefits associated with party affiliation. In this case, leaders face higher prospects of internal deposition and hence focus on minimizing it by purging competent ministers from the cabinet. While these competent ministers would improve the party's electability to the masses, this is not the most salient threat for a leader in this type of system. Nevertheless, when party members receive perks, leaders are not as easily deposed by their parties because party members cannot secure a stream of benefits under alternative leadership. This endows leaders with an 'incumbency advantage' over potential rivals, which allows them to focus on winning elections.

Just as in presidential systems, leaders in this parliamentary system win elections by keeping competent ministers in the cabinet. Partly for this reason – the other one being the potential for internal threats of deposition – parliamentary democracies present a large variation in cabinet tenure in office. In Australia, William McMahon occupied ministerial positions for more than 21 years between 1951 and 1972; he was also prime minister of Australia from 1971 to 1972. In contrast, Australian senator Glenister Sheil was minister of veteran's affairs for only two days in 1977. In Canada, the longest-serving minister of citizenship and immigration was in office from 2008 to 2013.

This type of political system where a leader faces internal and external threats also presents some of the most fascinating and dramatic stories of loyalty and betrayal. Anwar Ibrahim, Malaysian deputy prime minister and a political rising star in the late 1990s, was sent to prison on charges of corruption and sodomy – a very serious crime in Malaysia – after challenging the longest serving Malaysian prime minister. At the time of writing, Anwar is still in prison on charges of sodomy. In Malawi, another British colony that became independent in 1964, Prime Minister Hastings Kamuzu Banda surrounded himself with close allies and friends, many of whom shared a cell with him when he was in prison in 1959. However, disputes over the distribution of cabinet portfolios led to a cabinet insurrection and potential deposition of Banda as prime minister. Banda quickly dismissed his former friends and allies from the cabinet and effectively avoided his own dismissal. Many of the former ministers were later persecuted, and most of them left the country. Banda remained as leader of Malawi until 1994.

In his seminal study of the cabinet, Jean Blondel (1985) identified 'a ministerial condition' mostly characterized by ministers' temporary membership in the cabinet. I concur with Jean Blondel on the fact that in some cases, cabinet membership may be short and fleeting. In other cases, as I will show in the following chapters, government ministers and secretaries can hold on to office for decades. In these instances, stability and permanency characterize the ministerial condition. Next I will describe the empirical evidence that sustains my argument.

Foreign affairs: new data and empirical tests

The examples mentioned above were chosen to illustrate the nuances of the ministerial condition, which is determined by a complex interaction of ministerial competence and ambition, and a leader's tradeoff between internal and external political threats. Evidently, the degree of complexity of this interaction depends on political institutions. Everything else equal, the rules of ministerial survival in autocratic and democratic presidential systems are straightforward – in the former, loyalty and an apparent lack of competence practically guarantee many years in office, while in the latter, clear demonstrations of ability secure the leader's appreciation and consequently a long-lasting cabinet portfolio. Sometimes, this portfolio carries over multiple administrations – Robert Gates was US secretary of defense under the administrations of Presidents George W. Bush, a Republican, and Barack Obama, a Democrat. Maximizing ministerial tenure in democratic parliamentary systems is much more difficult.

The empirical tests of my theory require the collection of data on ministers' tenure in office, a measure of ministerial competence, and leaders' tenure in office. The latter has been extensively investigated and there are several datasets on their time in office, with *Archigos* (Goemans, Gleditsch, and Chiozza 2009) being the most popular one. As I will explain in Chapter 4, there are several databases on ministerial careers. These include the Blondel dataset (1985) – which covers the careers of thousands of individuals across 2,000 cabinet positions in 154 countries from 1945 to 1980 – as well as country-specific and regime-specific datasets. Unfortunately, these sources of information are not necessarily comparable or appropriate for valid comparative analysis – they place an emphasis on different aspects of ministerial politics, or are not updated, or do not offer sufficient variation in political institutions, or they simply do not highlight issues of competence. Hence, this book is also important for the study of elites and political survival in general because it introduces and systematically analyzes the tenure in office of more than 7,300 ministers of foreign affairs covering more than 180 countries spanning the years 1696–2004.

The Ministry of Foreign Affairs is one of the oldest and most important positions in any cabinet. As I explain in Chapter 5, it is closely connected to the development of the modern nation-state as defined by its self-determination and sovereignty over a territory defined by physical boundaries and that functions as the essential form of political organization in our current international system. Ministers of foreign affairs as their nations' top diplomats and representatives thus play a key role in the projection and implementation of their countries' policies in the international arena. In addition, they play important domestic political roles. For instance, they provide continuity to governments. Masuyama and Nyblade (2015) find that Japanese ministers of foreign affairs are the most reshuffle-resistant of all cabinet members. In a country where reshuffles take place almost every year, only 29 percent of cabinet members survive these cabinet changes. In contrast, between 1947 and 2011, 61 percent of all foreign ministers survived the reshuffles. In Pakistan, the ministry of foreign affairs is crucial for democratic stability; given Pakistan's tensions with India over the disputed territory of Kashmir, the army informally approves the appointment for the post of foreign minister (Mufti 2015).

Having said this, the missing part of the empirical puzzle resides in finding a measure of ministerial competence. In all honesty, there is no broadly accepted or objectively correct measure of ministerial competence, regardless of the area of activity. This notwithstanding, in Chapter 5 I develop a measure of ministerial competence that is applicable to ministers of foreign affairs. Of course, a minister of foreign affairs, like any other individual, may show competence in some specific tasks and not in others. Yet, it is safe to argue that foreign ministers are their nations' top diplomats and that diplomacy has an important role in the prevention of interstate war. In fact, I will argue that both diplomacy and war are part of the same bargaining process. In this light, I concentrate on ministers' ability to prevent hostilities through diplomacy. This measure of competence builds on a well-known theoretical result showing that governments can reach prewar bargains that leave them as well off as if they had fought a war while avoiding the costs of fighting, hence effectively preventing armed conflict (Fearon 1995). I argue that competent ministers of foreign affairs are simply more able to reach these *ex ante* bargains. In other words, I argue that competent foreign ministers produce a peace that yields the same goals of the war but without incurring the costs of fighting. In contrast, diplomacy led by an incompetent minister will lead to a peace that is not sustainable. The worst ministers of foreign affairs will lead their countries into wars that they will lose.

A test of these propositions is an econometric challenge. Recall that permanence in the cabinet depends on ministerial competence and ambition and a leader's incentives to stay in office. This suggests that permanency in office of both leaders and ministers is interdependent. Econometric models of time, also known as survival or event history models, are well known and have been used extensively in the social sciences, as they have in the empirical analysis of leaders' tenure (e.g., Bueno de Mesquita et al. 2003, 2004; Chiozza and Goemans 2003, 2004). They have also been used to explore the duration in office of cabinet ministers (e.g., Kerby 2009; Quiroz Flores 2009, 2015; Berlinski, Dewan, and Dowding 2010). The problem for inference, at least in the context of this book, is that the ministers and leaders depend for their tenure on each other; therefore, I cannot simply add a leader's time in office as an explanatory variable in my analysis of ministerial change. A model of simultaneous equations would be an ideal tool to explore this interdependence. Unfortunately, survival models that explore interdependence between two simultaneous, continuous time processes are not fully developed, at least not to sufficient standards.

To get around this problem, I rely on two solutions. First, I use an instrumental variable approach. Instrumental variables are a popular method to replace covariates that are correlated with a disturbance; such correlation violates at least one of the Gauss–Markov assumptions, thus causing biased estimates that invalidate inference in the linear model. This type of problem is also present in nonlinear models, such as survival models of time. In my analysis of the tenure of ministers, the tenure of leaders is endogenous because it depends on how long a minister has been in office. Although I describe the method of instrumental variables in detail in Chapter 6, I can say here that an instrumental variable is correlated with the endogenous variable – in this case leader's tenure – but not with the disturbance. My instrumental variable for leader's tenure is a leader's age, which is an indicator of actuarial risk and is correlated with the provision of private goods in small-coalition systems. For this reason, this approach – technically a probit model with instrumental variables – is only used in the context of nondemocratic countries. To overcome the lack of an instrumental variable applicable to countries with large-coalition systems, I use bivariate discrete survival models to explore the probability of leader and minister deposition conditional on their time in office. More specifically, I estimate a bivariate probit model of the joint probability of leader and minister change. This is a model where the duration processes of leaders and ministers are connected via their disturbances, which are draws from a bivariate distribution. This model, discussed in Chapter 7, allows for the estimation of the joint and conditional hazard rates of leaders and ministers.

The empirical tests provide evidence in favor of many of the hypotheses derived in this book. The results are quite strong for the cases of cabinet change in small-coalition systems, where leaders have incentives to depose competent ministers to prevent internal challenges to their leadership. These tests are developed in Chapter 6, where I explore a logarithmic transformation of years of peace as a measure of ministerial competence. Estimation results clearly indicate that competence measured as peacetime increases the hazard of ministerial deposition, thus meeting my theoretic expectations. Furthermore, I find that even when a minister leads her country into a war that is eventually lost, her prospects of replacement are unaffected. Indeed, in autocratic systems such as Iraq's under Saddam Hussein and Syria's under Assad, a minister who presides over the initiation of a war that is lost is not more likely to be deposed from office. The evidence in large-coalition parliamentary systems is more complex. On the one hand, the hazard rate of ministers increases as a function of their competence, measured as peacetime. This is consistent with expectations about the survival of ministers in cases of parties that do not provide perks to party members. The evidence of democratic, presidential systems is more mixed, although relatively consistent with some of my expectations about cabinet change in these systems.

Conclusion

Since Jean Blondel began to systematically analyze ministerial careers (1985), there has been a big increase in the number of empirical analyses of cabinet politics and an increasing methodological sophistication in the analyses, including first its connection to government stability and change, and more recently cabinet formation, cabinet duration and durability, and ministerial duration, and its link to broader aspects of politics such as democratic accountability and the implementation of domestic and international policy. This book contributes to this growing research agenda.

In the following chapters, I will discuss the literature on ministerial politics and careers (Chapter 2), develop my game theory model of cabinet change (Chapter 3), describe my data (Chapter 4), make a case for the importance of ministers of foreign affairs (Chapter 5), and lastly empirically analyze their tenure in office in nondemocratic and democratic systems around the world (Chapters 6 and 7). As mentioned before, this will contribute to our understanding of cabinet change, foreign affairs, and along with them, governmental stability and interstate war.

Notes

1 www.newyorker.com/news/news-desk/kim-jong-un-kills-the-old
2 www.theguardian.com/world/2015/oct/08/pinochet-directly-ordered-washington-killing-diplomat-documents-orlando-letelier-declassified
3 www.bbc.co.uk/news/world-middle-east-33521655

2 The study of cabinet change

Introduction

In 2011, a White House photographer took a now iconic photo of President Obama and his national security team monitoring the progress of the mission that killed Osama bin Laden. The decision to raid the compound in Abbottabad required painstaking analysis, and the operation itself was obviously dangerous and politically risky, particularly since American forces had to cross the Pakistan border without authorization from the Pakistani government. Given the potential political ramifications of the operation, it was not surprising to see Hilary Clinton, secretary of state, and Robert Gates, secretary of defense, in the Situation Room at that critical time in May of 2011. Both cabinet secretaries observed the operation in real time and were ready to provide advice to President Obama, commander-in-chief of the United States armed forces, and ultimately the figure responsible for the raid.

In the United States, the official mission of the cabinet is to provide advice to the president, and this was precisely what Clinton and Gates were doing that night of May 2011. Cabinet ministers, however, do much more than provide advice to a head of government. Cabinet secretaries are political agents who respond to their boss's instructions but who also pursue their own agendas. In this context, they have the ability and space to implement and manipulate policy, both domestic and international, often with historical consequences. To what extent they can do so depends on institutional characteristics and political incentives specific to a country or period in time.

To most of us, it is evident that cabinet ministers are key political and historical figures, and yet it has taken many years for scholars in the social sciences and the humanities to articulate and explain why and how the cabinet is important. This does not mean that we do not possess large amounts of information on cabinet ministers – the bookshelves of our homes, libraries, and bookshops are full of cabinet secretaries' memoirs and the official and unofficial texts of their biographers. From Henry Kissinger's *Diplomacy* (1994) to Richard Holbrooke's *To End a War* (1998), from Marjorie M. Farrar's analysis of Alexandre Millerand as French minister of war (1980) to Larry Eugene Jones's description of Alfred Hugenberg's participation in Hitler's cabinet (1992), and from Richard Loss's narrative of Dean Acheson's rise to US secretary of state (1974) to Hannah Arendt's *Eichmann in Jerusalem* (1963), there are innumerable accounts of life in the cabinet and other high-ranking executive positions.

This body of work, as important as it is, has not contributed to our general understanding of cabinet change or ministerial tenure for two reasons. First, as accumulated knowledge, it has not been systematic or always coherent. Second, it has failed to make general connections between political and economic institutions and the politics of the cabinet, including policy implementation and cabinet change. In the last few years, however, our approach to the cabinet has changed, and although we continue to buy and learn from political memoirs and biographies, researchers have produced a body of knowledge that has greatly improved our understanding of cabinet politics. This chapter describes and organizes this recent work, but not without first making another case for the importance of the cabinet.

Importance of the cabinet

The cabinet plays an essential role in the functioning of government, while cabinet change is central to accountability mechanisms and representative democracy (Dowding and Dumont 2009; Fischer, Dowding, and Dumont 2012). The study of cabinet change therefore contributes to our understanding of the duration of democratic and nondemocratic governments, and consequently to our comprehension of political transition. In fact, it is the fear of political change that shapes political leaders' incentives to replace their cabinet ministers. Autocrats are afraid of being replaced by their ministers in their own ruling coalition. All democratic leaders fear that voters will replace them with a challenger, while some democrats also fear that their own party will substitute them with a new party leader, probably a popular cabinet minister. What is crucial for the story in this book is that, in spite of the potential for internal deposition, leaders need their ministers to help them rule.

In the United States, the cabinet was first created as a source of advice to the president. The cabinet continues to fulfill this role, although specialized councils and offices such as, among others, the Council of Economic Advisers and the Office of National Drug Control Policy also inform presidents.[1] The role of the cabinet has now shifted more to domestic and international policy implementation. What is important in this relatively obvious role is that in implementing policy, cabinet secretaries in the US play the role of intermediaries between the White House, the bureaucracy, interest groups, and private corporations. In other words, cabinet members are agents of the president but also respond to powerful private interests; this feature is not as strong in other political systems. In this sense, a secretary is important for the implementation of the program of a particular president but is also important in the larger scheme of partisan politics and the role of private interests and the bureaucracy. An excellent example of the importance of cabinet secretaries in this context is the appointment of William S. Cohen as secretary of defense during the Clinton administration. The

Department of Defense is one of the pillars of the United States government. It is also the largest employer in the country, with 1.3 million individuals on active duty and a force of 742,000 civilian personnel.[2] The secretary of defense runs this enormous executive office and has control over the design and development of weapons systems and the acquisition of weapons programs (Lynn and Smith 1982). Given the significance of the appointment, it would be expected that a president would nominate a close ally. And yet, Clinton was compelled to choose Cohen, a Republican, in order "to secure the bipartisan support America's armed forces must have and clearly deserve."[3] Obama kept Republican Robert Gates as secretary of defense even though George W. Bush originally appointed him.

In parliamentary systems, however, the importance of the cabinet is quite distinct. First, cabinet members, unlike cabinet secretaries in presidential systems, are elected officials and members of the legislature. Hence, they act as agents of a prime minister – and potentially agents of private interests – but also respond to their constituents. In other words, they are elected representatives and members of the highest executive office in the country. This presents a completely different set of political incentives in most parliamentary systems: in order to remain as MPs and be part of the cabinet, ministers need to keep the loyalty of their constituents, and yet cabinet positions may come with the implementation of policies that could potentially alienate a minister's voters. In the 2015 British general election, several Liberal Democrats who were part of the coalition government of David Cameron lost their seats, including Business Secretary Vince Cable, Chief Secretary to the Treasury Danny Alexander, and Energy Secretary Ed Davey. As I write these lines, a Conservative majority forms the current British government.

Cabinets in parliamentary systems have a strong collective character that is not present in the cabinets of presidential systems. In coalition governments, this collective character might not be as strong as in single-party governments because cabinet portfolios are distributed according to the forces of coalition partners (King et al. 1990; Warwick 1994; Laver and Shepsle 1994; Diermeier and Stevenson 1999; Martin and Vanberg 2004). In spite of this, cabinet ministers in multiparty governments are crucial for the maintenance of the coalition and the implementation of policy. For instance, Nick Clegg, leader of the Liberal Democrats and deputy prime minister in the British coalition government of 2010–2015, was instrumental in raising tuition fees in England. Clegg had originally opposed an increase in tuition fees, but as his party joined the coalition government in 2010, they abandoned that pledge; the raise in fees led to massive student protests in the country. Clegg was instrumental in the emergence and survival of the first Cameron government, but he was portrayed in the election campaign of 2015 as an outsider who was easily manipulated, and his high-level participation in the coalition cost him the party leadership. The Liberal Democrats, on the other hand, experienced a decrease of fifty-seven MPs in 2010 to only eight in 2015.

In addition to their roles in policy implementation and government stability, cabinet members are important because they tend to succeed their leaders. Cabinet ministers are in a position of great influence and high visibility; they often are high-ranking party members and have links to bureaucracies, industry, and unions; they carry political power and enjoy political support both domestically and internationally. In general, cabinet ministers are in a unique position to succeed their bosses. Golda Meir was minister of labor and minister of foreign affairs before becoming prime minister of Israel. In Germany, Angela Merkel was minister of women and youth and minister of environment, nature conservation, and nuclear safety. Michelle Bachelet, two times president of Chile, served as secretary of health and secretary of defense. Taro Aso, prime minister of Japan, was first minister of internal affairs and communications from 2003 to 2005, and minister for foreign affairs from 2005 to 2007. Thabo Mbeki, the controversial president of South Africa from 1999 to 2008, was first deputy president – a cabinet position – from 1996 to 1999.

Are there any patterns in terms of who succeeds a leader and how they do so? Again, political institutions determine the transition from cabinet minister to leader. In some cases, a transition takes place according to formal and informal rules of political transition. On other occasions, this transition is illegal and violent. For instance, in presidential systems where chief executives are elected by popular vote and are subject to fixed terms in office (Carey 2008), leader transitions are often peaceful and lawful and coincide with leaders' ends of their terms in office. In the United States, Presidents Thomas Jefferson, James Madison, James Monroe, John Q. Adams, and Martin Van Buren all occupied the position of secretary of state. According to Lafeber (1977: 194): "Throughout the first century of American government, the ablest secretaries of state (Jefferson, Madison, John Quincy Adams, Seward) were, not coincidentally, also powerful domestic political figures." With the exception of Herbert Hoover, cabinet membership in the US did not lead to higher office in the twentieth century, although this might change in 2016, as former US secretary of state Hilary Clinton is the leading candidate on the democratic ticket. Only on a few occasions have cabinet secretaries replaced a president before his term in office came to an end. These transitions tend to be illegal and violent. In early–twentieth-century Mexico, Minister of Foreign Affairs Francisco Leon de la Barra and General Victoriano Huerta – another cabinet member – planned the deposition of democratically elected president Francisco Madero. In one of the most dramatic chapters of the Mexican Revolution, Madero and his vice president resigned and Leon de la Barra took over as provisional president, only to be succeeded by Huerta. Shortly after, Madero, his brother, and his vice president were all murdered.

In democratic parliamentary systems, prime ministers continuously face the prospects of being replaced by ambitious cabinet ministers. In parliamentary systems, prime ministers are selected to office by the legislature, and their terms in office are subject to legislative confidence (Carey 2008). Moreover, and even before prime ministers lose the confidence of the legislature, they may lose the confidence of their own party. The British Conservative Party has experimented with different sets of rules to elect the party leadership. Before 1965 the party elite selected the Conservative leader. A change in rules in 1965 gave Conservative MPs the power to elect the party leader. It is in this context that Margaret

Thatcher was able to defeat the incumbent party leader Edward Heath in 1975. The same set of leader selection rules facilitated her own deposition by the party in 1990. In 1998 the party reformed its rules in order to allow party members to elect their leader, although the actual selection of a leader is more complex and might require the pre-selection of candidates by Conservative MPs (Quinn 2012). Labour Party leaders have also been subject to internal challenges; Prime Minister Gordon Brown's leadership over the Labour Party was challenged by two former cabinet members.[4] In a letter to members of the Labour Party, Patricia Hewitt and Geoff Hoon argued that division within Labour was forcing the party to hold a secret ballot to choose alternative leadership.[5] If this secret ballot had taken place, Gordon Brown could have been deposed as leader of the party and prime minister.

More recently, Australian politics has provided us with excellent examples of how ministers can remove their party leaders. Australia is a parliamentary system that, in many respects, is similar to other Westminster-style governments. However, in terms of cabinet change, Australia stands apart due to the strongly factionalized nature of its leading political parties and the fact that, in the words of Dowding and Lewis (2015: 49): "a party leader, even when PM, can be removed at almost any time by a simple majority vote of the parliament party – demonstrating how strong the parties are relative to their leaders." Dowding and Lewis (2015) have found that three prime ministers were forced out of office by their own party between 1949 and 2010; a fourth was asked by Australia's governor general to step down due to a constitutional crisis. John Gorton stepped down in 1971 during a leadership challenge led by Foreign Minister William McMahon. Bob Hawke, prime minister from 1983 to 1991, was brought down by Deputy Prime Minister Paul Keating. The Labor governments in Australia between 2007 and 2013 were subject to constant leadership challenges: Kevin Rudd was replaced by his deputy Julia Gillard in 2010, who became Australia's first female prime minister. Gillard was in turn replaced in 2013 by Rudd, who had been appointed minister of foreign affairs and was regarded as a better electoral prospect (Dowding and Lewis 2015). In 2015, and only two years after taking office, the Liberal prime minister Tony Abbott was also forced out by his party.

Which agency problems?

I like to start my literature review on cabinet change with Jean Blondel's 1985 book *Government Ministers in the Contemporary World*. This is the seminal work on ministerial careers around the world and provides one of the most comprehensive examinations of cabinet ministers carried out over the course of a decade. There, Blondel examined the careers of thousands of cabinet ministers and analyzed their average time in office across countries, regions, and political systems. Most importantly, he presented a collection of potential explanations of the "ministerial condition," a term that describes the short tenure of cabinet ministers. These explanations can be summarized as follows:

> On the whole, these patterns of ministerial duration appear to be 'imposed' on the leaders by the traditions of the country and by the institutional structure indirectly, as well as by what appears to be a need to set up an effective and credible government.
>
> (Blondel 1985: 164–165)

As we have learnt more about politics in general and collected more data on cabinets and ministers, a growing collection of studies have greatly improved on Jean Blondel's initial explanation of the ministerial condition, which is in fact not as dismal as it seems. These explanations have covered a number of areas, which can be organized in multiple forms. For instance, in one of the first systematic quantitative studies of ministerial turnover, Dowding and Kang (1998) explore resignations and nonresignations of cabinet ministers in England from the Attlee to the Major governments. Both resignations and nonresignations – calls of resignations organized by the press, for example – are coded into one of eight categories: personal error, departmental error, sexual scandal, financial scandal, policy disagreement, personality clash, performance, and other controversies. Kang (2015) increased the list of resignation reasons to fifteen in his analysis of cabinet change in South Korea.

Dowding and Kang's aforementioned analysis (1998) concentrates on Britain, and therefore it does not explore how these reasons for resignation and nonresignation vary across types of parliamentary systems or other types of regimes, such as nondemocracies. Indeed, cabinet ministers across polities can resign for any of these eight reasons, but the propensity for replacement varies across regimes. The varying impact of political institutions on cabinet change can also be organized on a number of different forms. For instance, Fischer, Dowding, and Dumont (2012) look at regime type, constitutional and parliamentary rules, and party systems as institutional factors affecting ministerial durability. They also add a second dimension that captures the personal characteristics of cabinet ministers, such as education, age, and gender. As I explain in Chapter 4, current efforts to systematize data collection on ministerial careers also give these personal characteristics an important place in data gathering.

Fischer, Dowding, and Dumont (2012) summarize quite well the recent advances made in the formal and quantitative analysis of cabinet change. They cover ministerial durability across regimes and, in general, organize the determinants of durability mechanisms into three large classes: institutional characteristics of the environment, institutional framework of ministerial tenure, and political characteristics of the environment. The first class covers institutional characteristics of regime types (democratic and nondemocratic) and governmental systems (presidential and parliamentary), while the second class emphasizes strategic considerations of cabinet change and how firing and hiring decisions are closely connected. Lastly, they explore government types (single-party and coalition governments), party systems, and party politics, among other issues, all under the rubric of political characteristics of the environment. Notice that this is simply a different approach to understanding cabinet change – institutional characteristics, as well as personal characteristics of cabinet ministers, can all lead to resignations and nonresignations in the shape of ministerial error or policy disagreements, or any of the other categories first presented by Dowding and Kang (1998).

Dowding and Dumont (2009) take a slightly different approach and explore structural and strategic factors of cabinet change under the headings of ministerial 'hiring' and 'firing.' Again, notice that this is a different way of organizing the causes of cabinet turnover, as they explore constitutional and party factors, as well as strategic considerations of cabinet formation and termination. For instance, institutional and party constraints shape the hiring of ministers because they determine the size of the pool of potential ministers as well as specific portfolio allocation. Moreover, in countries where appointments are subject to legislature approval, as in the US (Quiroz Flores 2015), institutional limitations on hiring are an important consideration. Constitutional and party factors also determine the firing of ministers. For instance, up to 1960, Israeli prime ministers did not even have the legal authority to dismiss their cabinet ministers (Kenig and Barnea 2015). Dowding and Dumont (2009) begin to look at potential problems of agency behind the strategic reasons to replace ministers, including policy disagreement, scandals and corrective effects, and government revitalization. Lastly, it is important to note that 'hiring' and 'firing' are crucial because for every ministerial replacement, there needs to be a new appointment (Fischer, Dowding, and Dumont 2012).

So far, I have elaborated on the work of Dowding and Kang (1998), Dowding and Dumont (2009), and Fischer, Dowding, and Dumont (2012) because most research on cabinet change fits into their organization and understanding of the literature. This book is one exception, as it tells a story of how considerations of political survival shape leaders' incentives to replace their cabinet ministers. Yet, the book is based on the assumption that leaders cannot rule alone and therefore need to delegate authority to their cabinet ministers. In this light, my work here is more in tune with the approach recently undertaken by Dowding and Dumont (2015), where they highlight the important distinction between problems of agency rent and problems of moral hazard and adverse selection. Consequently, in the following pages I will spend considerable time describing their approach to agency issues and how the extant literature fits into that image of cabinet change.

I just mentioned that leaders need ministers to help them rule. As a consequence, ministers are strategically placed at the top of government agencies and departments to exercise influence over the formulation and implementation of policy (Modelski 1970). Moreover, ministers are responsible for the efficient administration of public affairs, which is a necessary condition for the maintenance of power and the coordination and implementation of policy (Cohen 1986; Huber 1998). This is not limited to democracies – military governments also rely heavily on ministers and civilian bureaucrats to run the government efficiently (Riggs 1981; Anene 1997). As leaders delegate in order to rule, they also create an opportunity for agency, that is, a space for the ministerial pursuit of goals that may not coincide with those of a leader (e.g., Fenno 1958; Laver and Shepsle

1994). This simple dynamic of executive delegation has opened up a growing literature on the agency problems caused by cabinet politics. These problems, known in the economics and political science literatures as principal–agent problems, are amplified or reduced by political institutions.

Principal–agent problems are typically caused by the delegation of tasks from a principal to an agent. In the context of this book, the principal is the leader, while the cabinet minister is the agent. This delegation takes place within a context of asymmetric information that often produces perverse incentives that might lead to what the literature labels as principal–agent problems. This is actually an important discussion, as different fields use different terms for the same analytical property of delegation. Dowding and Dumont (2015) distinguish among three sets of agency problems: agency rent, moral hazard, and adverse selection. Dowding and Dumont argue that agency rent might take two different shapes, shirking and shifting. This is a very useful terminology, as these two problems are elsewhere known as types of moral hazard. The latter, however, is quite distinct, and so is adverse selection.

In order to illustrate shirking and shifting more formally, consider the following single-shot game between a leader and a potential minister. A leader offers an individual the opportunity to join the cabinet as minister of foreign affairs and represent the leader in negotiations to settle an international dispute over territory. Assume that the leader's ideal settlement of the dispute is $L=1$ where $L \in [0, 1]$; this simply means that the leader's goal is to retain 100 percent of the disputed territory. The leader is willing to offer a contract to the minister that has two components, a salary and a bonus that is outcome dependent; this means that a minister will have a salary regardless of the outcome of the negotiations and a bonus that depends on the outcome of the negotiation. Of course, the potential minister is assumed to be already employed elsewhere and with an income. This is essentially an opportunity cost that can be represented, for instance, by the compensation that Robert McNamara received as president of the Ford Company before he joined the Kennedy cabinet as secretary of defense.

Now suppose the individual accepts the job and becomes minister of foreign affairs. In that role, her task is to represent the leader and carry out international negotiations to settle the international dispute. Ideally, the new minister will reach a settlement that produces $L=1$, which is the leader's goal. In this model, there are two set of reasons that might prevent the minister from reaching a settlement of $L=1$. The first set of reasons fall into the category of agency rent in Dowding and Dumont's interpretation of agency (2015), and they are caused by asymmetric information or hidden action. Let's consider shirking first. Negotiations are a long and difficult process, and it is probably the case that the minister's opponents also would like to keep the entire territory in dispute. In this case, the minister might not exert much effort and obtain a poor outcome. Maybe the minister is not particularly competent and therefore she could not negotiate a favorable settlement. Notice that shirking might take place even when both the leader and the minister perfectly coincide on the goal of the negotiations. Shifting differs from shirking in that the minister might have a completely different idea of what the final settlement of the dispute should be. More formally, the minister might have a goal of $M \neq L$, where $M \in [0, 1]$. In other words, a highly capable foreign minister might prefer to settle for less than 100 percent of the territory, even as she could potentially deliver the leader's preferred policy.

Why the minister is *unable* to negotiate a settlement that yields $L=1$ or *unwilling* to negotiate such a settlement is irrelevant, at least to some extent. In addition, the minister might not be able to reach the leader's ideal settlement due to stochastic factors. In other words, even a highly competent, hard-working minister with ideal position $M = L$, might not be able to successfully negotiate the dispute due to factors that are completely out of her hands. Regardless of the causes of a failure in negotiations, at least as seen from the leader's perspective, what is crucial for the model is that the leader observes only the outcome produced by the agent but does not observe her actions. Nevertheless, a rational leader can anticipate these potential problems of shirking and shifting and design a mechanism that eliminates, or at least minimizes, agency rent. For instance, a minister with an ideal settlement identical to the leader's might be persuaded to work harder under a better compensation package. In other words, a leader can offer a wage and an outcome based bonus that will secure the best work the minister can offer; this includes compensation that is proportional to the uncertainty produced by the stochastic factor mentioned above. This payoff simply needs to be larger or equal than the payoff that the minister would receive if she did not exert adequate effort to secure $L=1$. A compensation package that meets this condition is said to meet the incentive compatibility condition, that is, it provides conditions that give strong incentives to the agent to exert effort. Likewise, a highly competent, hard-working minister with an ideal settlement different than the leader's can be persuaded to abandon his own ideal position and use all her ability to try to secure the leader's objective. The compensation package that meets the incentive compatibility condition in the case of shifting will be a function of the distance between L and M, that is, the difference between the leader's and the minister's goals, and the level of uncertainty added by the stochastic component. This package can be easily topped up in case of potential shirking.

The incentive compatibility condition can be easily calculated using backwards induction, the well-known technique to find subgame perfect equilibria. This method allows the leader to design compensation packages to eliminate shirking and shifting. However, meeting the incentive compatibility condition is a necessary but not sufficient condition to produce an optimal contract. It could well be the case that the contract that eliminates potential shifting and shirking will not be large enough relative to what the potential minister could earn elsewhere. Recall that the individual who receives the cabinet offer is already on employment. Therefore, the leader needs to create a contract that meets the incentive compatibility condition but also leaves the minister as well-off as she would have been under alternative employment. A contract that fulfills this condition is known as a contract that meets the participation constraint. In short, a contract that meets both the incentive compatibility condition and the participation constraint will only attract a minister who will try to secure the leader's objective regardless of the level of effort or asymmetry in preferences. Rather informally, the agency rent problems can be easily solved if a leader offers enough compensation such that ministers, as agents of the leader, exert sufficient effort or abandon their own personal goals in case they differ from those of the leader.

I concur with Dowding and Dumont (2015) in describing these issues as agency rent problems. Nevertheless, it could be argued that agency rent problems described above meet the assumptions and implications of the 'canonical principal–agent model of moral hazard' often used in political science (Miller 2005). First, there is agent impact, that is, the agent's actions have an effect on the principal's payoff. In our example, this simply means that the minister's actions have consequences for the leader. Second, there is information asymmetry, that is, the principal observes only the outcome produced by the agent but not her actions. In other words, the leader cannot observe the actual negotiations carried out by the minister but only the result of the negotiations. Third, there might be an asymmetry in preferences, that is, the minister's ideal position over the territorial dispute could be different than the leader's. Fourth, the principal and the agent are rational individuals and the leader plays first in the sequence of moves. In other words, a minister cannot participate in the negotiations if the leader does not select that individual to be her agent in the first place. Fifth, the rules of the game are common knowledge. And lastly, the principal can impose a contract on the agent as a take-it-or-leave-it offer to participate in the game. In terms of the implications that follow from these assumptions, the contract that meets the incentive compatibility condition and the participation constraint is said to provide outcome-based incentives, as the size of the bonus is a function of the outcome of the negotiations. While the contract eliminates potential shirking and shifting, it does so at the expense of efficiency (Miller 2005), as the bonus is also proportional to the level of uncertainty caused by the stochastic component mentioned above.

Following Dowding and Dumont (2015), there are important differences between agency rent and moral hazard and adverse selection. Moral hazard as described by Dowding and Dumont refers to the more traditional set of incentives whereby agents engage in risk behavior once they have agreed to the terms of a contract. This form of moral hazard occupied headlines after the 2008 financial crisis and it referred to the recklessness of many financial institutions in their expectation of receiving huge government bailouts. Moral hazard is also a popular term in studies of international financial institutions such as the IMF – countries may have incentives to behave financially irresponsibly, as they may be able to access IMF rescue programs (Vreeland 2007). Recent research suggests that this problem might be more acute for allies of great powers such as the US or Great Britain, who tend to receive favorable treatment from the World Bank (Dreher, Sturm, and Vreeland 2009). In terms of cabinet politics, Dowding and Dumont refer to the moral hazard produced by collective cabinet responsibility in parliamentary systems, which gives incentive to ministers to behave irresponsibly in the knowledge that the entire cabinet, including the prime minister, will come to their rescue. This type of moral hazard, however, is not as ubiquitous in presidential systems partly because the cabinet is not really a collegial body there. Yet, as I will argue in the following chapters, moral hazard is quite pervasive in autocracies, as leaders have incentives to surround themselves with ministers who engage in illegal and even criminal behavior with few repercussions.

Lastly, it is important to distinguish adverse selection. Both in the economics literature as well as for Dowding and Dumont (2015), adverse selection presents principals with a different agency problem. In this setting, the problem does not arise from risky behavior but from the participation in a contract of inadequate agents who try to pass for adequate ones. Often, potential agents are drawn from a heterogeneous population in respect of certain characteristics required by the contract. For instance, recent graduates hoping to join the labor market have heterogeneous training – perhaps because some schools are better than others – which presents a problem for potential employers, as graduates with a poor education might try to pass as excellent graduates. Given this information asymmetry about the type of agents in the market, principals tend to offer low salaries to recent graduates, but this discards application by excellent students who expect compensation proportional to their training. This agency problem will occupy a central place in the following discussion, as the pool of potential cabinet ministers varies across political systems in terms of both size and quality.

Recent literature on cabinet politics explores cabinet change as a potential solution to agency problems. Some works refer to traditional problems of adverse selection and moral hazard, while others refer to shirking and shifting. In solving these problems, in equilibrium leaders will attract specific types of ministers or will force ministers to behave in a particular way regardless of their type. This suggests that there is an issue of identification of the causes of agency problems. As discussed by Dowding and Dumont (2015), it is difficult to know with certainty whether the actions of ministers are caused by shifting, shirking, moral hazard, or adverse selection. Practically all of these agency problems can shape the behavior of cabinet ministers and, without the ability to question the latter about the causes of their behavior, we can only guess whether a minister reached a particular settlement in an international dispute due to lack of effort, disagreement with the leader, poor diplomatic skills, or an inclination to engage in risky behavior. In the econometrics literature, this is known as a problem of identification, where an observed outcome could be the result of multiple data generating processes. Dowding and Dumont (2015) correctly argue that this is a pervasive methodological problem in analyses of cabinet change in parliamentary democracies. I believe that the problem persists across political systems.

Reducing agency: selection and dismissal

The problem of identification mentioned above presents challenges to both researchers of cabinet politics as well as politicians. Recall that in the model of agency rent discussed above, a leader can design a mechanism that meets the incentive compatibility condition and the participation constraint. In equilibrium, when these two conditions are met, ministers will always implement a leader's ideal policy. Clearly, this is not always the case: ministers implement their own preferred policies, respond to the wishes of actors other than their principal, and even manage to replace the leader. Out of the equilibrium path, a number of things can go wrong for both the leader and her ministers. In this light, it is important to ask, in addition to the asymmetric information that defines principal–agent models, what are the factors that prevent a leader from meeting the incentive compatibility condition and the participation constraint in a context of cabinet appointments? Perhaps more importantly, once a contract is active, what are the tools available to the leader to eliminate agency rent?

To begin with, the incentive compatibility condition and the participation constraint might not be met simply because the game is much more complex. As correctly described by Dowding and Dumont (2015), in parliamentary systems both the head of government and her cabinet ministers are agents of the voters, while ministers are also agents of the prime minister. Coalition governments increase the number of roles that ministers have, as they have to answer to voters, a prime minister, and their own party leaders. A similar type of complexity exists in semi-presidential systems, where a directly elected president might belong to a party that does not control parliament. Clearly, systems with ministers who answer to multiple principals are likely to experience very serious agency problems. In addition, in countries with strong private interests – for instance, in systems where electoral success depends on raising campaign funds, often from private donors – both leaders and cabinet secretaries are also agents of non-governmental forces (Fenno 1958). These political and economic forces can compel ministers to publicly show positions opposite to those of their leaders (Bertelli and Grose 2007) in a clear case of policy shifting. Of course, the dynamics in autocracies can be quite different, and in fact much more simple than in democracies. In 1878, Claus Spreckels, a businessman based in California, convinced the king of Hawaii to dismiss his entire cabinet in order to get approval for an irrigation system constructed and operated by Spreckels. The cabinet was dismissed and the new cabinet provided the rights for the irrigation system (Adler 1960).

In addition, the incentive compatibility condition and the participation constraint might not be met due to adverse selection. Naturally, a model will fail if it used to explain a situation it was not designed for. As unfair as this is to the model of agency rent, this is a useful discussion because it illustrates important aspects of cabinet politics. Having said this, adverse selection can be easily introduced if potential ministers, for example, have heterogeneous abilities to perform at the cabinet level. In a typical case of adverse selection, a potential minister might lie about her opportunity cost, that is, the income she would receive if she did not accept the leader's invitation to join the cabinet; perhaps that individual convinced the leader that her opportunity cost is high because she is talented, but in reality she might be impersonating a talented individual. This type of situation is feasible, particularly in politics, and it can lead to a situation where an apparently competent minister fails to perform adequately. Notice that in this case, meeting the incentive compatibility condition is useless, as it was designed for a completely different type of agent; the agent fails to perform due to her type being wrong for the type of contract designed by the leader and not by the incorrect design of the incentive compatibility conditions.

Great heterogeneity comes with increased adverse selection, which at the same time can lead to agency rent. Dowding and Dumont (2015) present an excellent example of this type of compound agency problem. According to the authors (Dowding and Dumont 2015: 13), Thatcher's cabinet reshuffles of 1981 could be traced to the fact that the prime minister "had little choice in her initial cabinet, which was full of Heathites (ministers in her predecessor's cabinet) or wets." This led to a situation where the 'wet' ministers had openly articulated their position on policy and challenged the prime minister's view on them. Interestingly, this case resembles the dynamics of other transitional governments that are forced to include cabinet members of previous administrations, sometimes with dire consequences.

The literature has highlighted two broad classes of solutions to agency problems: the careful selection of cabinet ministers and cabinet change. It is very important to note that these two tools, both theoretically and in politics, are actually quite different simply because selection takes place before the contract is executed, while replacement is applied once the contract is active. As trivial as this is, it constitutes an important distinction because leaders use these tools to solve different problems. By and large, as leaders select their cabinet, they reasonably aim at minimizing the effect of heterogeneous ministers and adverse selection (Kam and Indridason 2005). Once the cabinet is appointed, leaders might eliminate ministers who 'slipped through the cracks' of the selection process and are now implementing their own preferred policies. Even if leaders managed to eliminate all ministers with heterogeneous characteristics, or simply when all ministers have homogeneous characteristics, agency rent, as well as moral hazard, might still be present. At this point, only cabinet change can eliminate these problems.

Let's look at cabinet selection first. Careful cabinet selection is the initial tool that leaders use to minimize adverse selection and other agency problems. For instance, in modern parliamentary Japan, most cabinet ministers are recruited from the same set of prestigious universities (Tomita, Baerwald, and Nakamura 1981). In 1990s Mexico, a presidential system, most cabinet ministers had been classmates in prestigious PhD programs in the United States (Preston and Dillon 2004). In France, a semi-presidential system, leaders and cabinet ministers share an educational and social background (Dogan 1979). Unfortunately, institutional factors strongly shape two aspects of the selection process: the size of the pool of potential candidates, and the capacity to select candidates in such a pool.

First, the number of potential cabinet secretaries in presidential systems is larger than in parliamentary ones because potential ministers do not have to be members of parliament (Dogan 1979; Mann and Smith 1981; Tomita, Baerwald, and Nakamura 1981; King et al. 1990; Warwick 1994; Laver and Shepsle 1994, 1996; Diermeier and Stevenson 1999). In fact, some presidential systems actually prevent ministers from serving in the legislature due to strong separation of powers, as in the US. Likewise, in France, potential ministers with a place in the legislature must resign their seats and be replaced by their deputies if they want to serve in the cabinet. Yet, other presidential systems such as South Korea's allow ministers to be part of the cabinet while holding their legislative seats (Kang 2015). This effectively increases an already large pool of potential cabinet members in presidential systems. Some parliamentary systems have also implemented rules to increase the size of the pool of potential ministers. For instance, in Turkey, ministers do not have to be legislators to sit in the cabinet, although they should meet the requirement to run for election as a deputy (Mutlu-Eren 2015).

Altogether, larger pools give presidents considerable freedom to choose cabinet secretaries, thus facilitating recruitment and reducing potential adverse selection (Dowding and Dumont 2015). On the other hand, although the size of the pool might be orthogonal to the homogeneity of its members, it is reasonable to expect more heterogeneity in a larger pool of ministers, which increases the likelihood of adverse selection. In contrast, although the pool of ministers is smaller in parliamentary systems, the pool might be more homogeneous. Even if the pool of potential ministers were heterogeneous in a parliamentary system, taking the preferences of backbenchers into consideration during ministerial selection might reduce adverse selection (Kam et al. 2010).

Second, and holding the size of the ministerial pool constant, leaders face restrictions in the selection of their cabinet ministers. In the US, cabinet nominees must be confirmed by the Senate before they take office. Although the Senate tends to allow the president to form his cabinet without much trouble, the executive carefully selects nominees who will not be opposed by the Senate. And yet, the Senate has rejected nine cabinet nominations since 1789; the first rejection took place in June 1834, when President Andrew Jackson nominated Roger Taney as secretary of the treasury.[6] When the Senate is likely to reject a nomination, candidates often withdraw from the process; since 1801, twelve nominees have withdrawn their candidacies. Nevertheless, not all presidential systems face these restrictions. In Argentina and Chile, presidents enjoy considerable power and do not need to have their candidates approved by the legislature (Camerlo 2015; Siavelis and Baruch Galvan 2015). South Korea also has a presidential system, although it has some parliamentary features. For instance, ministerial appointments do not need legislative approval, and yet the legislature holds hearings that may invite a president to withdraw an appointment when a candidate has a poor public opinion record (Kang 2015).

In parliamentary systems with single-party governments, minister selection can be severely restricted by factionalized politics, as in Australia. According to Dowding and Lewis (2015), since the caucus of the Australian Labor Party has the right to pick the front bench, and because the party is highly factionalized, faction leaders tend to have an enormous influence in cabinet selection. These restrictions are even more stringent in parliamentary systems with multiparty governments, as cabinet portfolios are distributed according to the forces of coalition partners (King et al. 1990; Warwick 1994; Laver and Shepsle 1994;

Diermeier and Stevenson 1999; Martin and Vanberg 2004). In other words, coalition governments, particularly in parliamentary systems, further reduce the size of the pool of cabinet ministers (Berlinski, Dewan, and Dowing 2010).

This type of restriction imposed by coalition governments is particularly acute in Israel, where parties are heavily factionalized due to an electoral system with proportional representation and a divided society (Kenig and Barnea 2015). In fact, Israeli governments have been coalition governments, and cabinet allocation has been highly partisan across and within parties (Kenig and Barnea 2015). The size of the pool of potential cabinet ministers is a source of concern not only because it might reduce a leader's ability to minimize adverse selection, but also because it shrinks as leaders dismiss cabinet ministers. As I will explain in a moment, leaders dismiss ministers who perform poorly. However, as they continue to do so, leaders drain the talent pool of potential cabinet ministers (Dewan and Myatt 2010). This is a fateful condition, as this indicates that all governments are essentially destined to end at some point.

Coalition dynamics are not exclusive to parliamentary systems, and some presidents must also conform to the demands of coalition partners during cabinet selection, which reduces an otherwise large pool of ministers. Periods of democracy in presidential Chile have experienced both positive and negative effects of coalition governments. Pre-1973, coalition governments relied on fragile political alliances among participating parties, which led to unstable governments and cabinets. Yet, post-authoritarian Chile has experienced a long period of stable coalition governments, best exemplified by the *Concertación* that defeated the authoritarian regime of Pinochet. The demands on the *Concertación* were high because the success of the democratic transition depended on a smooth working relationship among coalition parties (Siavelis and Baruch Galvan 2015). Although the coalition succeeded in this, it also experienced obstacles because presidents did not have much space to choose ministers. This led to the creation of an alternative and controversial circle of advisers – popularly known as the *Segundo Piso* – who informally had ministerial status and that brought considerable tension to coalition politics (Siavelis and Baruch Galvan 2015).

Once the contract is active, leaders rely on reshuffles and cabinet replacement to minimize agency problems. The representative literature on this subject specifically argues that cabinet change is undertaken to eliminate adverse selection and moral hazard problems, even though they are actually referring to shirking and shifting. In order to avoid any confusion, in describing this literature I will refer to the substantive problems that cabinet change is supposed to solve, as opposed to their labels. The literature also places an emphasis on cabinet change in parliamentary systems; with a few exceptions (Camerlo and Perez-Linan 2015), this leaves agency problems in presidential systems slightly neglected. I will address presidential and nondemocratic regimes more rigorously in the next chapter.

Huber and Martinez Gallardo (2008) acknowledge that the selection process of cabinet ministers is imperfect. In their story, potential ministers have heterogeneous abilities as cabinet members; some individuals are talented, while others are not. Leaders fail to identify which individuals are capable to carry out their duties because ministers might have incentives to misrepresent themselves, or simply because this condition leads to a contract that does not attract high-quality candidates. What is crucial for the story is that the contract has been executed and the incompetent ministers have been identified due to poor ministerial performance. Cabinet change simply eliminates these poor performers.

As cabinet positions become available, leaders can match a new individual's ability with the demands of a particular portfolio and implement policy (Dewan and Hortala-Vallve 2011). Berlinski, Dewan, and Dowding (2010) also explore minister performance where prime ministers do not observe the tasks carried out by their ministers and only observe their policy outcomes or lack thereof. Specifically, leaders observe an individual minister's performance, as measured by resignation calls, as well as overall governmental performance, measured with the cumulative number of resignation calls. Berlinski, Dewan, and Dowding find that initial calls for resignation greatly increase a minister's risk of deposition, but this risk is decreasing in the number of cumulative resignation calls. This is a striking result, as it corroborates the importance of the collective character of cabinets in parliamentary systems but also a potential for moral hazard as defined by risky behavior.

As mentioned above, certain contracts might give agents incentives to engage in risky behavior. Risky behavior can lead to scandals. In May 2008, Maxime Bernier, Canada's minister of foreign affairs, left classified documents in his girlfriend's apartment. Although the scandal forced Bernier to resign, many other cabinet ministers refuse to leave office; this often has negative effects on a government's popularity. As an illustration, consider John Profumo, a British government secretary who lied to the House of Commons about an inappropriate relationship with Christine Keeler, his mistress and an acquaintance of the Soviet military attaché in London. The scandal quickly led to the demise of Harold Macmillan's government in 1963. Dewan and Dowding (2005) have shown that prime ministers correct for the negative effect of scandals by dismissing ministers. Understandably, ministers may then abandon risky behavior; unfortunately, this might also translate into the absence of policy innovation, as innovative ministers may face close scrutiny from opposition forces. In spite of this, Dewan and Myatt (2007) show that leaders can design mechanisms that promote innovation and build on the cabinet's collective character. In sum, the protection that ministers enjoy from collective government can facilitate risky behavior, and yet, under the right conditions, it can reduce moral hazard and promote policy innovation.

Kam and Indridason (2005) and Indridason and Kam (2008) are more concerned with cabinet change in the absence of poor ministerial performance or scandals. In fact, as I do in this book, they address ministers who have mixed motives in a context where leaders need to fend off internal challenges in order to maintain power. This is an important point I will return to when I develop my model of cabinet change in the next chapter. Meanwhile, these authors do recognize that the selection process is not perfect and that the wrong type of ministers might have managed to join the cabinet. Kam and Indridason (2005: 354) thus argue that reshuffles allow prime ministers to stay in power by replacing ministers when they are at most risk of losing office, that is, when "their intraparty, coalitional, and electoral positions become more precarious." In a subsequent analysis, Indridason and Kam (2008) extend the effects of ministers' mixed motives to a more specific deviation from the leader's ideal point on a policy space – for instance, spending. In this context, cabinet reshuffles reduce the incentives of ministers and bureaucrats to overspend. Although Kam and Indridason (2005), and Indridason and Kam (2008) tend to confuse moral hazard and adverse selection with agency rent, the effect of cabinet change on minimizing ministerial drift has been indirectly validated by Shotts and Wiseman (2010), who argue that the particular threat of minister replacement is a powerful tool to force convergence between the actions of an imperfect agent – who may be carrying out an investigation in an area relevant to her agency – with the preferences of a leader.

The work described above tacitly assumes that leaders have the ability and freedom to replace and reshuffle their ministers. This might not always be the case; the scale and timing of reshuffles is determined by constitutional provisions (Schleiter and Morgan-Jones 2009), as well as by elections, administrative impact, and the parliamentary timetable, among others factors (Alderman and Cross 1987). Moreover, Indridason and Kam (2008) remind us that leaders of coalition governments face great restrictions on their ability to replace ministers. Doing so might bring the government to an end, which is partly why coalition dynamics are the center of studies of government duration and change (King et al. 1990; Warwick 1994; Laver and Shepsle 1994, 1996; Diermeier and Stevenson 1999).

In presidential systems, some presidents have faced institutional restrictions to their ability to dismiss cabinet secretaries. The US cabinet emerged out of the Senate's refusal to advise the president in executive matters (Fairlie 1913). Yet the Senate has had a massive influence on the cabinet; I already mentioned the Senate's power over cabinet nominations. In terms of cabinet change, the Senate had the capacity to protect cabinet secretaries from unilateral presidential dismissal up to 1887 and it still has the prerogative to impeach cabinet secretaries. Today presidents are quite free to select and deselect cabinet secretaries, at least institutionally, but no research has been undertaken on the informal restrictions to a president's ability to dismiss cabinet secretaries. This type of limitation to ministerial dismissal was also present in Israel, at least until 1981. Kenig and Barnea (2015) tell us that up to 1960, Israeli prime ministers did not have the legal authority to dismiss their cabinet ministers. The Knesset changed this provision and in 1962 allowed the PM to dismiss cabinet members in cases of blatant violation of the collective responsibility principle that is so intrinsic to parliamentary governments. Only in 1981 did the Prime Minister in Israel gain the right to freely replace ministers (Kenig and Barnea 2015).

Conclusion

Cabinet change can be a very useful tool, albeit one that should be used carefully. As suggested by Thomas (1998: 200): "A smooth reshuffle will enhance the prime minister's reputation while a bungled exercise will damage it." In this chapter I have discussed the relevant literature that explains two issues in cabinet politics: agency problems, and solutions to these problems. The agency problems fall rather coarsely into one of three large classes of problems: agency rent, moral hazard, and adverse selection. Solutions to these problems can be explored as careful ministerial selection and cabinet change.

There seems to be some confusion on the labels of agency problems, which emerge because principals delegate tasks to agents. In this book, I consider leaders delegating policy to cabinet ministers. The latter can shirk and not exert effort while doing their job. They can also have different policy preferences than their leaders, thus causing policy shifting. Unfortunately, leaders cannot really prevent these problems, as they happen due to partial or no observability of a minister's actions. As correctly argued by Dowding and Dumont (2015), the literature refers to these problems as moral hazard and adverse selection, even though these are actually quite different. Moral hazard is simply the risky behavior of agents caused by imperfections in their contract or some other aspects of their relationship with the principal. Adverse selection is caused by heterogeneous agents on relevant characteristics.

There are two points that I would like to make in this discussion. First, and also as correctly pointed out by Dowding and Dumont, these problems are not mutually exclusive. Adverse selection can cause shifting, but not all shifting is caused by adverse selection. Moreover, the latter can be solved and yet there is potential for shirking. This leads to the second point: it is quite difficult to identify the cause of the agency problem. Indeed, a policy implemented by a minister that differs from the ideal point of a leader in that policy space might be caused by adverse selection, shifting, or shirking. Most studies of cabinet change fail to make this important distinction.

Perhaps this is not a serious problem, at least not at the level of politics as it is practiced rather than studied. Of course, all ministers will go through a rigorous selection process before they are called to the cabinet. However, the process of selection is strongly restricted by political institutions that determine the size of the pool of ministers, as well as their heterogeneity in relevant characteristics, such as competence. But all selection processes are faulty and agents might 'slip through the cracks.' Once a minister is in the cabinet, a leader can observe only the outcome of their actions and learn about their abilities and preferences over policy. The problem is that, at this point, ministers are already in the cabinet, and solving any agency problems requires a reshuffle or a dismissal. Again, political institutions will determine to what extent leaders can use cabinet change to eliminate agency problems. Moreover, cabinet change might become a problem itself, as it drains the pool of potential ministers.

The model developed in the next chapter is also based on the premise of delegation. The latter, however, presents an opportunity to show competence and loyalty, and based on their realizations, a leader will decide whether to keep the minister in the cabinet or replace her. In other words, cabinet change in this book is not a necessary a tool to solve agency problems as discussed in this chapter, but a tool to enhance a leader's prospects of staying in office. It does so by keeping ministers who help provide public goods, when public goods are necessary; or by firing ministers who have the ability to provide these goods, as these ministers are potential challengers. Thus, cabinet change is a tool to minimize internal and external threats that leaders face.

Notes

1 Cabinet secretaries in the US are also important because they are high on the list for the presidential line of succession; although the top of the list is occupied by the vice president, the speaker of the house of representatives, and the president *pro tempore* of the Senate, the secretaries of state, treasury, and defense, and the attorney general are next in line.
2 www.defense.gov/About-DoD (accessed Jan. 24, 2016).
3 http://history.defense.gov/Multimedia/Biographies/ArticleView/tabid/8347/Article/571281/william-s-cohen.aspx (accessed May 30, 2012).
4 Alan Cowell, 'Senior Labour insiders want secret ballot on Brown,' Jan. 6, 2010. www.nytimes.com/2010/01/07/world/europe/07britain.html
5 'Hoon and Hewitt letter in full,' Jan. 6, 2010. www.politics.co.uk/feature/legal-and-constitutional/hoon-and-hewitt-letter-in-full-$1351593.htm
6 United States Senate, '1801–1850. June 24, 1834: First cabinet rejection,' www.senate.gov/artandhistory/history/minute/First_Cabinet_Rejection.htm

3 Political survival and cabinet change

Introduction

> Prime Ministers need to be good butchers; they must be able to dispense with the services of even their closest colleagues when required.
> Graham Thomas, in *Prime Minister and Cabinet Today* (1998: 7)

The previous chapter discussed the literature on cabinet politics and specifically on cabinet change. In delegating tasks to their ministers, leaders open an opportunity for ministerial agency. Leaders anticipate these problems and implement rigorous ministerial selection procedures to eliminate problematic ministers. Nevertheless, all selection processes are faulty, and undesirable ministers might 'slip through the cracks.' Once this has taken place and the cabinet is formed and active, leaders use reshuffles and dismissals to eliminate agency problems. The literature has explored these issues very thoroughly in parliamentary democracies, and to a less extent in presidential ones. Cabinet politics in nondemocracies remains slightly neglected, although new research has begun to explore cabinet politics in autocracies.

My goal in this chapter is to develop a model of cabinet change that is applicable to all forms of political systems, democracies and nondemocracies, presidential and parliamentary systems, as well as systems with different party organizations and specific types of autocracies. The unifying theme across political regimes is the combination of a minister's competence and loyalty and her leader's ambition and need to hold on to power. Under different settings, these factors will produce cabinet change. As I will show in a moment, the predictions of the model can be quite counterintuitive and yet very significant for our understanding of cabinet change.

A model of cabinet change

The citizens of a nation care about three aspects of government performance: ministerial competence, policy positions, and policy coherence. In the game we consider a simplified government composed of a leader (l) and a single minister (m_1).[1] The incumbent government implements policy and generates public goods.

From these outcomes the citizens learn about the ability of government ministers, the overall policy position of the government, and the level of policy discord between the leader and her ministers. The leader decides whether to replace the existing minister m_1 with a new minister m_2. By doing so, the leader wipes away part of her government's legacy – whether it be good or bad – and replaces the known minister with a relatively unknown quantity. After a cabinet change, the incumbent leader faces reselection by first the party and then by the public. Although leaders might care about competence, policy, and policy coherence, we assume that their predominant concern is to retain office. Since our focus is comparative, we examine how institutional differences affect this interplay among cabinet changes, party retention, and elections.

Ministers are responsible for running and managing their ministries. Managing a department, however, is not an easy task. Robert Reich, secretary of labor during the Clinton administration, described his feelings after an initial meeting with Lynn Martin, George H. W. Bush's outgoing secretary of labor (Reich 1997: 43–44): "As I walk out of [Lynn Martin's] office it suddenly strikes me: I'm on my own from here on. There's no training manual, no course, no test drive for a cabinet secretary." George Dern, US secretary of war from 1933 to 1936, explained his position as a new member of the cabinet as follows:

> I was like a sea captain who finds himself standing on the deck of a ship that he has never seen before. I did not know the mechanism of my ship; I did not know my officers – even by sight – and I had no acquaintance with the crew.
>
> (Fenno 1959: 225)

All ministers differ in their managerial capacity. Competent, capable ministers are likely to produce high levels of public goods and run their bureaucracies efficiently. In contrast, less competent ministers risk more scandals, failed policies, and wasted resources. We assume that all politicians have a level of ministerial competence a, which, for convenience, is assumed to be distributed according to a standard uniform distribution. As ministers serve in office, the citizens update their beliefs about the ministers' competence. Those who run their office well and produce many public goods are revealed to be competent; therefore, they are likely to produce more public goods in the future. Although this updating could be explicitly modeled, for simplicity we assume that the voters learn ministerial and leader competence. The relative benefit of a competent government is α. Thus, if the expected competence of the leader and minister are a_l and a_{m1}, then citizens receive benefits worth $\alpha(\lambda a_l + (1-\lambda)a_{m1})$, where $\lambda \in [1/2, 1]$ reflects the importance of the leader relative to a minister. If a member of the government is replaced, either through a reshuffle, internal party deposition, or an election, then the competence of the new cabinet member is unknown. Until they have their abilities revealed, untried cabinet members have expected competence of $1/2$, since their ability is uniformly distributed on $[0, 1]$.

40 Political survival and cabinet change

The model assumes that ministers can be dismissed by the leader. Without any doubt, this is usually the case across current political systems. This characteristic, however, is the culmination of particular national historical processes, which suggests that ministers were not always subject to the will of their leaders. In Britain, during the early years of cabinet formation in the 1830s, the prime minister did not even have the power to appoint ministers (Thomas 1998). In the United States, the Senate had the power to protect a secretary from unilateral presidential action. Only until 1887 was the US president able to fully control the dismissal of cabinet secretaries. Yet, the US Senate still has the power to impeach them. This power has been materialized at least on one occasion, when Secretary of War William W. Belknap was impeached in 1876. The Senate initiated proceedings against two other secretaries: Attorney General Harry M. Daugherty, due to his involvement in the Teapot Dome scandal of 1922, and Secretary of the Treasury Andrew Mellon, due to conflicts of interests (Cohen 1988). Both were forced to resign by their respective presidents.

Politicians and citizens care about policy. Each person has an ideal point z_i on the closed interval -1 to 1. We assume that the citizens are evenly distributed over this interval such that the median voter has ideal point $z_v = 0$. The incumbent party is assumed to be on the right wing, with its members uniformly distributed on the unit interval $[0, 1]$. The median party decision maker is located at $z_R = 1/2$. By analogous construction, the opposition party contains party members with ideal points between -1 and 0.

The effective policy of the government depends upon the preferences of its members. If the leader has ideal point z_l and the minister has ideal point z_{m1}, then the effective government policy is $\frac{z_l + z_{m1}}{2}$. We assume quadratic preferences such that a person with ideal point z_i receives a policy payoff $-p\left(z_i - \frac{z_l + z_{m1}}{2}\right)^2$ of from the implementation of government policy, where $p > 0$ is the salience of policy position.

The effective government policy position reflects internal cabinet bargains. It also requires implementation by multiple members of government. Even if both the leader and minister agree to a common policy, each will try to shift it toward their ideal point at the implementation stage. On average these shifts will cancel out. However, the discord created by their attempts to manipulate policy according to their ideal points leads to policy inefficiency. Voters dislike divided cabinets for precisely this reason. The loss from policy discord is $\sigma(z_l + z_{m1})^2$; the greater the disagreement within the cabinet, the greater the cost of policymaking and the less efficiently policy is implemented. The parameter σ reflects the salience of policy discord.

The citizens and party elites care about competence, policy, and discord payoffs. In addition, we assume that party elites receive office benefits related to their standing in the party. Specifically, they receive a payoff of φ from remaining privileged members of the ruling party. Leaders are predominantly office seeking and they seek to maximize their tenure in office.

In this model, political leaders face retention decisions by both the party and the masses. In democratic systems, the mass retention decision takes the form of an election in which the voters compare the expected policy, policy discord, and competence of the incumbent party with that of the opposition. Elections often also occur in nondemocratic systems, although they are rarely free and fair. This does not mean that the incumbent is completely free from the risk of deposition by the masses. Rather, this means that it is much harder for the masses to depose the incumbent and so they are less likely to take such action unless conditions are dire. However, revolutions do occur. We refer to this stage as an election by the voters, although in nondemocratic systems it might entail protest and rebellion. To model the extent to which the incumbent is beholden to the masses, we assume that citizens pay a cost $D - \chi$ to replace the incumbent, where D is a fixed cost that reflects the overall difficulty of removing the incumbent and χ is a random variable that reflects variations in these costs and the relative benefits of the incumbent and opposition on dimensions other than those explicitly modeled. The variable χ is drawn from a distribution $F(x)$ at the time of the election, such that $F(x) = \Pr(\chi < x)$. The voters base their decision to retain the incumbent on the relative benefits they expect to receive from the incumbent relative to the opposition, and the cost of removing the leader. The decision of the median voter characterizes the decision of a majority of the voters and therefore the outcome of the electoral stage depends upon the median voter's decision.

Leaders can also be deposed by the ruling party. In democratic systems, this takes the form of internal party leadership battles, which often entail elections within the party membership or within the parliamentary members of the party. The equivalent mechanism within nondemocracies is a coup. The members of the party can replace the incumbent leader with another leading politician from the party. The decision is made by members of the party elite. We assume that the median member of this group has policy ideal point $z_R = 1/2$. The party elites pay a cost $\Lambda - \mu$ to depose the incumbent, where Λ represents the average cost of internal deposition and μ is a random variable which represents the variance in this cost: $E[\mu] = 0$ and μ is distributed $G(x) = \Pr(\mu < x)$.

In addition to the cost associated with replacing leaders, party elites potentially jeopardize their access to privileges within the party when leader change occurs. New leaders can reorganize the hierarchy of the party, promoting some members and demoting others.

To capture this risk, suppose that there are S potential candidates for each elite party position and that these elite party members receive benefits φ. If the party decision is decided by a small group of elite party members, then φ is likely to be large. However, if the mass membership votes, few of these members receive perks and so φ is small. Bueno de Mesquita et al. (2003) refer to S as the selectorate, the pool of potential supporters from which a winning coalition is drawn. Here the situation is slightly more complex, as the leader requires support at both the party and mass levels. Since a new leader reorganizes the party to promote her friends, the existing party elite cannot be certain of being included in the new leader's inner circle. If they are excluded, they lose the rewards of being an elite influential member of the party. Since there are S potential candidates for the each elite position, the expected benefits for the existing party elite under a new leader is φ/S. Naturally, the nature of internal party competition shapes S. In a parliamentary system, senior party member are often restricted to the party's members of parliament, so S is comparatively small. In presidential systems, party elites are drawn from a wider pool, and so S is larger. The pool from which the elite is drawn can also vary greatly in nondemocratic systems. For instance, in military juntas, elite membership is typically restricted to a small number of senior military officers. In contrast, S is much larger in a corrupt electoral system, as virtually anyone can, with a very small probability, be promoted to executive office.

In this model, voters have the power to remove parties from government, whereas the party leadership has the power to replace a leader. A leader has the power to remove any of her cabinet ministers. Since each decision depends on a large number of parameters, the analysis is relatively complicated. Therefore, the following sections begin by considering some limiting cases.

Autocracies

The first limiting case assumes that elections are noncompetitive. This is representative of political systems best represented by autocracies, such as military juntas, monarchies, and corrupt electoral regimes. In this case, the key assumption is that the voters' cost of deposing a leader is so large that the probability of being reelected to office is very close to 1.[2] Thus, a leader dismisses a minister only when it reduces the probability of internal party deposition.[3] The probability of internal deposition depends, partly, on the elite party members' access to privileges. Naturally, if elite party members do not remove the leader, they will enjoy a stream of benefits with certainty. However, if they decide to remove the leader, then their access to these benefits is probabilistic. The probability depends on the size of the pool of potential elite party members for each elite position, which we denoted S. The size of the pool, and therefore loyalty toward a leader, varies across autocracies. For instance, in a military junta, elite membership is limited to a small number of senior military officers, whereas in systems with corrupt elections the pool is much larger. Since S is small in political systems ruled by a military junta, there is not much loyalty toward a leader. This is because any new leader faces the same pool of potential junta members. Systems based on rigged elections have a larger pool of potential elite party members. Therefore, the probability that these members receive benefits from a new administration is relatively small. In turn, leaders in these systems have more loyal elite party members.

Under these assumptions, and after some algebraic manipulation, a leader deposes a minister if $\alpha\left(\frac{1}{2}\right)(2\lambda-1)(2a_m-1)-\frac{1}{8}(4\sigma-p)(2z_l-1)(2z_m-1)>0$.[4] Recall that a minister's competence is a random variable uniformly distributed between 0 and 1. Clearly, this expression decreases as the minister's competence a_m declines. This suggests that, *in autocracies, leaders tend to keep incompetent ministers in their cabinet in order to increase their own tenure in office.* As an illustration, suppose that competence in the provision of goods is the only factor that determines whether a party will depose a leader. Thus, a leader deposes her minister if $\left(\frac{1}{2}\right)(2\lambda-1)(2a_m-1)>0$. Evidently, if a_m is below the average (i.e., 1/2), then the expression on the left is negative, which indicates that a leader will keep a minister who performs poorly. In contrast, the leader replaces ministers whose production is above average to reduce the threat from internal rivals.

Policy and policy discord also influence internal party competition and so affect turnover of cabinet members. Effective government policy depends upon the position of both the minister and the leader. On the basis of policy preferences, the leader enhances her position if the effective government policy is close to the party elite median position (0.5). Therefore, if the leader is on the left wing of the party, a right-wing minister will help her survive the internal party selection process. However, retaining ministers from the opposite wing of the party increases policy discord. Policy and policy discord have opposing effects on the incentive to dismiss a minister – which one dominates depends upon the relative salience of the two factors p and σ.

Incompetence in the cabinet: Ethiopia and Iraq

Since leaders keep incompetent ministers in the cabinet, these governments are associated with poor performance. Robert Mugabe and his cronies have ruled Zimbabwe at least since 1987 in spite of a failing economy with an inflation rate in the millions of percentage points. Henry Kifordu (2015) has documented the tenure of cabinet ministers in Nigeria who, though accused of corruption, manage to hold on to office in spite of the weakening condition of the country.

The strategic selection of incompetent ministers in autocracies is well illustrated by a passage by Ryszard Kapuscinski in his book about Haile Selassie, emperor of Ethiopia for forty-three years:

> The King of Kings preferred bad ministers. And the King of Kings preferred them because he liked to appear in a favorable light by contrast. . . . Instead of one sun, fifty would be shining, and everyone would pay homage to a privately chosen planet. . . . There can be only one sun.
>
> (Kapuscinski 1989: 33)

Haile Selassie's strategy did not promote the welfare of the people. However, it enabled him to survive for forty-three years as emperor until he was overtaken by decrepitude.

44 *Political survival and cabinet change*

In 1995, former US secretary of state James A. Baker III reflected on the survival of Saddam Hussein in political office following his defeat in the 1991 Gulf War (Baker 1995: 442): "To this day he remains in control of his country, while the administration that defeated him in a textbook case of diplomatic and military skill is no longer in power." In spite of the clear defeat suffered at the hands of allied forces in 1991, Tariq Aziz and Saddam Hussein, as well as many of Hussein's relatives, such as Ali Hassan al-Majid, otherwise known as 'Chemical Ali,' managed to rule Iraq until 2003, when the Iraqi government was toppled by an invasion led by the United States.

This fear of internal deposition in autocracies can be reduced and more competent ministers retained only if there is a commitment mechanism whereby ministers can be excluded from holding the top job. In this regard, many leaders pick a second in command who is for some reason ineligible or unlikely to become leader. For instance, Saddam Hussein of Iraq chose Tariq Aziz as his second in command. Aziz was the international spokesman of the regime, and as such had the difficult task of defending his leader's policies. According to Krasno and Sutterlin (2003: 109), during negotiations with the United Nations, Aziz played a prominent role where "his competency, linguistic fluency, and total loyalty to Saddam Hussein were known quantities before [Executive Chairman of the United Nations Special Commission (UNSCOM)] Rolf Ekeus, and subsequently Richard Butler, came face-to-face with him on UNSCOM matters." Evidently, Aziz's background could not be matched by any other Iraqi minister. Nevertheless, since Aziz, originally named Mikhail Yuhanna, was an Assyrian Christian, he would have had problems as a leader of a predominantly Muslim country. In the Byzantine empire, it was common for the emperor to employ eunuchs as administrators. The emperor could not be 'spoiled,' which meant that eunuchs were not political rivals. The empire benefited from the retention of high-quality ministers (Norwich 1997).

Presidential democracies

The second limiting case assumes that party elites find it difficult to depose a leader. This is representative of democratic presidential systems, where leaders face little prospects of internal party deposition during their administration. In this case, the key assumption is that the party's cost of deposing a leader (Λ) is large so that the probability of being internally deposed is very close to 0.[5] Therefore, the leader decides whether to make changes to the cabinet on the basis of maximizing electoral support. In particular, she dismisses a cabinet member if the probability of reelection with the new minister is larger than the probability of reelection with the original minister.[6] Under these assumptions, and after some algebraic manipulation, a leader deposes her minister if

$$-\left(\tfrac{1}{2}\right)\alpha(1-\lambda)(2a_m - 1) - \tfrac{1}{12}p\left(6z_l z_m - 3z_l + 3z_m^2 - 1\right) + \tfrac{1}{13}\sigma\left(3z_l - 6z_l z_m + 3z_m^2 - 1\right) > 0.$$

It is worthwhile separating this expression into its constituent parts. Leaders are relatively immune from internal party deposition. Thus, in terms of competence, they replace their cabinet members when $-\left(\frac{1}{2}\right)\alpha(1-\lambda)(2a_m - 1) > 0$. This expression is decreasing in ministerial ability, which implies that *leaders in presidential democracies keep capable ministers and replace those who perform poorly*. A competent cabinet enables the leader's party to win the election. Democratic presidential systems promote the retention of competent cabinets, although the difficulty of internal party replacement makes it difficult to replace poorly performing leaders.

Policy and policy discord also affect cabinet changes. On the basis of policy, leaders increase their chances of survival when their cabinet has a minister from the moderate wing of the party. This is true whether the leader is a moderate ($z_l = 0$) or an extremist ($z_l = 1$). However, offsetting this effect is policy discord. Since voters dislike policy disagreements within the cabinet, leaders have an incentive to retain ministers with similar policy positions to their own. If the leader is moderate ($z_l = 0$), then policy and policy discord motives converge to reinforce each other. The leader retains a moderate minister and replaces those from the extreme of the party. If the leader is more extremist ($z_l = 1$), then the policy and policy discord incentives are contradictory. In this case, the leader is more likely to retain a moderate minister if the policy effect is more salient (σ small) and more likely to retain a fellow extremist as minister if the discord effect is more significant (σ large).

Competent cabinets: the US and Mexico

The theory suggests that incompetent ministers are quickly replaced in democratic presidential systems. The Teapot Dome scandal in the United States presents a perfect example of this type of dismissal. In the early 1920s, the Department of the Navy transferred oil reserves at Teapot Dome, Wyoming, and Elk Hills, California, to the Department of the Interior. The secretary of the interior, Albert Bacon Fall, leased the properties to two businessmen without competitive bidding, thus causing a Senate investigation. Fall was found guilty and was sentenced to one year in prison. Subsequently, the secretary of the navy, Edwin Denby was removed from the cabinet. In the words of Mark Sullivan (Fenno 1959: 224): "[Denby's] record demonstrated him to be ludicrously unfit for his post. The man merited neither tears nor prosecution. He deserved to be laughed out of the Cabinet."

In order to avoid dismissing an incompetent minister, presidents often seek capable and qualified secretaries in the first place. According to Fenno (1959: 35), US president Warren G. Harding stated in his acceptance speech that "[our] vision includes more than a Chief Executive; we believe in a Cabinet of the highest capacity, equal to the responsibilities which our system contemplates."

The cabinet assembled by President Kennedy and his team best reflects the emphasis on competence at the top of government. This is the subject of David Halberstam's classic book *The Best and the Brightest* (1972), which begins with

46 *Political survival and cabinet change*

the description of an encounter between President-elect Kennedy and Robert A. Lovett, a "representative of the best of the breed." The purpose of this December 1960 meeting was to recruit Lovett as a cabinet member. Although Kennedy failed to do so, both men discussed potential secretaries for the Kennedy administration. By the time Kennedy took office in 1961, he had assembled a cabinet that was composed of the best America had to offer, at least according to Halberstam. Robert McNamara, who became secretary of defense, was the president of Ford Motor Company. McGeorge Bundy, national security adviser, was dean of the Harvard Faculty of Arts and Sciences. Dean Rusk, who became secretary of state, was president of the Rockefeller Foundation. As described by Halberstam, members of the Kennedy cabinet (Halberstam 1972: 41): "Carried with them an exciting sense of American elitism, a sense that the best men had been summoned forth from the country to harness this dream to a new American nationalism."

When Robert Rubin resigned as secretary of the treasury in 1999, President Clinton announced that Lawrence Summers would replace him. Clinton described Summers as "brilliant, able, and deeply" knowledgeable. Clinton added that "rarely has any individual been so well-prepared" to take over the Department (Mitchell and Buerkle 1999). In Mexico, during the initial phases of the transition to democracy, President Carlos Salinas de Gortari selected a cabinet that consisted of academic stars (Preston and Dillon 2004). This team led Mexico to its first democratic election since the 1920s and negotiated the North American Free Trade Agreement (NAFTA).

Parliamentary democracies

The analysis of parliamentary democracies is more complicated because leaders face both internal and external threats of deposition. Leaders seeking to remain in power must trade off between these competing risks. For instance, retaining competent ministers helps win elections. However, it also increases the risk of internal party deposition. Leaders therefore face a dilemma: to remove a competent minister in order to prevent internal deposition but increase the prospects of electoral defeat, or to keep the minister and risk deposition by the party. Since there are competing incentives in the case of parliamentary democracies, the section begins by focusing on the impact of leader and minister competence.

Figure 3.1 plots the probability that the voters retain the incumbent party as a function of government competence and whether a cabinet change has occurred. The horizontal axis refers to the competence of the original minister, a_{m1}. There are six lines in the graph. The graphs are constructed assuming F() and G() are standard normal distributions, $\Lambda = 0$, $D = 0$, $\lambda = 3/4$, $\alpha = 2, \sigma = 0$, $p = 1$, $z_1 = 1/2$ and $z_{m1} = 1/2$. The three upward sloping lines correspond to reelection probabilities if no dismissal occurs and the election is contested by a government composed of the original leader and minister ($F(Q_1)$). The three different types of lines correspond to different levels of leader competence. Specifically, the black solid lines refer to the case of an incompetent incumbent leader ($a_1 = 0$);

Political survival and cabinet change 47

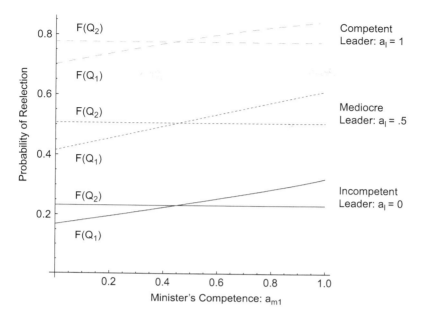

Figure 3.1 A leader's probability of reelection

the red dotted lines refer to a moderately competent incumbent leader ($a_1 = 1/2$); and the blue dashed lines refer to a highly competent incumbent ($a_1 = 1$). The flat lines in Figure 3.1 correspond to electoral probabilities if the leader dismisses the minister (i.e., $F(Q_2)$). These lines are flat because the new minister's competence does not contribute to the government's quality at the time of the election, since it is (relatively) unknown.

As expected, the voters reelect more competent governments, so the blue dashed lines are higher than the red dotted lines, which are higher than the solid black ones. The reelection probabilities when the minister is retained and when the minister is replaced are equal at $a_{m1} = 1/2$, as this is the expected competence of any new minister.

A key component of the party's decision to retain or replace its leader is "electability." Competent leaders with competent ministers are more likely to be reelected. It is therefore not surprising that competent leaders are more likely to be retained by their party. This is shown in Figures 3.2 and 3.3. These figures plot the probability that the leader is retained by the party depending upon whether the leader has retained her original minister or replaced her with a new one (ρ_1 or ρ_2, respectively). The latter case, in which the known minister is replaced by a relatively unknown minister, corresponds to the flat lines in the figure. The figures use the same legend as Figure 3.1. When the leader retains the minister, the probability that the party keeps its leader (ρ_1) decreases in the competence of the minister. This is demonstrated by the downward sloping lines in Figures 3.2

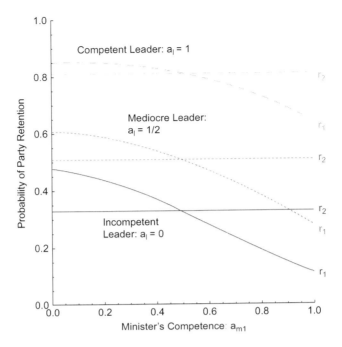

Figure 3.2 A leader's probability of party retention: no private goods

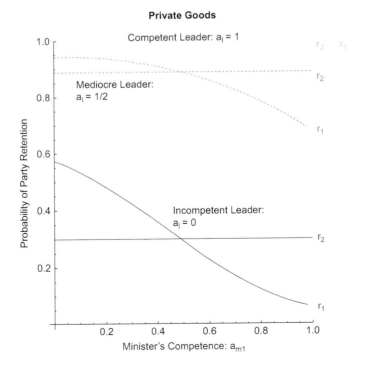

Figure 3.3 A leader's probability of party retention: private goods

Political survival and cabinet change 49

and 3.3. Competent ministers make attractive leaders. To survive the party retention step, leaders have incentives to remove competent ministers and retain incompetent ones. This was the incentive that dominated in the autocratic case. Yet, retaining incompetent ministers reduces the party's electability. To increase the party's electability, the leader should retain competent ministers.

Electability is a key factor in the party's leadership decision. Nevertheless, it is not the only significant factor. The election procedure within the party affects the party's retention decision, and therefore the leader's decision to dismiss a cabinet member. The members of the party who pick leaders often have important positions within the party; and they might lose the perks associated with their positions should a new party leader reorganize the party. In the model, these perks are worth φ. There are S potential candidates to fill each party seat. When the perks are valuable, the party members who receive them are reluctant to pick a new leader. Figures 3.2 and 3.3 show the difference these private goods make. Figure 3.2 assumes the party-level decision makers receive few private goods, $\varphi = 0$. In contrast, the influential party-level decision makers in Figure 3.3 receive substantial private goods, $\varphi = 5$ and $S = 2$.

Party election procedures affect leader retention and cabinet change. The British Conservative Party has used a variety of rules to choose party leaders. Prior to 1965 there was no routinized election procedure. Rather, the leader was chosen by a consensus of the party elite. In 1965 the selection rule was changed to allow for the election of the party leader by the Conservative Members of Parliament. It was through the use of this rule that Margaret Thatcher challenged and defeated the incumbent party leader Edward Heath in 1975. Having become prime minister in 1979, she was herself deposed by the party in 1990. In 1998 the party further reformed its rules such that the party leader is now chosen by the mass membership of the party.

The actual electoral procedures used by the Conservatives are complicated and can involve numerous runoff elections (see Heppell 2008: appendix for a full description). However, within the context of the model, the selection rule in the Conservative Party shows a clear progression. Since 1998, the selection has been made by the mass membership of the party. Few of these individuals receive private benefits or perks due to their standing in the party. As a result, they risk little when they replace the party leader. This case is illustrated in Figure 3.2. Incompetent leaders are removed with a high probability. Government electability is thus the dominant incentive in the choice of party leader. In the last ten years, the Conservatives have had four party leaders, and perceptions of low electability have precipitated their removal (Heppell 2008).

It is important to note that in the 120 years prior to the rules change in 1965, the Conservatives have had only ten party leaders, and the party leadership has been contested only three times (in 1911, 1923, and 1957). In each of these three cases, the contest followed the resignation of the sitting party leader. This situation is more reminiscent of Figure 3.3. Party elites chose the leader. These elites enjoyed the benefits and perks of high office. If they switched party leader, then these elites risked jeopardizing their access to perks. This made it easier for the party leader to survive, as can be seen in the comparison of Figures 3.2 and 3.3. In the second figure, moderately capable leaders ($a_1 = 1/2$) have high party

50 Political survival and cabinet change

survival probabilities, while in the absence of private goods their survival rate in the party competition is around 50 percent. This is not to say that electability was irrelevant in the second circumstance. In fact, low competence leaders stand little chance of surviving even when the leadership choice is made by privileged party insiders. Although these insiders jeopardize their private benefits by replacing the leader, they will lose many of these perks anyway if the party is defeated at the election. Although the pre-1965 period did not experience the leadership contests observed over the last ten years, prime ministers with failed policies resigned. For example, Anthony Eden and Neville Chamberlain resigned after the failed foreign policies of the Suez invasion of Egypt in 1956 and the appeasement of Nazi Germany in the late 1930s, respectively.

To survive, leaders need to be retained by the party and reelected by the voters. Ministerial competence affects these decisions in opposite ways. Whether leaders replace their cabinet members depends upon whether or not it enhances their overall survival. This decision is shown in Figures 3.4 and 3.5. These graphs plot the overall probability of the leader surviving if she retains her minister minus the probability of her survival if she dismisses a minister: $p_1 F(Q_1) - p_2 F(Q_2)$. If $p_1 F(Q_1) - p_2 F(Q_2)$ is positive, then the leader retains her minister. However, when it is negative, she replaces the minister.

Figures 3.4 and 3.5 show both similarities and differences. In the first case, the members of the party choosing the leader receive few perks and so the leader

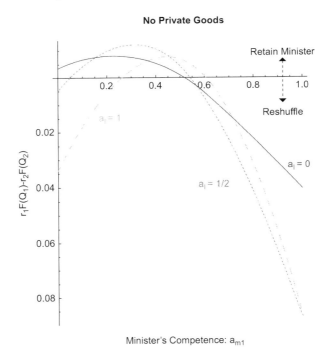

Figure 3.4 Probability of cabinet change: no private goods

Political survival and cabinet change 51

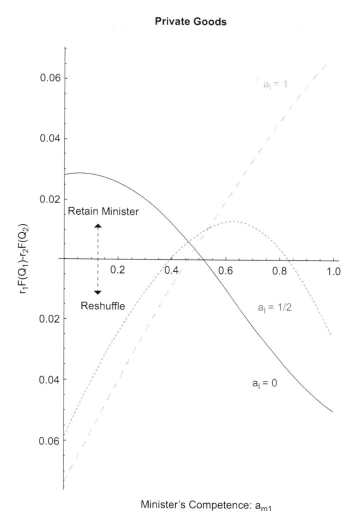

Figure 3.5 Probability of cabinet change: private goods

is not advantaged in the leadership election. As a result, all leaders replace highly competent ministers to prevent them from becoming rivals in the party competition. Nonetheless, leaders also have an incentive to replace highly incompetent leaders to improve the party's electoral prospects. Hence, leaders retain those ministers with moderate ability. These ministers present relatively small leadership threats and yet are not disastrous for the party's electability. The range of ministers that a leader retains depends upon the leader's ability. The more capable the leader becomes, the less she has to worry about rivals and the more she can focus on improving the party's electability. As can be seen in Figure 3.4, as the competence of the leader improves, the range of ministers that the leader retains shifts to the right, which means that she retains more competent ministers.

In Figure 3.5, the incumbent leader is advantaged in the party election because of the private goods that internal party decision makers receive. This advantage indicates that the party leader has less to fear from internal party rivals, and so *the range of ministers that each leader retains shifts to the right*. This shift toward retaining more competent ministers is most dramatic for more competent leaders. The party election advantage that accrues from private goods is small for the least competent type of leader, since under such a leader the party elites are likely to lose their perks anyway at the main election.

Beyond the big changes in 1965 and 1998, the Conservatives in Britain have tinkered with their party electoral rules on a number of occasions. Usually, these changes have followed in the wake of perceived failures using the previous rule. Each of the rules faces a tradeoff. Opening the leadership election to the mass party membership made it easier to replace a poorly performing leader, which is good for both the party's electability and performance in office. However, such gains come at increasing the incentives for party leaders to stymie the careers of potential rivals. Naturally, this reduces the average quality of cabinets, which at the same time reduces party electability and performance. There is significant variation in party rules both within and across parliamentary systems (Weller 1994). For instance, the British Labour Party allows about 4 times more people to participate in leadership elections than the Conservative Party. Shifting the party's leadership election rules emphasizes one benefit at the expense of the other. However, it cannot simultaneously promote the ease of leader removal and the retention of competent ministers.

Dismissing rivals: India, Malawi, and Malaysia

In most parliamentary systems, the cabinet is the pool of future prime ministers. Often, cabinet ministers wait for their turn to become prime ministers. However, highly competent ministers may not have incentives to wait and therefore can become serious threats to a leader who is not prepared to voluntarily give up her position as national leader. This can have deadly consequences. On the one hand, leaders who do not depart voluntarily may end up in prison or in exile, to say the least. On the other hand, and for this very reason, leaders might use a number of tools to prevent internal depositions; this includes ruthless cabinet changes and reshuffles, but also the imprisonment of cabinet members and even the creation of new political parties.

In India, both Jawaharlal Nehru and Indira Gandhi manipulated the tenure of their cabinet ministers in order to achieve government stability and control over their parties. Prime Minister Gandhi in fact opted for breaking up the party when she faced an internal challenge posed by a former cabinet minister who was favored to become president. According to Sisson:

> In her efforts to mobilize support and undercut her opposition within the party, Mrs. Gandhi employed a strategy of frequent ministerial turnover and

even more frequent reallocation of ministerial responsibilities. In contrast to the pattern of ministerial egress through policy difference or death that characterized the Nehru cabinets, Mrs. Gandhi's cabinets have been reconstituted for the purpose of augmenting prime ministerial power.

(Sisson 1981: 151)

The tenure of Mahathir bin Mohamad, the longest serving prime minister of Malaysia, is one of the best illustrations of a successful solution to the dilemma of internal depositions. Mahathir ruled multi-ethnic, multicultural Malaysia from 1981 to 2003. Anwar Ibrahim, a rising star and leader of the youth section of Mahathir's party, the United Malays National Organization (UMNO), was a key member of the cabinet. Ibrahim had been in charge of the Ministries of Culture, Youth and Sports in 1983, Agriculture in 1984, Education in 1986, and Finance in 1991; and he seemed to be the natural successor to Mahathir, who promoted him to deputy prime minister in 1993. In 1997, Ibrahim acted as acting prime minister for two months while Mahathir was abroad during a two-month leave. This proved to be a unique opportunity for Ibrahim. According to Hwang (2003): "Anwar's two month tenure as acting prime minister proved him a capable leader and seemed to confirm his position as Malaysia's prime-minister-in-waiting."

In spite of the public displays of political affection, there were important differences between Mahathir and Ibrahim. According to Hwang (2003), Mahathir had started to contain Ibrahim's political advances, whether real or imagined, since 1995, when Mahathir prevented Ibrahim's allies from becoming part of the cabinet during a reshuffle. After the 1997 financial crisis in Asia, then-Finance Minister Ibrahim favored restrictive economic policies while Mahathir pushed for more expansionary ones in order to benefit his allies in both the marketplace and UMNO.

As tensions between the two leaders increased, thousands of letters accusing Ibrahim of being a homosexual and sodomite began to circulate across Malaysia and during party assemblies. On September 2, 1998, Ibrahim was detained on charges of corruption and sodomy and thrown into prison for six years. Mahathir had managed to extend his tenure in office by dismissing and literally sending to prison a potential challenger. According to Hwang:

Mahathir effectively pre-empted any possible challenge from him by sacking [Anwar] from the ruling party as well as the government.... By doing this, Mahathir not only eliminated any prospect of Anwar's challenge to his national leadership but also demonstrated that he could guarantee the protection of his cronies.

(Hwang 2003: 306)

Malawi also presents an excellent example of the strategic deposition of ministers in parliamentary systems. The country gained independence from Britain in 1964. As the country moved toward independence, Britain progressively introduced local politicians into the government structure. During this process, Hastings

Kamuzu Banda became the leading political figure in the country and its first prime minister. As leader of the Malawi Congress Party and prime minister, Banda surrounded himself with close allies and friends, many of whom had shared a cell with him when he was imprisoned in 1959. Several cabinet members turned out to be highly competent and popular both domestically and internationally. However, Banda had started to accumulate power within the cabinet by nominating ministers to trivial portfolios while he captured more important positions. A full cabinet was first installed in 1962. Shortly after, Banda dismissed his first cabinet minister. This produced strong reactions among other cabinet members, as Banda did not provide an explanation for the dismissal (it turned out that the dismissed minister was an alcoholic). In this context, Banda gave a speech at the airport upon his return from a meeting of the Organization of African Unity in 1964. According to Baker, Banda stated:

> [We will] have strange funny people here very soon, Ambassador from this country, Ambassador from that country, and they will be trying to corrupt people in the party, and they will be starting with Ministers and Members of the National Assembly. So I want you to be vigilant.
>
> (Baker 2001: 93)

This quickly prompted the cabinet ministers to try to stop Banda from concentrating more power. By September 1964, after failing to force Banda to agree to specific demands in regard to the allocation of cabinet positions, several cabinet ministers decided to depose him. Banda, however, preempted their action by dismissing them from the cabinet. Many of the former ministers were later persecuted, and most of them left the country. Banda remained as leader of Malawi until 1994.

Conclusion

Political leaders face both internal and external threats to their tenure as leaders. To survive, they must both win elections and prevent internal threats of deposition. This chapter explores how leaders strategically retain and fire ministers when confronted with these dual threats. Moreover, the analysis characterizes the types of behavior we expect to observe under different political institutions. It also allows us to make comparisons across these systems, as the composition of the cabinet is likely to have an impact on the provision of goods.

In autocratic systems elections are not fair. Therefore, the more salient threat to a leader's survival is from within a leader's own party or ruling coalition. Given that the salient threat is internal and not mass based, leaders take action to ameliorate the challenge posed by rivals. In particular, leaders remove highly competent leaders and retain those less able. By doing so, the leader not only places herself in a favorable light, but also keeps ministers who have little prospects of retaining ministerial power under alternative leadership, and so are loyal to her. On average, this results in poorer government performance. Autocratic governments are led by paranoid leaders and their incompetent but loyal ministers. Of course, this applies as long as leaders intend to stay in office, which is one of the central tenets of this book. However, in a few cases, autocratic leaders might consider abandoning power, which has consequences for performance. For instance, Mufti (2015) argues that caretaker and military governments in Pakistan do not care much for loyalty emanating from cabinet members because they are simply not interested in holding on to power.

In democratic presidential systems, the main threat for a leader's tenure is electoral defeat. Political parties typically find it hard to replace the president, at least compared with parliamentary systems. Given the low salience of internal threats of deposition, leaders focus on maximizing their chances of being reelected to office by the masses. To improve electability, they dismiss incompetent ministers and retain capable ones. This results in a larger provision of public goods and national wealth. However, while presidential systems encourage the promotion of capable ministers, there are limited mechanisms to remove poorly performing presidents.

Parliamentary systems provide a mechanism whereby the party can remove an incompetent leader. On the one hand, this increases the performance of a prime minister relative to a president, who is relatively immune from internal party deposition. On the other hand, since prime ministers realize they are at risk of being replaced by talented ministers, they might stunt the careers of such potential rivals. Hence, while parliamentary government makes it easier to remove poorly performing leaders, it does so at the cost of recruiting less capable ministers.

In terms of expected performance, presidential systems dominate autocratic ones. Presidents retain competent leaders and sack poorly performing ones, while autocrats do the opposite. Further, incompetent presidents are likely to be removed by the electorate, while poorly performing autocrats are not. While the party might remove such an autocrat, these party competitions are generally less competitive than mass elections. Further, the replacement pool is of low quality. The comparison between parliamentary and presidential systems is less clear. As we say in the discussion of party leadership election rules, making leader removal easier encourages the leader to dismiss cabinet members in order to reduce the internal party threat posed by capable ministers. Parliamentarianism improves prime ministerial quality but at the cost of lowering cabinet quality.

Appendix
Game theory model of cabinet change

Leaders, party elites, and voters play the following game.

Game

1. Performance: The leader (l) and minister ($m1$) govern. Everyone sees the policy positions as leader and minister and everyone learns about their abilities to produce public goods.
2. Cabinet Change: The leader decides whether to replace a minister. If she does so, then a new minister ($m2$) takes office. This untried minister has ideal point $z_{m2} \sim U[0, 1]$ and competence $a_{\pi 2} \sim U[0, 1]$.
3. Internal Party Competition: The party observes a random variable μ associated with the costs of deposing the incumbent. The party elite then decides whether to internally depose their leader at cost $\Lambda - \mu$. If they do so, then the minister (either $m1$ or $m2$) becomes leader. The new leader then draws another minister, m_3 from the pool of potential candidates. This untried minister has ideal point ($z_{m3} \sim U[0, 1]$ and competence $a_{m3} \sim U[0, 1]$).
4. Mass Political Competition: The voters observe a random variable χ and decide whether to retain the incumbent party or replace it with the opposition at a cost $D - \chi$.

Subgame perfect equilibrium

The following characterizes the subgame perfect equilibrium of the game by analyzing decision making at each stage of the game.

Cabinet change, internal party politics, and elections

Electoral decisions

The voters receive payoffs according to the expected competence, policy, and policy discord of the leaders of the party they elect. They also pay electoral costs if they replace the ruling party. Suppose the voters elect the opposition party. In this case, the opposition party leader and minister (represented by ol and om) form the government. The opposition's competence (a_{ol}, a_{om}) and policy positions (z_{ol}, z_{om}) are unknown. However, given their distribution, the median voter's expected payoff from electing the opposition is $\alpha \lambda E[a_{ol}] + \alpha(1 - \lambda)E[a_{om}] - E\left[p\left(\frac{z_{ol}+z_{om}}{2}\right)^2\right] - \sigma E[(z_{ol} - z_{om})^2] - D + \chi = \frac{\alpha}{2} - p \int_{-1}^{0}\int_{-1}^{0}\left(\frac{z_{ol}+z_{om}}{2}\right)^2 dz_{ol} \, dz_{om} - \sigma \int_{-1}^{0}\int_{-1}^{0}(z_{ol} - z_{om})^2 dz_{ol} \, dz_{om} - D + \chi = \frac{\alpha}{2} - \frac{7}{24}p - \frac{1}{6}\sigma - D + \chi$. The first term corresponds to the expected competence of an opposition government; the second term corresponds to the expected policy payoff; and the third term corresponds to the expected losses through policy discord. The final terms $(-D + \chi)$ relate to the cost of replacing the incumbent.

The voters' reward from retaining the incumbent depends upon their knowledge of the cabinet's ability and policy positions. If the original leader and minister comprise the cabinet, then their policy positions and competence are known (case 1). The median voter's payoff from retaining these known entities is therefore $\alpha(\lambda a_{al} + (1 - \lambda)a_{am1}) - E\left[p\left(\frac{z_l+z_{m1}}{2}\right)^2\right] - \sigma(z_l - z_{m1})^2$. These terms correspond to government competence, policy position, and policy discord. The voters retain the government if $\alpha(\lambda a_{al} + (1 - \lambda)a_{am1}) - E\left[p\left(\frac{z_l+z_{m1}}{2}\right)^2\right] - \sigma(z_l - z_{m1})^2 \geq \frac{\alpha}{2} - \frac{7}{24}p - \frac{1}{6}\sigma - D + \chi$. Given the distribution of χ, this occurs with probability $F(Q_1)$, where $Q_1 = \alpha(\lambda a_{al} + (1 - \lambda)a_{am1}) - E\left[p\left(\frac{z_l+z_{m1}}{2}\right)^2\right] - \sigma(z_l - z_{m1})^2 - \frac{\alpha}{2} + \frac{7}{24}p + \frac{1}{6}\sigma + D$.

If a shuffle or an internal party deposition has occurred, then the voters know comparatively less about the incumbent government. Suppose the leader has replaced a minister, but she has been retained by the party. At the election, the incumbent cabinet is composed of l and $m2$ (case 2). In this setting the leader's characteristics are known, but the minister's are relatively unknown. The median voter's payoff from retaining the incumbent is $\alpha\lambda a_l + \alpha(1 - \lambda)E[a_{m2}] - E\left[p\left(\frac{z_l+z_{m2}}{2}\right)^2\right] - \sigma E[(z_l - z_{m2})^2] = \alpha\lambda a_l + \alpha(1-\lambda)\frac{1}{2} - p\int_0^1\left(\frac{z_l+z_{m2}}{2}\right)^2 dz_{m2} - \sigma\int_0^1 (z_l - z_{m2})^2 dz_{m2} = \alpha(\lambda a_l + (1 - \lambda)\frac{1}{2}) - p(\frac{1}{4}z_l + \frac{1}{4}z_l^2 + \frac{1}{12}) - \sigma(z_l^2 - z_l + \frac{1}{3})$, where the terms correspond to competence, policy position, and policy discord, respectively. Therefore, the probability that the incumbent party wins the election is $F(Q_2)$, where $Q_2 = \alpha(\lambda a_l + (1 - \lambda)\frac{1}{2}) - p(\frac{1}{4}z_l + \frac{1}{4}z_l^2 + \frac{1}{12}) - \sigma(z_l^2 - z_l + \frac{1}{3}) - \frac{\alpha}{2} + \frac{7}{24}p + \frac{1}{6}\sigma + D$.

Suppose the party promotes the minister $m1$ to leader. This means that $m1$ picks a new (and therefore unknown) minister $m3$ (case 3). The median voter's payoff from retaining this government is $\alpha\lambda m_1 + \alpha(1 - \lambda)E[a_{m3}] - E\left[p\left(\frac{z_{m1}+z_{m3}}{2}\right)^2\right] - \sigma E[(z_{m1} - z_{m3})^2]$
$= \alpha(\lambda m_1 + (1 - \lambda)\frac{1}{2}) - p(\frac{1}{4}z_{m1} + \frac{1}{4}z_{m1}^2 + \frac{1}{12}) - \sigma(z_{m1}^2 - z_{m1} + \frac{1}{3})$. In this scenario, the incumbent party wins the election with probability $F(Q_3)$, where $Q_3 = \alpha(\lambda m_1 + (1 - \lambda)\frac{1}{2}) - p(\frac{1}{4}z_{m1} + \frac{1}{4}z_{m1}^2 + \frac{1}{12}) - \sigma(z_{m1}^2 - z_{m1} + \frac{1}{3}) - \frac{\alpha}{2} + \frac{7}{24}p + \frac{1}{6}\sigma + D$.

Finally if a dismissal has occurred, hence bringing $m2$ into the cabinet, the party can also promote $m2$ to party leader (case 4). Therefore, the median voter's payoff from retaining this incumbent government is $\alpha\lambda E[a_{m2}] + \alpha(1 - \lambda)E[a_{m3}] - E\left[p\left(\frac{z_{m2}+z_{m3}}{2}\right)^2\right] - \sigma E[(z_{m2} - z_{m3})^2] = \frac{\alpha}{2} - p\int_0^1\int_0^1 \left(\frac{z_{m2}+z_{m3}}{2}\right)^2 dz_{m2} \, dz_{m3} - $

58 *Political survival and cabinet change*

$$\sigma \int_0^1 \int_0^1 (z_{m2} - z_{m3})^2 \, dz_{m2} \, dz_{m3} = \frac{a}{2} - \frac{7}{24}p - \frac{1}{6}\sigma.$$ In this case, the probability of reelection is $F(Q4)$, where $Q4 = \frac{a}{2} - \frac{7}{24}p - \frac{1}{6}\sigma - \frac{a}{2} + \frac{7}{24}p + \frac{1}{6}\sigma + D = D$.

Internal party deposition

The party elite can replace the incumbent leader. Several factors affect their decision. First, changing the leader alters the "electability" of their party. Second, a new leadership alters the competence, policy, and policy discord of the government. This is precisely why a change in leader affects electability, although the median voter and median party elite member view the policy benefits of the government differently. Third, party elites potentially jeopardize their access to rewards as influential party members, as the new party leader might choose to replace them.

If the opposition party wins the election, then the opposition party leader and minister (represented by ol and om) form the government. Thus, the party elite median member's payoff is $\alpha \lambda E[a_{ol}] + \alpha(1-\lambda)E[a_{om}] - E\left[p\left(\frac{1}{2} - \frac{z_{ol} + z_{om}}{2}\right)^2\right] - \sigma E[(z_{ol} - z_{om})^2] = \frac{a}{2} - p \int_{-1}^{1}\int_{-1}^{1}\left(\frac{z_{m1} + z_{m2}}{2} - \frac{1}{2}\right)^2 dz_{m2}\, dz_{m1} - \sigma \int_0^1 \int_0^1 (z_{m1} - z_{m2})^2 \, dz_{m2}\, dz_{m1} = \frac{a}{2} - \frac{25}{24}p - \frac{1}{6}\sigma$.

If the median party elite retains the leader (l) and minister ($m1$) and the party wins the election, then its payoff is $\alpha(\lambda a_l + (1-\lambda)a_{m1}) - E\left[p\left(\frac{z_l + z_{m1}}{2} - \frac{1}{2}\right)^2\right] - \sigma(z_l - z_{m1})^2 + \varphi$. The terms correspond to the value of government competence, policy, policy discord, and private rewards as members of the party elite. The expected value of retaining l and $m1$ depends upon these payoffs weighted by the electoral probabilities: $F(Q_1)(\alpha(\lambda a_l + (1-\lambda)a_{m1}) - E\left[p\left(\frac{z_l + z_{m1}}{2} - \frac{1}{2}\right)^2\right] - \sigma(z_l - z_{m1})^2 + \varphi) + (1 - F(Q_1))(\frac{a}{2} - \frac{25}{24}p - \frac{1}{6}\sigma) = F(Q_1)(\alpha(\lambda a_l + (1-\lambda)a_{m1}) - E\left[p\left(\frac{z_l + z_{m1}}{2} - \frac{1}{2}\right)^2\right] - \sigma(z_l - z_{m1})^2 + \varphi - (\frac{a}{2} - \frac{25}{24}p - \frac{1}{6}\sigma)) + (\frac{a}{2} - \frac{25}{24}p - \frac{1}{6}\sigma)$.

It costs the median party elite $\Lambda - \mu$ to depose the incumbent and promote $m1$. If the party does so, then the party wins the next election with probability $F(Q_3)$ and receives benefits $\alpha(\lambda a_{m1} + (1-\lambda)a_{m3}) - E\left[p\left(\frac{z_{m1} + z_{m3}}{2} - \frac{1}{2}\right)^2\right] - \sigma E[(z_l - z_{m1})^2] + \frac{z}{5}$. Therefore, the expected payoff from deposing the party leader is $F(Q_3)$ $(\alpha \lambda m_1 + \alpha(1-\lambda)\frac{1}{2} - p(-\frac{1}{4}z_{m1} + \frac{1}{4}z_{m1}^2 + \frac{1}{12}) - \sigma(z_{m1}^2 - z_{m1} + \frac{1}{3}) + \frac{z}{5}) + (1 - F(Q_3))(\alpha(\lambda a_{m1} + (1-\lambda)\frac{1}{2}) - p(-\frac{1}{4}z_{m1} + \frac{1}{4}z_{m1}^2 + \frac{1}{12}) - \sigma(z_{m1}^2 - z_{m1} + \frac{1}{3}) + \frac{z}{5} - (\frac{a}{2} - \frac{25}{24}p - \frac{1}{6}\sigma)) + (\frac{a}{2} - \frac{25}{24}p - \frac{1}{6}\sigma) - (\Lambda - \mu)$.

The median party elite retains the party leader if the expected value of doing so is greater than the expected value of promoting $m1$. This occurs with probability $P_1 = G\, (F(Q_1)(\alpha(\lambda a_l + (1-\lambda)a_{m1}) - p\left(\frac{z_l + z_{m1}}{2} - \frac{1}{2}\right)^2 - \sigma(z_l - z_{m1})^2 + \varphi - (\frac{a}{2} - \frac{25}{24}p - \frac{1}{6}\sigma)) - F(Q_3)\,(\alpha \lambda m_1 + \alpha(1-\lambda)\frac{1}{2} - p(-\frac{1}{4}z_{m1} + \frac{1}{4}z_{m1}^2 + \frac{1}{12}) - \sigma(z_{m1}^2 - z_{m1} + \frac{1}{3}) + -(\frac{a}{2} - \frac{25}{24}p - \frac{1}{6}\sigma)) + \Lambda$.

The median party elite's decision changes if a cabinet change has occurred, since comparatively less is known about the prospective party rival ($m2$). If the party retains the leader, then the median party elite's payoff is $F(Q_2)$ $(\alpha(\lambda a_1 + (1-\lambda)\frac{1}{2}) - p(\frac{1}{4}z_I + \frac{1}{4}z_I^2 + \frac{1}{12}) - \sigma(z_I^2 - z_I + \frac{1}{3}) + \varphi - (\frac{\alpha}{2} - \frac{25}{24}p - \frac{1}{6}\sigma)) + (\frac{\alpha}{2} - \frac{25}{24}p - \frac{1}{6}\sigma)$.

However, if the party replaces the leader, then the median party elite's expected payoff is $F(Q_4)\,[(\frac{\alpha}{2} - \frac{7}{24}p - \frac{1}{6}\sigma + \frac{\varphi}{5}) + (1 - F(Q_4))((\frac{\alpha}{2} - \frac{25}{24}p - \frac{1}{6}\sigma) - (\Lambda - \mu)) = F(Q_4)[\frac{\alpha}{2} - \frac{7}{24}p - \frac{1}{6}\sigma + \frac{\varphi}{5} - (\frac{\alpha}{2} - \frac{25}{24}p - \frac{1}{6}\sigma)] + (\frac{\alpha}{2} - \frac{25}{24}p - \frac{1}{6}\sigma) - (\Lambda - \mu)]$.

The party leader is retained when the former is greater than the latter, which occurs with probability $\rho_2 = G(F(Q_2)(\alpha(\lambda a_{a1} + (1-\lambda)\frac{1}{2}) - p(-\frac{1}{4}z_I + \frac{1}{4}z_I^2 + \frac{1}{12}) - \sigma(z_I^2 - z_I + \frac{1}{3}) + \varphi - (\frac{\alpha}{2} - \frac{25}{24}p - \frac{1}{6}\sigma)) - F(Q_4)(p + \frac{\varphi}{5}) + \Lambda$.

Cabinet change

The analysis above characterizes the probability that the incumbent leader survives the internal party selection and the election. We assume that the leader is primarily motivated to retain office. If she retains minister $m1$, then her probability of survival is $\rho_1 F(Q_1)$. Alternatively, if she dismisses a minister and replaces $m1$ with $m2$, then her probability of survival is $\rho_2 F(Q_2)$. The leader decides whether to replace a cabinet member so as to maximize her probability of survival.

The subgame perfect equilibrium of the game follows directly from the above characterization of decision making at each stage.

Proposition

In the subgame perfect equilibrium of the game, the leader dismisses a minister if $\rho_2 F(Q_2) > \rho_1 F(Q_1)$; otherwise she retains minister $m1$.

If the government is composed of l and $m1$, then the median party elite retains the party leader iff $(F(Q_1)(\alpha(\lambda a_{al} + (1-\lambda)a_{am1}) - p(\frac{z_I + z_{m1}}{2} - \frac{1}{2})^2 - \sigma(z_I - z_{m1})^2 + \varphi - (\frac{\alpha}{2} - \frac{25}{24}p - \frac{1}{6}\sigma)) - F(Q_3)(\alpha\lambda m_1 + \alpha(1-\lambda)\frac{1}{2} - p(-\frac{1}{4}z_{m1} + \frac{1}{4}z_{m1}^2 + \frac{1}{12}) - \sigma(z_{m1}^2 - z_{m1} + \frac{1}{3}) + \frac{\varphi}{5} - (\frac{\alpha}{2} - \frac{25}{24}p - \frac{1}{6}\sigma)) + \Lambda \geq \mu$.

If the leader has previously reshuffled, then the median party elite retains the party leader iff $(F(Q_2)(\alpha(\lambda a_{al} + (1-\lambda)\frac{1}{2}) - p(-\frac{1}{4}z_I + \frac{1}{4}z_I^2 + \frac{1}{12}) - \sigma(z_I^2 - z_I + \frac{1}{3}) + \varphi - (\frac{\alpha}{2} - \frac{25}{24}p - \frac{1}{6}\sigma)) - F(Q_4)(p + \frac{\varphi}{5}) + \Lambda \geq \mu$.

The median voter uses the electoral strategy characterized in the section for electoral decisions, where Q_1, Q_2, Q_3, and Q_4 are also given in that section, whereas ρ_1 and ρ_2 are defined above.

Notes

1 In the United States, cabinet members must be confirmed by the Senate. Generally, Senate confirmation is not considered an issue, particularly at the beginning of a new administration. However, since the 1980s, the Senate has not confirmed potential secretaries on at least eight different occasions (Cohen 1988).
2 This means that $F(Q_1) \approx F(Q_2) \approx 1$.
3 That is, when $\rho_2 > \rho_1$.
4 For the complete derivation of all results, see Quiroz Flores and Smith (2011).
5 This means that $\rho_1 \approx \rho_2 \approx 1$.
6 That is, if $F(Q_2) > F(Q_1)$.

4 Data on foreign ministers

Introduction

In the previous chapter I presented a game theory model where competition for mass support and competition within the ruling elite determine leaders' incentives to replace their cabinet ministers. Political institutions further shape these incentives. In autocratic countries, leaders replace competent ministers in order to minimize the threat of internal deposition. In democratic, presidential systems, competent cabinet secretaries are not a threat to leaders; therefore, only mediocre secretaries are dismissed from the cabinet. The survival of ministers is most complex in democratic, parliamentary systems because leaders need competent ministers to provide public goods and win elections, as long as they are not competent enough that they become internal challengers.

The rest of the book is devoted to test these predictions. In order to do so, I need information on leaders' tenure in office, ministers' tenure in office, and a measure of ministerial competence. There are several datasets and a large number of empirical studies of the tenure of leaders in office (e.g., Bueno de Mesquita and Siverson 1995; Goemans 2000a, 2000b, 2008; Bueno de Mesquita et al. 2003, 2004; Chiozza and Goemans 2003, 2004; Smith 2008; Bueno de Mesquita and Smith 2009; Quiroz Flores and Smith 2013). This chapter discusses some of the available datasets on cabinet ministers and explains in detail the database of foreign ministers used in the rest of the book. This new database covers the tenure of 7,311 ministers of foreign affairs in 181 countries from 1696 to 2004.

The number of cabinet positions

In 1985, Jean Blondel published *Government Ministers in the Contemporary World*, perhaps the largest completed empirical work on cabinet politics – it examines the careers of thousands of individuals across 2,000 cabinet positions in 154 countries from 1945 to 1980. In the twenty-first century, what is the distribution of cabinet positions across countries? What subject areas do they cover? Is the number of positions constant over time and within countries? As I will argue in the next sections, these are important questions because, in the absence of large datasets of ministerial careers that facilitate comparative analysis, researchers may need to choose a limited set of cabinet positions for empirical analysis.

Most cabinets are built around five basic functions of government – Interior, Defense, Foreign Affairs, Finance, and Justice. However, cabinets can cover a wide array of dimensions. The executive power in Afghanistan has a Ministry of Martyrs and Disabled People, while the United States has a Department of Veterans Affairs. India, Pakistan, and Turkmenistan have a Ministry of Textiles or Textile Industry. Australia has a Ministry for Immigration and Border Protection, whereas the US Department of Homeland Security oversees such issues. Oil-rich Kuwait has a Ministry of Oil, whereas Nigeria has a Ministry of Petroleum Resources. In Mexico, PEMEX, an independent agency of the federal government, is in charge of all oil-related processes. New Zealand has a Ministry of Maori Development, whereas Singapore has a ministry of Muslim Affairs. Malta has a Ministry for Gozo, the second largest island in the country.

According to the CIA's directory of Chiefs of State and Cabinet Members of Foreign Governments, in February 2009 the average number of cabinet positions by country was 21.8.[1] In other words, heads of state had an average team of twenty-two ministers to help them rule a country. At the same time, there is high variance in the number of cabinet positions. In fact, the standard deviation for this sample of countries is 9.98 cabinet seats. Figure 4.1 presents the distribution of cabinet positions for 200 countries in February 2009. This distribution is unlikely to have changed over the last few years.

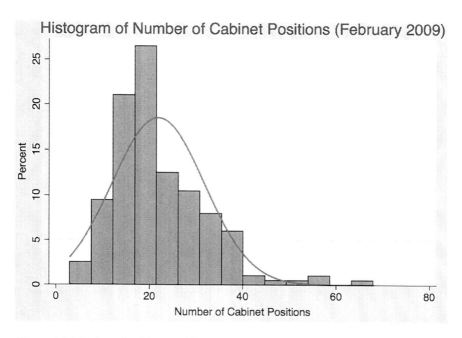

Figure 4.1 Number of cabinet positions, February 2009

62 *Data on foreign ministers*

As mentioned before, there is large variation in the number of cabinet positions across countries. Table 4.1 presents illustrative cases of the number of ministers according to the percentiles in the data.

Although this is an informative table, it is difficult to identify any patterns in the number of cabinet positions. Dissimilar countries like Guatemala and Uzbekistan have fourteen cabinet positions, while Slovenia and Jamaica have eighteen cabinet seats each. Cabinets in similar presidential systems like Mexico and Venezuela also have very different sizes: Mexico has nineteen ministers, while Venezuela has twenty-nine. Perhaps this variation in the number of cabinet positions depends on the size of a country's population. Table 4.2 presents the number of ministers per 100 thousand people in selected countries.

Evidently, once population is taken into account, the number of cabinet positions across countries presents different characteristics. Countries with large populations such as China, India, Russia, Brazil, Indonesia, Japan, and Mexico have a small number of ministers relative to their population. Countries with small populations such as St. Kitts and Nevis, Palau, Liechtenstein, and San Marino have a much larger number of ministers relative to their population.

The number of cabinet positions across countries is quite large. It also varies over time, as illustrated by the case of Pakistan, where leaders can extend and shrink the cabinet according to different political circumstances. Not only is the cabinet made of federal ministers and more junior ministers of state, the president is in a position to appoint five additional individuals who have the status of minister but do not need to be members of parliament. More crucial to this discussion is that the number of cabinet positions varies according to the types of governments; according to Mufti (2015), caretaker and martial law governments have small

Table 4.1 Number of cabinet positions for selected countries, February 2009

Country	Number of Cabinet Positions	Percentile
Uganda	68	Max
Jordan	28	75
Finland	19	50
Tajikistan	15	25
Monaco[2]	5	Min

Table 4.2 Number of cabinet positions per 100,000 people, February 2009

Country	Number of Cabinet Positions per 100 Thousand People	Percentile
St. Kitts and Nevis	42.3	Max
Oman	1.19	~75
Sri Lanka	.27	~50
Mozambique	.12	~25
China	.001	Min

cabinets, while elected governments have larger cabinets. Data provided by Mufti show that the Qureshi caretaker government that ruled Pakistan from July to October of 1993 had the smallest cabinet, with only twelve positions. In contrast, the second Gilliani government between 2008 and 2011 had the largest cabinet, with sixty-two positions! Mufti in fact argues that the allocation of cabinet positions in Pakistan is a form of patronage, and as such, it increases in size about two years before an election in order to provide candidates – then promoted to the cabinet – with additional incumbency advantage. Of course, not all leaders enjoy such latitude with their cabinet. From 1894 to 1994, the number of cabinet positions in Argentina was constitutionally fixed at eight (Camerlo 2015), while the size of the cabinet was also fixed in Chile (Siavelis and Baruch Galvan 2015). The number of cabinet positions in Argentina after 1994 later on increased to sixteen.

Evidently, there is a large variation in the number of cabinet positions. The implication is that not all cabinet positions are equally important. In the US, the secretaries of state, treasury, and defense, along with the attorney general (the Big Four), are closely tied to the president and occupy top places in the presidential line of succession – first in line is the vice president, followed by the speaker of the House of Representatives, the president pro tempore of the Senate, and then the Secretary of State, Treasury, Defense, and the Attorney General. The Department of Homeland Security has gained a more important role over the last decade. Now, if we take the budget of cabinet offices as an indicator of significance – political, economic, or social – the picture is quite different. In the US, discretionary spending largely determines the budget of executive offices and federal agencies; in 2014, the actual base discretionary funding added up to US$1,030.8 billion.[3] The Department of Defense absorbed US$496 billion, that is, 48 percent of the discretionary agency funding. The Department of Health and Human Services occupies second place with a discretionary budget of US$79.8 billion, equivalent to 7.7 percent. The State Department has a budget of US$42.9 billion, the Treasury has US$12.7 billion, and the Department of Justice has US$27.3 billion. According to this picture, three of the Big Four are actually not that big and are in fact surpassed by departments with significant social impact, such as Veterans Affairs and Education.

In Mexico, another presidential system, the budget for the executive branch in 2015 was 1,087,136.1 million Mexican pesos (Mex$), which at a rate of US$1 for Mex$18.3, this is equivalent to US$59.4 billion. In Mexico, the Departments of Education, Health, and Social Development are the largest sources of expenditures, with a combined of Mex$543,283 million, almost 50 percent of the budget. However, the Department of the Interior has been historically the most influential executive office – the secretary is the president's key political agent in domestic politics, and at least during the years of dominance of the PRI (Institutional Revolutionary Party), almost all presidents were succeeded by their secretaries of the interior. To illustrate how important this office is, it had a 2015 budget of Mex$74,485.2 million, while the Department of Defense had a budget of Mex$71,265.4 million. In a country where the Department of Defense has done the bulk of the fighting in the war against drugs for the last ten years, the budget of the Department of the Interior is actually quite large.[4]

As an example of a parliamentary system, the UK cabinet has twenty-two positions, including the prime minister. Anecdotally, it is safe to say that the most important departments are the Chancellor of the Exchequer, the Home Department, the Foreign and Commonwealth Office, the Ministry of Defense, and the Ministry of Justice. Notice that unlike the US, the Home Office in the UK is immensely influential, and for the fiscal year of 2015–2016, it had an expenditure limit of £10.2 billion. In contrast, the Ministry of Defense had an expenditure limit of £28.1 billion, the Foreign Office a limit of £1.8 billion, and Justice a limit of £6.3 billion. The National Health Service (NHS) as part of the Department of Health is by far the largest source of expenditures, with a ceiling of £111.9 billion, which corresponds to 35 percent of the total budget of £316.1 billion.[5] This type of organization is also present in parliamentary Israel. According to Kenig and Barnea (2015), the most important cabinets are Foreign Affairs, Finance, Internal Affairs, and – given Israel's position in the Middle East – Defense. These Big Four positions are followed by ministries with very large budgets, such as Health and Education, and economic portfolios such as Transport and Trade. Lastly, and this is quite crucial in the context of coalition governments, there are several ministers without portfolios, who contribute to the maintenance of the coalition.

This discussion suggests that there are two challenges for the empirical analysis of cabinet ministers. First, there is a large number of cabinet positions; this number varies across countries and time. Second, not all cabinet positions are equally important across countries. In this light, the next section of the chapter describes how different studies of cabinet politics have overcome these problems.

Current available datasets

Clearly, a full empirical analysis of cabinet politics requires data on all cabinet positions for all countries for a long period or time. In the absence of such data, empirical studies of cabinet change have concentrated on a set of executive offices and ministries, or a geographical region or country, over a limited period of time. As mentioned before, the Blondel dataset (1985) covers the careers of thousands of individuals across 2,000 cabinet positions in 154 countries from 1945 to 1980. These are the data at the heart of Blondel's *Government Ministers in the Contemporary World*, one of the largest completed empirical works on cabinet politics. Jean's work is the seminal study of cabinet politics. It is a source of inspiration for many researchers of cabinet politics and continues to serve as the original reference for studies of the cabinet.

As researchers have updated the database of ministerial careers, several recent works have used large databases that include multiple countries, often in parliamentary systems. For instance, Kam and Indridason (2005) use data on all cabinet positions from five parliamentary democracies: Britain, Ireland, Canada, Australia, and New Zealand. Their dataset is quite extensive and covers the years 1958 to 2002. Huber and Martinez Gallardo (2008) extended this empirical analysis and explored cabinet turnover in nineteen parliamentary democracies between

1945 and 1999: Australia, Austria, Belgium, Canada, Denmark, Finland, France, Germany, Iceland, Italy, Ireland, Luxembourg, the Netherlands, New Zealand, Norway, Portugal, Spain, Sweden, and the UK. Given the larger coverage of countries, the authors explored the nine most important cabinet portfolios in these countries according to an index that reflects the time each portfolio was occupied by a minister. They combined this index with Laver and Hunt's (1992) expert survey of cabinet portfolios in order to choose the most adequate cabinet positions for their empirical analysis.

These empirical analyses and databases have contributed greatly to our understanding of cabinet politics. However, these works tend to omit variables that might be crucial to test hypotheses that allow us to identify a potential case of agency, such as adverse selection, moral hazard, or agency rent. For instance, an empirical analysis of cabinet change in presidential democracies would benefit from information about the political background of cabinet secretaries. US presidents sometimes appoint cabinet members from opposing political parties —President Clinton appointed Republican William S. Cohen as secretary of defense, while President Obama also appointed another Republican, Robert Gates, as secretary of defense. Although this might strengthen stability at the Department of Defense, particularly during times of war, it could potentially lead to adverse selection and policy shifting. Ernesto Zedillo, president of Mexico between 1994 and 2000, experienced such problems when he appointed Antonio Lozano Gracia as attorney general. Lozano Gracia was a member of the leading opposition party and prosecuted members of the same political elite that had supported Zedillo; unfortunately he presented poor investigations that eventually led to his dismissal.

In this sense, Jean Blondel's work (1985) is also important because his database is quite rich and includes detailed information on cabinet ministers on approximately sixty different variables. Obtaining this information for a large number of countries requires a huge effort that can only be completed with the help of a network, as I will explain in a moment. Meanwhile, scholars of cabinet change have collected these data for selected countries. An early study by Dowding and Kang (1998) explores resignations and nonresignations of cabinet ministers in England from the Attlee to the Major governments. More recently, Samuel Berlinski, Torun Dewan, and Keith Dowding have developed one of the most complete databases of ministerial careers in the UK. These data have evolved over the years and now cover all British ministers from 1945 to 2007. In order to explain ministerial resignation, Dewan and Dowding (2005) explore data on individual ministers from 1955 to 1998. A related article on the length of ministerial tenure extends the database from 1945 to 1997 and includes information on tenure, educational background, age, gender, and previous political and ministerial experience, among other variables (Berlinski, Dewan, and Dowding 2007). This database also appears in Berlinski, Dewan, and Dowding (2010), where they explore ministers' hazard rates as a function of an individual minister's performance as measured by resignation calls, and overall governmental performance as measured by the cumulative number of resignation calls. I like this dataset because it includes a new measure of ministerial performance based on resignation calls collected from *The Times*. As I will explain in the following chapters, producing a measure of competence is crucial for an analysis of cabinet change. Berlinski, Dewan, and Dowding have now extended the database further and cover ministers from 1945 to 2007 in their book *Accounting for Ministers: Scandal and Survival in British Government, 1945–2007* (2012). Kam et al. (2010) use an innovative dataset of MPs' ideal points to explore cabinet selection in the UK, including shadow cabinets, and how the inclusion of backbenchers' preferences might reduce potential agency problems.

Other democratic parliamentary systems have also been carefully covered. Indridason and Kam (2008) look at cabinet ministers during the Fraser and Hawke administrations in Australia; altogether, the database covers the years 1975 to 1993. Dowding and Lewis (2012) and Dowding, Lewis, and Packer (2012) have an even larger database that covers Australian cabinets from 1949 to 2010. It includes information on 339 individuals in the cabinet. Kerby (2009), on the other hand, explores the appointment of MPs to cabinet positions in Canada in a database that covers 1935 to 2008. In this database, out of 2,688 MPs covered, 401 were actually appointed to the federal cabinet. As with other country-specific databases, Kerby's data include information on age, gender, education, and even legal training. Kerby (2011) has also explored ministerial careers in Canada from 1867 to 2006. This dataset of ministers includes information on 587 cabinet members and 787 actual ministers, since individuals have served in multiple cabinets. The dataset is also very rich and contains information on ministers' age, gender, legal background, and political experience, as well as some other crucial variables such as whether they challenged party leadership. Ministerial career data for Japan, the country with the largest parliamentary record outside of Europe, are also quite extensive and detailed. For Pakistan, Mufti (2015) presents innovative data covering ministerial careers from 1973 to 2013. The data and her analysis are based on interviews that present a fascinating picture of cabinet politics in a political system that has oscillated from parliamentary democracy to autocracy.

With the exceptions of Argentina (Camerlo 2015), Chile (Siavelis and Baruch Galvan 2015), Russia (Semenova 2015), and South Korea (Kang 2015), presidential systems have not been adequately covered by empirical studies, and detailed databases of the careers of cabinet secretaries focus mostly on the United States. The appointment of cabinet secretaries and cabinet-level officers in the US is a top priority. However, US presidents also nominate agency heads, deputy secretaries, and ambassadors, among many other executive heads. Patterson and Pfiffner (2001) have identified at least 1,125 full-time positions subject to presidential appointment and Senate confirmation; a president makes another 490 nominations for part-time positions that also require Senate approval. In this context, the most comprehensive database of US cabinet secretaries was collected by Stuart Jordan, Dave Lewis, Nolan McCarty, and Kelly Chang. The dataset focuses on executive nominations and time to the Senate's confirmation, as well as tenure in office for cabinet secretaries since the end of the eighteenth century to 2003; the database is unique because it also covers the nomination and tenure of US undersecretaries and other high-ranking officials. Of course, this is not the only database of US cabinet executives in the US. Cohen (1986, 1988) has explored cabinet careers up to 1984 and his database includes information on secretaries' sector of recruitment, sector of de-recruitment, age at time of appointment, and other relevant variables. Given the potential for agency, Bertelli and Grose (2007) use data on 298 congressional testimonies of secretaries of labor, commerce, and agriculture from 1991 to 2002 in order to explore ministerial shift. The authors find that between 1991 and 2002, labor secretaries took public positions that disagreed with the president 21 percent of the time, while agriculture secretaries did so 22 percent of the time, and commerce secretaries did it 31 percent of the time.

Lastly, scholars with an interest in specific aspects of cabinet politics have collected new datasets that cover multiple types of political systems. Borrelli (2002, 2010) has explored the selection and exclusion of women in the US cabinet, which has a history of gender imbalance. In an effort to empirically explore the potential gendered nature of cabinets across countries, Escobar-Lemmon and Taylor-Robinson (2009) investigated the career paths of men and women in cabinet positions across 18 Latin American countries from 1980 to 2003. The authors found that cabinets in this region were in fact gendered institutions, as they were constructed to reinforce gender differences. Krook and O'Brien (2012) extended the coverage to 117 countries for August 2009 and constructed a 'gender power score' that weights the number of women appointed to prestigious cabinet positions. Using this measure, they find that the recent changes to women's access to power are explained by political variables rather than social ones.

It is evident that empirical studies of cabinet politics have turned to different techniques to test hypotheses. These works have contributed to our understanding of cabinet change in particular countries, time periods, or issues. However, in terms of cabinet change as a field of study, we lack a systematic and coherent dataset of ministerial careers for valid comparative analysis. Blondel's empirical analysis of ministerial careers (1985) systematically collected information on sixty different variables. The Selection and Deselection of Political Elites (SEDEPE) research network has made the Blondel (1985) dataset available online. This network is also encouraging researchers to continue collecting data on cabinet ministers in order to widen the scope of previous empirical work according to a systematic procedure conducive to comparative analysis. In order to do so, the network has made a codebook available to researchers that will guide them in their data collection efforts. In the spirit of Blondel's codebook, the SEDEPE Codebook places an emphasis on a large number of variables that will contribute to the empirical analysis of ministerial careers across countries and political systems. So far, members of the SEDEPE network have contributed to two edited volumes of ministerial politics, *The Selection of Ministers in Europe* (Dowding and Dumont 2009) and *The Selection of Ministers around the World* (Dowding and Dumont 2015).

Members of the SEDEPE network are getting closer to providing a comparable dataset of ministerial careers. In the meantime, without consistent data for a large number of countries and cabinet positions, it is difficult to draw conclusions from an analysis of ministries that are not necessarily comparable. Part of the problem is that cabinet hierarchy differs across countries. As mentioned above, the Big Four cabinet positions in the US are simply much more important than the other eleven executive departments. However, the Department of the Interior in Mexico is the most important cabinet position in the country, and although this position exists in the United States, it is not part of the Big Four. For this reason, some studies are based on an index that reflects the importance of particular cabinet positions (Huber and Martinez Gallardo 2008). Yet, this type of exercise has not been extended to presidential systems and even less to autocratic regimes. In this light, this book takes a different approach to the study of cabinet change. Rather than creating an arbitrary index that is useful for all types of political regimes, it focuses on a single cabinet position – the Ministry of Foreign Affairs.

Data on ministers of foreign affairs

This book explores cabinet change by focusing on a single cabinet ministry: Foreign Affairs. Ever since the modern state emerged, it has been defined and understood, both theoretically and in practice, as an entity that is rather well defined by its geographical borders, its sovereign right to tax its citizens, and its ability to conduct relations with other states. In fact, the modern state succeeded as a form of political organization because it was comparatively much more efficient at taxing, fighting, and in general protecting its borders than alternative polities, such as urban leagues or city-states (Spruyt 1996). The power and influence of ministries that control a country's treasure, provide justice, secure internal order, and regulate interactions with other states directly emanate from the state's sovereign right and ability to tax its citizens and, in exchange, its responsibility to protect citizens from themselves and others beyond its borders. As long as the state is the basic unit of analysis in this particular international system, it is valid to assume that the ministry of foreign affairs is a window to the politics of cabinet change.

Indeed, ministers of foreign affairs occupy a central position in an administration. All things considered, they are the highest-ranking diplomatic representatives of a country. They shape foreign policy and coordinate thousands of employees stationed around the globe. They represent their countries, participate in international organizations, and serve as negotiators and third-party interveners during international disputes. In the words of George Modelski (1970: 143): "Foreign ministers are not, as a rule, the principal architects of foreign policy but they are, frequently, the principal foreign policy advisers in relation to the governmental decision process, hence strategically placed for exercising influence over that process."

I am particularly interested in the role that ministers of foreign affairs play in the occurrence of interstate war. Specifically, I want to know how the competence of a foreign minister may or may not contribute to the initiation of hostilities between countries. For this reason I compiled a database on the tenure of foreign ministers. The dataset has information on 7,311 foreign ministers in 181 countries, spanning the years 1696–2004. It includes the specific day, month, and year in which 4,911 foreign ministers took and left office. For the remaining ministers, only the years in which they took and left office were recorded. Many records also include the minister's date of birth and death. Ministers holding office up to 2004, as well as ministers from countries that ceased to exist (e.g., Yugoslavia), were recorded as right-censored.[6]

The main source of records on foreign ministers is Spuler, Allen, and Saunders' (1977) *Rulers and Governments of the World*. Spuler, Allen, and Saunders' three volumes list the duration in office of most political leaders and several ministers since Roman times up to the 1970s. Unfortunately, Spuler, Allen, and Saunders' records offer details about the European powers, a few former British colonies, and other countries that have had an important role in international politics. In order to solve this missing data problem, the records were complemented with three additional sources. The first source is B. Schemmell's data (www.rulers.org) on foreign ministers as provided on the website *Rulers of the World*.[7] This website contains a list of political leaders in most countries since 1700, as well as a list of several ministers and their time in office. The second source is Peter Truhart's (1989) *International Directory of Foreign Ministers, 1589–1989*. This book contains data on a large cross-section of ministers that served nations that achieved independence after the Second World War, as well as several developing countries up to 1989. Data for the 1990s were collected from governmental websites.

The data collection involved reading all records for each country for each minister and recording the day, month, and year in which the minister took and left office. Each minister was assigned a unique identification number. It is important to note that the same individual could have the position of minister of foreign affairs on different occasions. In these cases, each term the minister served in a different administration has a different identification number. In a few cases the sources had different information about the tenure of ministers, probably because countries may have different groups that claim to be the legitimate government. In these instances, Spuler, Allen, and Saunders' *Rulers and Governments of the World* (1977) is used as reference.

As mentioned above, the dataset has information on the careers of foreign ministers in 181 countries from 1696 to 2004. The dataset presents some significant patterns. First, European nations have a larger number of foreign ministers simply because they emerged earlier in the modern international system. For instance, the data cover France from 1696 to 2004, Britain from 1697, the US from 1781, Portugal from 1785, and Denmark from 1797. Young nations that gained independence recently are obviously covered for fewer years: coverage for Belize begins in 1981, Slovenia in 1990, the Czech Republic in 1992, and Eritrea in 1993. Some of these countries emerged from other nations; for instance, Czechoslovakia is covered from 1918 to 1992 while Austria-Hungary is covered from 1848 to 1918. Latin American countries are also well covered by the dataset, as many of them reached independence in the nineteenth century: coverage for Chile begins in 1810, Peru in 1821, Brazil in 1822, Mexico in 1830, and Argentina in 1835, to mention a few. Poland and Lithuania are some of the oldest countries in Europe, and the confederation that they formed in the sixteenth century was one of the largest unions ever created on the Continent. For historical reasons, coverage for Poland and for Lithuania begins only in 1918. Overall, countries are covered for a mean of 74.5 years and a variance of 3255.5 years. The smallest coverage is for Eritrea, with 12 years, and the largest for France, with 309 years.

It is reasonable to assume that older countries have a larger number of foreign ministers. This, in fact, is not the case. The country with the largest number of foreign ministers is Peru, with 269 individuals who have occupied this cabinet position in a total of 184 years of coverage. Second place is occupied by Greece with 238 foreign ministers from 1833 to 2004. Interestingly, Spain and its former colonies, which are also relatively old countries, have a large number of foreign ministers. In this database, Spain has 213 foreign ministers from 1814 to 2004. Chile, Mexico, Paraguay, Costa Rica, and Colombia have 216, 210, 181, 165, and 162 ministers of foreign affairs respectively. France, Britain, the US, and Denmark have some of the most extensive coverage in my database, and yet they only have 194, 109, 94, and 62 ministers of foreign affairs. The only exception is Portugal, which is covered since 1785 and has 235 ministers of foreign affairs.

In order to be more systematic and take into consideration the age of countries, it is more useful to look at the number of ministers of foreign affairs per year; this is simply the number of foreign ministers divided by the number of years covered by country. According to this new variable, Peru has the highest ratio, that is, 1.46 foreign ministers per year. Greece, Congo-Brazzaville, Mexico, Paraguay follow with 1.38, 1.24, 1.2, and 1.1 foreign ministers per year respectively. Other Latin American countries also have high ratios of ministers per year, which confirms the argument I made above. However, there are other countries with very high ratios: Jordan, Iraq, Cambodia, Papua New Guinea, and Rumania have ratios of 1.04, .97, .88, .83, and .79 respectively. This is indicative of large turnover, particularly since the mean number of foreign ministers per year is .45. The country with the smallest ratio is Bahrain, with .02; this means that in a hundred years, Bahrain has had just less than three ministers of foreign affairs. Brunei has a larger ratio of .04 foreign ministers per year.

What explains this large variance in the number of ministers per year across countries? Why is it the case that, all else equal, some nations experience larger turnover of leadership at the key ministry of foreign affairs? This book gives an answer to these questions by exploring the rate at which foreign ministers are deposed from office. This rate of deposition represents the velocity at which these individuals leave office. This rate is quite low in some countries, such as Bahrain, Brunei, the UAE, North Korea, and Singapore, and quite high in countries such as Peru, Greece, Japan, Haiti, and Italy.

One systematic method to explore this rate of deposition entails keeping track of the number of ministers who are in office at some point in time t, and counting how many of them have lost office at some other point in time $t+1$. As an illustration, take the fifteen post-Soviet states: Armenia, Azerbaijan, Belarus, Estonia, Georgia, Kazakhstan, Kyrgyzstan, Latvia, Lithuania, Moldova, Russia, Tajikistan, Turkmenistan, Ukraine, and Uzbekistan. For illustration purposes, assume that each country appointed a minister of foreign affairs on January 1, 1992, just a month after the USSR was dissolved in December 1991. Clearly, in January 1992 there are fifteen foreign ministers. As time goes by, some of these ministers will lose office and will be replaced with new ones. If we stop the clock on January 1, 2002, ten years after the countries became independent, we can simply count the proportion of ministers who were replaced within their first year in office, the proportion of ministers who were replaced within their second year in office, and so on and so forth. Notice that this is an account for all ministers who have been in office between January 1, 1992 and January 1, 2002; these are likely to be more than fifteen ministers, as some of the original ministers might have been replaced. This method thus simply tracks the proportion of ministers who are still in office at any point in time; it is assumed that no minister can stay in office forever, and therefore this proportion is decreasing over time. This type of counting is at the heart of a method known as the Kaplan–Meier (KM) estimate of the survivor function, where the survivor function is interpreted as the proportion of ministers who are still in office at a point in time. As an introduction to the data on ministers of foreign affairs, Figure 4.2 presents Kaplan–Meier nonparametric estimates of the survivor function of foreign ministers along with its 95 percent confidence interval.

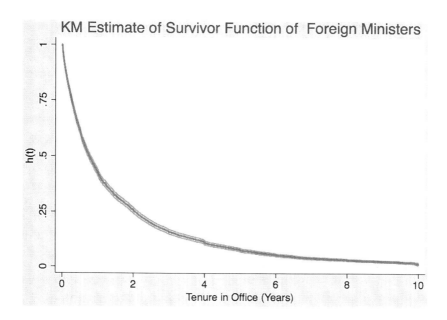

Figure 4.2 Survivor function of foreign ministers, 1696–2004

Figure 4.2 presents a very interesting picture. First of all, it is important to note that at time zero, 100 percent of ministers are in office; this is equivalent to saying that, in our example above, all fifteen ministers of foreign affairs were in office on January 1, 1992. However, only one year after taking office, 50 percent of all ministers had already been replaced. In our example above, this indicates that 50 percent of all foreign ministers in all fifteen countries in our period of study were replaced by the time they reached their first year in office. This applies to the original ministers who took office in January 1992, but also to all other ministers who may have replaced them. In other words, 50 percent of all ministers, whether they took office in 1992 or afterward, did not make it past their first year in office. By the second year in office, only 25 percent of all ministers were still in the cabinet. This means that 75 percent of all the ministers in all the countries in our period of study did not make it past their second year in office. Figure 4.2 is an excellent illustration of the ministerial condition (Blondel 1985): the tenure in office of foreign ministers is in fact quite short.

An even better picture of foreign ministers' tenure in office is given by their hazard rate. A hazard rate presents the rate at which ministers lose office at different periods in time. In our example above, if a large proportion of ministers lost office very early in their term, while the surviving ministers managed to stay in office for extended periods of time, the overall hazard rate would be very high at the beginning but then it would decrease over time – this simply indicates that ministers experience high rates of deposition at the beginning of their term, say, one year, but that this rate drops after one year in office. In contrast, if the same number of ministers is replaced constantly over time, then the hazard rate would be relatively flat. In a different case, if more and more ministers are replaced as time goes by, this would produce an increasing hazard rate. In other words, the hazard rate represents the rate of ministerial replacement conditional on time in office. Although the hazard rate presents tenure in office in a format that might be quite different than the survivor function, they are actually closely related, and one can be derived from the other, at least mathematically. Figure 4.3 presents the hazard rate for the ministers of foreign affairs and its 95 percent confidence interval.

Although the actual hazard rate on the left axis of Figure 4.3 is not easily interpreted, at least substantively, its shape over time gives us an excellent picture of the rates of deposition of ministers of foreign affairs. The peak at the far left side of the figure indicates that foreign ministers lose office at very high rates at the beginning of their term. However, to the right of that peak, the hazard rate experiences a huge drop. This clearly suggests that if ministers manage to survive their very initial period in office, their rate of deposition is actually decreasing over time. In other words, ministers are easily replaced at the beginning of their terms, but as they accumulate tenure, they are increasingly difficult to depose. As I will show in the next few chapters, the foreign ministers who hold on to office for long periods of time represent countries with small winning coalitions, such as the USSR, Kuwait, and Czechoslovakia. This is illustrated by Table 4.3, which presents a list of the foreign ministers with the longest tenure in office.

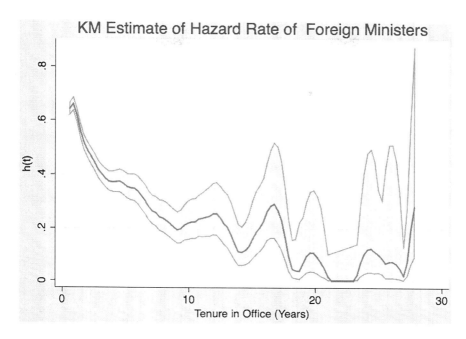

Figure 4.3 Hazard rate of foreign ministers, 1696–2004

Table 4.3 The Hall of Fame of foreign ministers

Name	Country	Years in Office
Prince Varoprakar	Thailand	39
Joseph Bech	Luxembourg	33
Sheikh Sabah Al Ahmad	Kuwait	29
Arnold Green	Estonia	29
Andrey Gromyko	USSR	29
Aleksandr Gorchakov	Russia	27
Joseph, Count Beroldingen	Wuerttemburg	26
Hermann, Baron Mittnacht	Wuerttemburg	25
Raul Sapena Pastor	Paraguay	21
Giuseppe Motta	Switzerland	21
Jean-Baptiste Colbert, Marquis	France	20
Behar Shtylla	Albania	18
Halvard Lange	Norway	18
Edvard Benes	Czechoslovakia	18
Otto Divlev, Baron Rosenørn	Denmark	18

This pattern of long ministerial tenure in autocratic countries is consistent with the literature on leader survival, which indicates that leaders in autocracies have longer tenure in office than their counterparts in large-coalition systems (e.g., Bueno de Mesquita et al. 2003). As I mentioned in the Introduction to this book, leaders stay in office by providing a mix of public and private goods to their political supporters. In countries with large winning coalitions, such as Canada and Norway, leaders provide a larger mix of public goods, such as national security and a healthy environment. In countries with small winning coalitions, such as North Korea and Burma, leaders provide more private goods than public ones. Different political systems are associated with a different likelihood of obtaining goods, either public or private. Keeping the size of the selectorate constant, an individual's likelihood of obtaining goods provided by the leader is higher in a country with a large winning coalition than in a country with a small winning coalition. This has important consequences for the survival of leaders.

Political supporters in countries with large coalitions are not very loyal – not only are they relatively more likely to form part of a new coalition under a new leader, but the latter will provide a large mix of public goods, which, by definition, can be consumed by everyone regardless of their political allegiance or status in the country. Hence, supporters in democracies depose their leaders at a high rate that does not depend on a leader's tenure in office. In other words, a leader's likelihood of deposition is always relatively high and constant over time. In contrast, political supporters in small-coalition countries are very loyal – since they are relatively less likely to form part of a new coalition under a new autocrat and because the private goods provided by the latter cannot really be shared. This loyalty is weak during a leader's early term in office because both the leader and her supporters have yet to confirm mutual support. Once they are committed to the exchange of political support for private goods, leaders in autocracies are incredibly difficult to depose. Leaders in small-coalition systems stay longer in office than their counterparts in large-coalition countries for this reason.

This same pattern applies to foreign ministers in autocratic countries. To see how, Figure 4.4 presents the hazard rate of foreign ministers by the size of the winning coalition. Although I will elaborate on the measurement of these institutions in Chapter 6, it will suffice to say here that the dashed line corresponds to countries with very inclusive political systems where the size of the winning coalition is equal to 1, while the solid line corresponds to less inclusive regimes where the size of this coalition is less than or equal to .75. This variable is effectively an indicator of how democratic a political system is.

As with political leaders, the figure shows that in very inclusive political systems, the foreign ministers' rate of deposition – although oscillating – is relatively constant over time, while in less inclusive systems it drops over time. This indicates that foreign ministers in countries that resemble democracies lose office at the same rate over time. In contrast, ministers in less inclusive systems have a decreasing rate of deposition over time. Although this pattern does not take

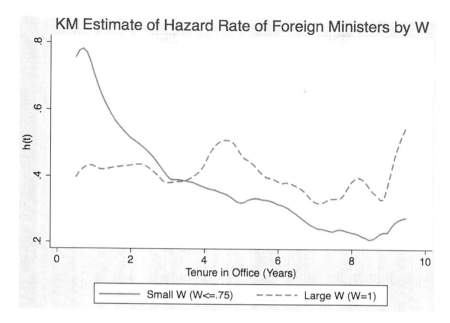

Figure 4.4 Hazard rate of foreign ministers by W

into consideration issues of competence, it does speak to the nature of political loyalty across political systems. As I argued previously (2009), ministers' loyalty is an unknown quantity as they enter office. Of course, potential ministers have been thoroughly screened in the selection process, which, as discussed in Chapter 2, might reduce adverse selection. However, the selection of ministers is never perfect and leaders only learn their ministers' true allegiance once they are in office. As discussed before, researchers have argued that cabinet change eliminates agency problems in the aftermath of cabinet formation (Kam and Indridason 2005; Huber and Martinez Gallardo 2008; Indridason and Kam 2008; Berlinski, Dewan, and Dowding 2010).

As leaders learn their ministers' allegiance, often at the beginning of their terms in office, ministers face great risks of depositions. This is precisely the time when most purges take place (Bueno de Mesquita et al. 2003), as well as most coups. Leaders do not know whether to count on the support of their ministers, and therefore might have incentives to purge them. Since ministers can anticipate this, they might strike preemptively and try to remove the leader. Leader transitions are thus very unstable times in autocracies. Yet, if the new leader and the ministers overcome this period of uncertainty, they can then commit to a very stable, solid, and long-lasting relationship marked by the long tenure of leaders and their ministers. The figures above are evidence in favor of this theory of cabinet change.

Conclusion

This chapter discussed data on ministerial careers and introduced my database on foreign ministers. Since Blondel (1985) began to collect systematic information on the characteristics of ministers around the world, a number of studies have followed up by collecting information on specific countries, regions, and time periods. These works are invaluable and some of the authors of those studies have organized a collective effort to gather data in a more systematic form in order to facilitate comparative analysis. This is represented by the work of the SEDEPE network. While this database is ready, I turned to the analysis of the tenure of 7,311 ministers of foreign affairs in 181 countries, spanning the years 1696–2004. Currently, this is the largest available database of foreign ministers.

In the next chapter I will elaborate on the importance of foreign ministers. So far I have based my decision on the fact that as long as the state is the basic unit of analysis in this particular international system, the Ministry of Foreign Affairs will be one of the key ministries across the planet. Perhaps this will encourage others to continue updating the database, particularly along the lines suggested in the SEDEPE Codebook, as it includes variables on the personal characteristics of ministers that will help us understand cabinet change and ministerial careers.

Notes

1 The directory is available online at www.cia.gov/library/publications/resources/world-leaders-1/
2 Technically, the Vatican has the smallest number of cabinet positions – 3.
3 www.whitehouse.gov/sites/default/files/omb/budget/fy2016/assets/budget.pdf
4 www.transparenciapresupuestaria.gob.mx/es/PTP/PPEF_2016
5 www.gov.uk/government/publications/summer-budget-2015/summer-budget-2015#budget-policy-decisions
6 There is no reliable information about the resignations of foreign ministers. This dissertation assumes that if the ministers are not right-censored, they fail. Although ministers do resign from their positions, it is reasonable to assume that in general they try to stay in office for as long as possible.
7 These data are publicly available at www.rulers.org/

5 Foreign affairs, diplomacy, and war

Introduction

> Diplomacy is hard work; but when we work hard, diplomacy can work, and not just to defuse tensions, but to achieve results that advance our security, interests and values.
>
> Hilary Clinton in her statement to the Senate Foreign Relations Committee on January 13, 2009[1]

I argued that an empirical test of the implications of the game theory model of Chapter 3 requires three variables: leaders' tenure in office, ministers' tenure in office, and a measure of ministerial competence. The previous chapter discussed data on leaders and presented an overview of the existing databases on cabinet ministers. It also described an original database of the tenure in office of ministers of foreign affairs, which I will use to test the implications of my argument. The last piece of the puzzle is a measurement of the competence of ministers of foreign affairs. Creating this measure is by no means easy or completely comprehensive because ministers of foreign affairs have a multiplicity of roles, both domestic and international. For instance, the appointment of the minister of foreign affairs in Pakistan is closely connected to civil-military relations (Mufti 2015) and the Kashmir conflict. The role of the US secretary of state is much more connected to international politics than domestic politics. Yet, in spite of the variation in the role of foreign ministers across countries, they all meet the same basic function: they are their nation's highest ranking diplomats.

In this light, I explore competence in foreign affairs as the ability to avoid interstate war. I build this argument on a well-known theoretical result in the international relations literature showing that governments can reach prewar bargains that leave them as well-off as if they had fought a war while avoiding the costs of fighting. I extend this logic and contend that competent ministers of foreign affairs are simply more able to reach these *ex ante* bargains. Consequently, and all else equal, governments run by competent ministers of foreign affairs should be associated with longer-lasting periods of peace relative to governments run by mediocre ministers. In the following paragraphs, I will elaborate on the precise connection between competence and war occurrence and how this fits into a theoretical framework of rational war. The most important

78 *Foreign affairs, diplomacy, and war*

lesson of this chapter, however, is that since incompetent ministers are omnipresent in autocratic governments, I expect the latter to be associated with interstate conflict, at least relative to democratic governments. In this sense, I am proposing a new link between cabinet change and one of the most robust patterns in international relations, the democratic peace.

A summary of theoretical expectations

In Chapter 3 I used a game theory model to examine policy performance, the turnover of cabinet ministers, and the survival of political leaders across different institutional settings. One key assumption in the model is that leaders try to maximize their tenure in office. However, leaders can be replaced by their own peers and the masses. The type of political system determines the specific procedure and cost of leader deposition. In autocratic systems, leaders are usually deposed by their own peers, often by means of a coup. The masses can also depose an autocrat, but the costs will be high and probably marked by violence; this reduces the likelihood of external deposition. In democratic systems, leaders are deposed by the masses by means of elections. In addition, leaders can be deposed by their party members in parliamentary systems, but not in presidential ones, or at least not at the same rate. In this context, cabinet members play a strategic role in the survival of leaders. On the one hand, competent ministers are needed to win the support of the masses because they contribute to an efficient provision of public and private goods. On the other hand, competent ministers can effectively contribute to the deposition of a leader, either by means of a coup in autocratic systems or by internal party elections in democratic ones. Based on this logic, cabinet change becomes a pillar of political survival.

This argument can be easily summarized in two sets of hypotheses. The first set focuses on the survival of leaders.

1. In autocratic systems, leaders maximize tenure in office by dismissing competent ministers.
2. In democratic presidential systems, leaders maximize tenure in office by dismissing incompetent ministers.
3. In democratic parliamentary systems where the party elite does not receive perks, leaders tend to keep moderately competent ministers. When the party elite receives perks, leaders can afford to have more competent ministers.

The second set focuses on the survival of ministers or, from another perspective, on the probability of cabinet change.

1. In autocratic systems, competent ministers are more likely to be dismissed from office than incompetent ones.
2. In democratic presidential systems, competent ministers are less likely to be dismissed from office than incompetent ones.

3   In democratic parliamentary systems where the party elite does not receive perks, moderately competent ministers are less likely to be deposed than highly incompetent or highly competent ministers. When the party elite receives perks, relatively more competent ministers are less likely to be deposed than highly incompetent or highly competent ministers.

International relations, war, and diplomacy

The causes of interstate war are a central, even defining, theme in international relations. At least since Thucydides discussed the Peloponnesian War, international relations scholars and researchers have developed theories to explain the emergence and duration of war. Over the last fifty years, realist and neorealist theories of war, as well as the rationalist explanations of war that are so closely connected to them, dominated the field. Nevertheless, as time went by and the line between international relations and comparative politics faded, it became rather clear that the understanding of interstate conflict could not be separated from an analysis of domestic politics. In this sense, our explanations of interstate war have come almost full circle – as Kenneth Waltz (1959) dismissed the individual and state levels of analysis to focus on the characteristics of the international system and their effect on war, we have brought back domestic political institutions and leader incentives to initiate and end interstate conflict as key causes of international conflict. This book falls within this tradition.

In order to connect the role of ministers of foreign affairs and cabinet change with the occurrence of conflict, I need to elaborate on some of the key theories of war and particularly the argument presented by Kenneth Waltz in *Man, the State, and War* (1959). I do so for pedagogical purposes but also because the scientific approach at the core of Waltz's analysis has provided, at least indirectly, some of the methodological foundations of this book. In *Man, the State, and War*, Waltz refers to three levels of analysis as conceptual spaces where the causes of war might reside: individuals, states, and the international system. The first image is more substantive than methodological: war is related to human nature. The second level places an emphasis on the internal characteristics of states, such as political institutions, organization of the economy, and its elites. Lastly, the third level is based on the characteristics of the international system, which is anarchic and populated by unitary nation-states that differ not in their functions but in their capabilities and power. The causes of war on this last level of analysis are further developed in Waltz's *Theory of International Politics* (1979), which ultimately connects the distribution of power in the anarchic international system to the occurrence of war – to put it simply, a lack of balance of power leads to interstate conflict. In contrast, power transition theories of war argued that international conflict arises when dissatisfied states achieve power parity with the hegemon that maintains the status quo (Lemke 2002).

While the theory of war advanced by Waltz (1959, 1979), as well as more sophisticated versions of it (e.g., Niou and Ordeshook 1986; Fearon 1995; Powell 1999), dominated the scientific study of interstate conflict, researchers began to rediscover the link between national political institutions and war. This work was partly motivated by two striking patterns: that democracies tend not to fight other democracies – also known as the democratic peace – and that democracies win wars at higher rates than nondemocracies (Reiter and Stam 2002). There are a number of mechanisms that link domestic political institutions to war, and describing all of them would only distract from my interest on leaders, ministers, and war. In its simplest form, the connection between democracy and war lies in citizens' ability to replace their leaders. Assuming that voters punish elected officials in the case of defeat, democrats only fight wars that they can win. This implies that democrats choose their fights very carefully and since this logic applies to all democrats, the latter tend not to fight each other. Democrats do fight autocrats, but only if they are likely to win.

Since this book approaches cabinet change from a political survival perspective, and as I explore ministerial competence in the area of international affairs, I am particularly interested in the effect of national political institutions on leaders' incentives to initiate wars and how that affects the likelihood of holding on to office. Some of the seminal work in this area is Bueno de Mesquita and Lalman (1992), Bueno de Mesquita, Siverson, and Woller (1992), and Bueno de Mesquita and Siverson (1995). Ultimately, this body of work led to Bueno de Mesquita et al.'s *The Logic of Political Survival* (2003), which was originally conceived as a theory of war that connected domestic political institutions and leader survival. In an extension to their original work, Bueno de Mesquita et al. (2004) assume that victory in war is a public good separate from other political benefits acquired during the conflict, such as territory and wealth, or extracting policy concessions. War is also costly, and leaders must divert resources funded through taxation; this is costly for political supporters of leaders in large-coalition systems, but it is even more taxing for the supporters of autocrats, as both benefits and costs are highly concentrated in these political systems. Although supporters might be compensated in the aftermath of war, the outcome of the conflict is probabilistic. As long as the odds of winning a war are not overwhelming, Bueno de Mesquita et al. (2004) find that democratic leaders exert greater selectivity in fighting wars than their counterparts in small-coalition systems. Additionally, and conditional on the occurrence of war, they find that leaders in large-coalition systems exert greater effort in winning wars than their autocratic counterparts.

This research has been further complemented by analyses of the effect that different types of depositions have on leaders' incentives to implement policy (Chiozza and Goemans 2003, 2004; Goemans 2008; Debs and Goemans 2010). For instance, if leaders anticipate that they will be replaced in an irregular – perhaps even violent – manner, they might engage in diversionary war (Goemans 2008). Diversionary war is simply the initiation or continuation of war for the purposes of staying in office in the anticipation of a likely deposition (Downs and Rocke 1994). Leaders engage in this type of risky behavior for several reasons. In a classic treatise on risky behavior in a principal–agent setting, Downs and Rocke (1994) argue that although principals – in this case, voters – can reduce adventurism in war, they might precipitate a 'gambling for resurrection' effect whereby a leader might continue fighting a war that cannot be won because termination might lead to agent replacement. Croco (2011) further argues that war initiation can contribute to risky behavior: leaders who initiate war may want to back down, but the potential for domestic punishment in the case of defeat or a poor war settlement might force them to continue fighting. In contrast, leaders who take office during the conflict face more forgiving domestic audiences and are therefore in a better position to end hostilities.

Altogether, this discussion suggests that risky behavior in terms of war initiation and continuation is rational, although motivated by different problems. More than this, risky behavior is in fact strategic. Rational models of war have argued that conflict is caused by private information and incentives to misrepresent it (e.g., Fearon 1995), among other factors that I will elaborate on in a moment. Nevertheless, war can also take place in settings with full information whereby leaders introduce additional risk in a rational gamble that can bring disastrous consequences (Goemans and Fey 2009). Optimistic actors can also precipitate war by engaging in risky behavior in order to reveal credibility or obtain better terms of peace (Slantchev and Tarar 2011). It is very important to note that this risky behavior is strongly motivated by the effect of domestic political institutions. If leaders did not fear deposition, either internal or external, they might not have incentives to initiate war or even continue fighting. It is precisely because domestic institutions shape the rate and form of leader deposition that leaders engage in risky behavior, including diversionary war, gambles for resurrection, or the introduction of additional risk into the conflict.

Diplomacy is important in this theoretical framework for methodological and substantive reasons. The previous discussion indicates that even in an anarchic international system, the occurrence of war cannot be separated from the actions of individuals and the domestic political institutions that constrain their behavior. In particular, the political imperatives to hold on to office (e.g., Bueno de Mesquita et al. 2008; Debs and Goemans 2010) shape a leader's actions that might lead to war, as I just explained above. What I would like to highlight here is that this literature clearly places leaders as the main drivers of international conflict. Diplomacy as interpreted in this book also makes a case for the individual as the unit of analysis in international relations. Specifically, I emphasize the role of ministers of foreign affairs and their personality, charisma, and ambition, but most of all their ability, competence, and loyalty toward a leader. For instance, Richard Holbrooke, the famous US diplomat who negotiated the Dayton Agreement for Bosnia in 1995, was known to yell and his usual negotiation strategy, according to journalist George Packer, was "to deploy cajolery, flattery, criticism, analysis, implied threat, teasing humor, fibs – any means at his disposal – to exert his will on a counterpart. Usually, he prevails."[2] Ralph Bunche, architect of the armistice agreements signed in the aftermath of the 1948 war between Israel and its neighbors, and the 1950 Nobel Peace Prize winner, "in a virtuoso display of personality, stamina, and skill, successfully negotiated the four armistice agreements and gave the Middle East seven years' respite from war, as well as the vital first step towards a peaceful settlement" (Urquhart 1998: 21). In short, if diplomacy is taken into consideration, it must be based on the individual as the unit of analysis.

Substantively, diplomacy is important because it forms part of the same bargaining process as war. Let's start with war as bargaining. Filson and Werner (2002: 819) remind us: "Our explanations for war termination, however, tended to rule out the possibility that diplomacy can continue even after the fighting starts and therefore cannot account for negotiated settlements of war." However, numerous wars have ended in a negotiated settlement, which suggests that bargaining and diplomacy also take place while nations engage in hostilities. In a context where 'war is the continuation of policy by other means,' researchers argue that war is part of a bargaining process whereby sides reveal information on capabilities, expectations of victory, and their sensitivity to bear the costs of fighting, among others. In this approach, war ends when participants find a negotiated settlement that is preferable to the continuation of war (Wittman 1979; Werner 1998; Wagner 2000; Goemans 2000b; Filson and Werner 2002, 2004, 2007; Slantchev 2003; Mattes and Morgan 2004). The use of force is therefore interpreted as a tool of diplomacy – fighting is another form of communication and learning that, just like more traditional diplomacy, can be used to avoid and terminate wars. For instance, in an excellent application of this theoretical framework, Filson and Werner (2007) explore leaders' sensitivity to the costs of fighting and a potential defeat. In their account, leaders sensitive to costs such as war casualties might feel obligated to end a conflict and accept defeat, while leaders sensitive to defeat might engage in protracted and costly wars. Diplomacy through the use of force exposes leaders' sensitivities and might force them to accept defeat. The connection to domestic political institutions, although not fully explored, is fascinating, as sensitivity to costs and defeat might vary across and within political systems, as first indicated by Chiozza and Goemans (2003, 2004), Goemans (2008), and Debs and Goemans (2010). This should determine both the initiation of war as well as its conduct and duration.

I agree with Filson and Werner (2002, 2004, 2007) that war is a type of diplomacy. At the same time, I also argue that diplomacy has teeth and is part of the same bargaining process as war. In fact, diplomacy as is traditionally understood – that is, as a set of negotiations undertaken to avoid full-scale war – is never isolated from the potential use of force. For example, as Iran negotiated the downgrade of its nuclear activities in exchange for the lifting of international sanctions, Robin Wright from *The New Yorker* noted: "Throughout the diplomacy, the Defense Department continued contingency planning."[3] This included continued support to Iran's enemies in Yemen and Syria, and development of bunker-buster bombs adequate to penetrate the type of facilities that safeguarded Iran's nuclear facilities. According to Mares (2001), this type of diplomacy with teeth, or militarized interstate bargaining, as he labels it, is ubiquitous in Latin America. This militarized interstate bargaining is best illustrated by the competition between Brazil and Argentina in South America, which was marked by the diplomatic settlement of small disputes but also by an arms buildup undertaken in case diplomacy failed (Mares 2001).

In this framework, 'tough diplomacy' is central to defusing international crises. In a recent exercise to classify interstate wars and trace their potential causes, Valeriano and Vasquez (2010) and Vasquez and Valeriano (2010) argue that power politics on the eve of conflict are central for our understanding of war. The authors refer to these activities as alliance formation but also participation in arms races. Alliances are important pillars of the international system and have been considered as tools to balance power and threats (Walt 1987). Some of them are still active in spite of their age, such as the bilateral alliance between England and Portugal, first established in 1386, which was crucial during the Napoleonic Wars. Others are based on colonial commitments, such as the alliance between the US and the Philippines. Other alliances involve multiple partners, such as NATO and the Inter-American Treaty of Reciprocal Assistance. Whether alliances defuse international crises or actually facilitate conflict, it is safe to assume that alliance formation, and consequently the practice of power politics, cannot really take place without diplomacy.

Traditional diplomatic efforts are more evident in the settlement of wars. The creation of the Council of Foreign Ministers (CFM) is an excellent example of the role of diplomacy in war settlements. As one of the conclusions of the Potsdam Conference of July-August 1945, the US, the UK, and the Soviet Union agreed to establish the CFM with the explicit purpose of preparing peace settlements. The CFM was composed of the foreign ministers of the US, the UK, and the Soviet Union, as well as China and France. The Council's priority was a treaty of peace with Italy, Rumania, Bulgaria, and Finland, but also the preparation of a settlement with Germany. Although the Council encountered profound challenges in meeting its goals, particularly in terms of German reunification, it met several times with significant success, such as helping to end the blockade of Berlin in 1949.

In short, diplomacy is important for substantive reasons because it forms part of the same bargaining process as war. As mentioned above, the literature on war as bargaining identifies hostilities as a specific tool of diplomacy that facilitates communication and the revelation of preferences and capabilities. In this sense, war is a type of 'tough diplomacy.' Diplomacy also plays a role before hostilities take place, and in fact is often undertaken in order to avoid the fighting. Although this traditional form of diplomacy might be more evident than its fighting form, it should accomplish the same goal: a settlement that is acceptable to the parties. The point I would like to make here is that as traditional diplomacy fails and tough diplomacy settles in, *ex post* inefficiency emerges. In a classic examination of interstate war, Fearon argues that

> [as] long as both sides suffer some costs for fighting, then war is always inefficient ex post – both sides would have been better off if they could have achieved the same final resolution without suffering the costs.
> (Fearon 1995: 383)

According to Fearon (1995), countries are unable to reach a settlement due to private information and incentives to misrepresent it, commitment problems, and issue indivisibilities. Commitment problems are represented by countries' inability or unwillingness to maintain the terms of a settlement, while issue indivisibilities refer to issues that are simply not subject to compromise or negotiation. Although foreign ministers are in theory able to convince a country that a settlement will hold or that their country is willing to negotiate even the most precious of possessions, Fearon does not consider these issues as real obstacles to a potential settlement; instead, he is more concerned with diplomacy's inability to overcome them. In short, diplomacy does not play a role in reducing commitment problems and issue indivisibilities. I argue that diplomacy and a minister's diplomatic skills play a key role in the effect of private information and incentives to misrepresent it.

Ministerial competence and interstate war

In the previous section, I argued that diplomacy is important for our understanding of interstate war for methodological and substantive reasons – it highlights the individual as the unit of analysis and forms part of the same bargaining process as interstate war. In practice, however, diplomacy needs little justification. In her statement to the Senate Foreign Relations Committee on January 13, 2009, Hilary Clinton, as Barack Obama's nominee for secretary of state, noted:

> The President-elect has made it clear that in the Obama Administration there will be no doubt about the leading role of diplomacy. One need only look to North Korea, Iran, the Middle East, and the Balkans to appreciate the absolute necessity of tough-minded, intelligent diplomacy.[4]

Diplomacy, however, is mostly practiced by ministers of foreign affairs rather than their leaders. For instance, the rules that established the CFM explicitly described the team members for each delegation: the foreign minister, a high-ranking deputy to replace the minister in case of absence, and a small staff of technical advisers. Laurent Fabius, France's minister of foreign affairs, rather than Françoise Holland, was the central player in the development of the 2015 Paris Climate Change Agreement, perhaps the most ambitious climate change deal in decades. According to *The Guardian*, Fabius had "the key role, finding out from other governments their targets and concerns, forming a bridge between nations that have historically had differences, and liaising closely with the UN to understand how the unwieldy process can be managed."[5]

Ministers of foreign affairs take the leading diplomatic roles for a number of reasons. First, many of them are actually members of the Foreign Service and are trained in diplomacy and negotiation. In contrast, most national leaders do not have credentials as diplomats. Second, they are the gatekeepers for the ultimate executive decision makers in their country; this gives them room to operate and credibility to argue that they lack the power to accept the terms of a settlement, which serves as a technique for further negotiation. In some cases, this strategy is even used by envoys and special representatives, who serve as gatekeepers for the foreign minister. Lastly, foreign ministers take the lead because negotiations can be long and time-consuming. At the end of the day, this is partly why leaders delegate to their ministers. The July 2015 deal between Iran and several world powers that limited the country's nuclear activities in exchange for lifting international sanctions presents an excellent illustration of the role of ministers of foreign affairs in lengthy negotiations.

Since 2006, Iran had been negotiating the downgrade of its nuclear activities – including the removal of centrifuges and the elimination of enriched uranium, among others – with the US, the UK, France, China, Russia, and Germany. The formal agreement was announced on July 14, 2015 and sanctions were lifted in January 2016 after the International Atomic Energy Agency confirmed that Iran had restricted its nuclear activities. Although the deal involved six different countries, the diplomatic efforts were driven by Iran and the US, and particularly by the Iranian foreign minister, Mohammad Javad Zarif, and the US secretary of state, John Kerry. According to Robin Wright, Zarif had been playing a pivotal role since 2003, while Kerry started to play a more active role after the Sultan of Oman offered to host cover diplomacy between the countries in 2011.[6] Wright goes on to describe negotiations marked by cooperation, setbacks, and shared meals in Oman, Geneva, and Vienna, among other details of the meetings between the ministers. Although the leaders of the major powers – most significantly US president Barack Obama and Iranian president Hassan Rouhani – announced the deal in July 2015, the most important nonproliferation agreement of current times was actually shaped by the foreign ministers of the US and Iran over the course of twenty-two months of negotiations.

Leaders might set the general direction of a country's foreign affairs, and yet the example above clearly shows that foreign ministers have sufficient agency to shape foreign policy. This is precisely what motivated Modelski (1970) to analyze foreign ministers in the first place; they have sufficient power to shape policy. The potential for agency is also illustrated by Richard Holbrooke's role as Barack Obama's special representative to Afghanistan and Pakistan. According to George Packer from *The New Yorker*, not only did Holbrooke insist on receiving the title of *special representative* rather than *special envoy*, but along with it "[he] would create a rump regional bureau with the State Department, carved out of the Bureau of South and Central Asia, whose Afghanistan and Pakistan desks would report to him."[7]

The potential for agency is an important point. As highlighted in previous chapters, the relationship between a leader and a minister can be understood as an interaction between a principal and an agent. In Chapter 2, I elaborated on the distinction between problems of agency rent, moral hazard, and adverse selection; all of them can lead to a deviation from a leader's ideal point in a policy space. In this chapter, I want to concentrate on competence as the result of the poor selection of ministers (adverse selection) or the result of perfect selection of ministers who engage in unobserved behavior (rent). More specifically, I assume that the extent to which the actions of ministers differ from the ideal policies of leaders is determined by ability and not by political or ideological incongruence between them. In other words, it is not the case that leaders and ministers have different ideal points on the diplomatic arena, but rather that the minister is not competent enough to implement the leader's ideal policy. I am willing to do this for two reasons. First, the connection between internal and external threats to a leader's rule are heavily dependent on competence – able ministers in autocracies and certain parliamentary democracies are dismissed so they cannot challenger the leader, while democratic presidents keep their competent ministers in the cabinet because they do not present a threat. Second, if ministers have strong feelings about their leader's policy preferences, they can always resign. For instance, Robin Cook felt particularly proud of his role as minister of foreign affairs during the time of the policy of containment after the first Iraq War.[8] However, as Tony Blair began entertaining the idea of invading Iraq, Cook distanced himself from the government and resigned in March 2003. This suggests that ministers of foreign affairs who do not resign over decisions to fight a war are equally responsible for it.[9] As I argued above, recent research shows that the initiation of conflict has an important effect of war continuation (Croco 2011).

Having established that ministers of foreign affairs have the space to implement foreign policy with some degree of agency but that this agency is not caused by ideological differences but competence, I argue that *highly competent foreign ministers can solve the puzzle of war by securing a peace that yields the same goals of the war but without incurring the costs of fighting*. In contrast, incompetent ministers might produce two undesirable situations: a peace that does not yield the same goals of the war – and therefore a peace that is not an equilibrium – or interstate war. The worst and most incompetent of ministers will lead their countries to a war that they will lose. How can ministers solve the puzzle of war? Clearly, there is information that is strategic and revealing that it could weaken a country's position during a crisis; this is precisely why countries have incentives to misrepresent it (Fearon 1995). Nonetheless, there is information that can be disclosed without adverse effects and it is precisely here that the competence of a minister of foreign affairs plays a key role: highly competent ministers should be able to disclose private information without debilitating their country's position.

The story of Belize's independence from Britain provides an excellent example of the role of competent ministers of foreign affairs in preventing interstate conflict. Belize is a former British colony that was known as British Honduras; the territory, albeit located in Spanish colonial lands, had been historically populated by British settlers. Until recently, Mexico and Guatemala claimed sovereignty over large portions of Belize, although Guatemala has claimed the territory much more vigorously. Guatemala, Mexico, and the UK had held meetings and negotiations at least since the late nineteenth century, but they always failed to settle the matter.

As former colonies became independent in the postwar era, a potential solution to the dispute over Belize gained momentum in the 1960s, even as Guatemala was ruled by authoritarian military leaders fighting a brutal civil war. When Guatemalan president Julio Cesar Mendez Montenegro took office in 1966, he appointed Emilio Arenales as the country's minister of foreign affairs. Arenales was a trained diplomat and a former president of the UN General Assembly who used his diplomatic skills to carry out secret negotiations with his British counterparts; he was particularly adept at negotiating with the British while convincing the hawkish Guatemalan military establishment of the need for a diplomatic settlement. This difficult diplomatic effort culminated with the Webster Proposals of 1968, which for the first time provided a realistic draft treaty to settle the dispute between the UK and Guatemala. This was no small goal, particularly since Guatemalan elites – and the ruling military – were growing increasingly conservative, violent, and nationalistic. Unfortunately, Arenales was terminally ill and the British knew it. As his condition deteriorated, negotiations gained pace and yet they could not be completed because he died in 1969.

Arenales was replaced by a talented foreign minister, Alberto Fuentes Mohr, who occupied the position until 1970. Unfortunately, Fuentes Mohr did not have the diplomatic skills, the international reputation, or the adequate domestic political circumstances to continue negotiations. As Julio Cesar Mendez Montenegro left the presidency in 1970, so did Fuentes Mohr, who was detained by the new government of Colonel Carlos Manuel Arana Osorio and then forced into exile. Arana Osorio was the first of a series of brutal Guatemalan military commanders who had an almost reckless approach to Belize. Although meetings with the UK formally continued in the early 1970s, Guatemala no longer had a talented foreign minister who could negotiate with the British while keeping the hawkish military rulers at bay, as Arenales had done in the late 1960s. Rumors of a Guatemalan invasion of Belize forced the UK to send the aircraft carrier HMS Ark Royal and a naval air squadron to 'show the flag' over Belize in 1972. Negotiations over Belize resumed after the incident, but a second international crisis in 1975 further delayed a potential settlement and Belize's prospects for an independence safe from Guatemalan aggression (Quiroz Flores 2003). By then, it was clear to the UK, the Belizean political elite, and Belize's allies that the road to Belizean independence would be completed without an agreement with Guatemala. Belize gained independence in 1981 with broad international support.

As with most observational data, we can only speculate on what could have happened to the territorial dispute between Belize and the UK if Arenales had stayed in office. Maybe Belize would have gained independence earlier. Maybe sections of Belize would have been absorbed by Guatemala. Unfortunately, in the case of Belize and Arenales, we cannot observe the counterfactual. As I will explain in the next chapter, we can work around this using quantitative analysis. In the meantime, there is another example of an incredibly talented foreign minister who not only protected his country from aggressive neighbors but also managed to enlarge his country's territory in a peaceful manner. I am referring to Jose Maria da Silva Paranhos, Baron of Rio Branco, Brazilian diplomat, and minister of foreign affairs from 1902 to 1912. As I will explain in a moment, his work as foreign minister perfectly represents the ability to produce a peace that yields the same goals as a war but without incurring the costs of fighting.

In order to explain Rio Branco's contribution to Brazil's territorial expansion, I need to briefly elaborate on Brazil's unique place in the Americas. Brazil was the largest Portuguese possession in the New World, which was mostly controlled by Spain. The 1494 Treaty of Tordesillas had organized Spanish and Portuguese possessions around the planet, including in the Americas. Yet, there were areas in this massive continent that were populated by both Spanish and Portuguese settlers, exactly as it happened in Belize. For instance, Brazil's current state of Acre, its westernmost state, lies at the confluence of large waterways and massive natural resources that were claimed by both Bolivia and Peru, although they were mostly exploited by the Portuguese (Ganzert 1934). This area was beyond the boundary established by Tordesillas, and therefore Spain had to sign new treaties with Portugal in 1750 and 1777 to stop the latter's westward advance. At the turn of the nineteenth century, and as Brazil gained independence in 1822, it based its claim over Acre on the principle of *uti possidetis de facto*, that is, its ability to claim the land, as it already possessed it. In contrast, Bolivia and Peru turned to international law and the old treaties between Spain and Portugal.

As the century went by and the parties could not agree to a settlement, Bolivia tried to impose jurisdiction in this area now heavily populated by Brazilian nationals, who ended up rising against Bolivian authorities in 1903. It is precisely at this time that Rio Branco played a key role in the territorial dispute. Rio Branco had been appointed foreign minister in 1902; by then he had accumulated credentials as a formidable negotiator in the international arbitrations that settled disputes between Brazil and Argentina in 1895 and Brazil and France over French Guyana in 1900 (Lafer 2000). In a series of moves that included lifting Brazilian sanctions on Bolivian trade, recognizing sections of Bolivian territory in the area, and compensating an Anglo-American conglomerate in exchange for their concessions in the territory, Rio Branco signed in Petropolis a boundary treaty with Bolivia in 1903 (Ganzert 1934).

The Petropolis treaty brought additional complications into the negotiations with Peru, which also claimed part of Acre. By 1904 both Brazilians and Peruvian settlers had engaged in small skirmishes. Again, Rio Branco used his diplomatic skills to sign two agreements with Peru in 1904; the first stopped all hostilities between the parties, while the second called for an arbitral tribunal (Ganzert 1934). The tribunal, as well as Brazil and Peru, continued to negotiate a potential settlement until 1909. Negotiations could have stopped then, as the Peruvian minister was on leave and no successor could be found; according to Ganzert (1934: 446): "This was a case in which Rio-Branco's long and continuous service as foreign minister enabled him to keep alive negotiations that otherwise might have been dropped." Rio Branco signed a settlement with Peru in 1909.

Rio Branco did not stop there. Brazil had ten neighbors, and many had disputes over territory. He continued to settled more disputes with the UK over British Guyana in 1904, Venezuela in 1905, the Netherlands over Dutch Guyana in 1906, Colombia in 1907, and Uruguay in 1909 (Lafer 2000). Altogether, Rio Branco had used diplomacy, international law, and arbitration to give Brazil an additional territory the size of France (Mares 2001). Perhaps more importantly, he had contributed to the formation of Brazilian continental identity, the institutionalization of Brazil's foreign service, and a Grotian diplomatic ethos and style that carried over to the twentieth and the twenty-first century (Lafer 2000). In this sense, I concur with Lafer (2000: 214) on the extraordinary diplomatic performance of Rio Branco: "As Rubens Ricúpero asserts, it is difficult to find, in the history of international relations, a negotiating performance and an exclusively peaceful patter similar to the Brazilian one in the establishment of national borders."

Rio Branco and Arenales are archetypes of diplomatic competence. Nevertheless, both died in office and therefore it is not possible to explore to what extent they fit with my theory of cabinet change – as competent ministers in less than perfect democracies they should have been replaced by their leaders, particularly Rio Branco, who was very popular and had held office under four different Brazilian presidents. In the following chapters I will systematically analyze whether foreign ministers' competence leads to dismissal under different political systems. Meanwhile, I would like to elaborate on some cases where a minister's competence has come into question and how his performance led to war. Under certain political circumstances, being incompetent, or at least appearing so, might be an excellent political strategy.

Let's start with Lord Clarendon, British foreign secretary from 1853 to 1858. George William Frederick Villers, Earl of Clarendon, was appointed secretary of state for foreign affairs in 1853 by Lord Aberdeen just as Britain, France, Sardinia, and the Ottoman empire prepared to fight Russia in the Crimean War. The Crimean War is a complicated story of great-power competition mixed with religious motives whereby Russia, as self-described protector of the Orthodox church, tried to secure protection of its subjects and their access to Christian places of worship under the control of the Ottoman empire. As Russia occupied the Danubian Principalities – what is now Romania – in July 1853, a conference of ambassadors met in Vienna to negotiate a potential settlement of the conflict between the Russian and Ottoman empires. This agreement, proposed jointly by Britain, France, Austria, and Prussia, and known as the Vienna Note, was crucial because it had been accepted by the tsar, whose intransigence had become a significant obstacle to peace.

In Britain, Lords Aberdeen and Clarendon "decided that [the Turks] 'must' accept the note, a view that should be conveyed '*in strong terms, privately to Stratford*'" (Lambert 1990: 45). Lord Stratford was Britain's special envoy to Turkey and adviser to the Turkish government. Although it has been argued that Stratford apparently managed to convince the Ottoman officials to reject the settlement, in a case of Clarendon's poor oversight of the diplomatic corps, the fact is that the Vienna Note was destined to fail because it largely ignored the preferences of Turkey (Lambert 1990), while allied military presence in the area also weakened a potential settlement (Herkless 1975).

It is the case, however, that there was an opportunity to use diplomacy to avoid the hostilities of October 1853, marked by ruthless combat in the Crimean peninsula. It is also the case that Clarendon was a cabinet minister in a coalition government led by Prime Minister Aberdeen but that included Viscount Palmerston, a towering figure of British foreign policy, in the position of home secretary. Clarendon was caught between Palmerston and Aberdeen and often appeared as a wavering figure. And yet he held on to office until 1856, two years after the Crimean War had ended. This fits my theory of cabinet change in parliamentary democracies – I argued that both very competent and very incompetent ministers are replaced by their leaders, as the former cannot provide the public goods necessary for the leader's reelection, while the latter are potential political challengers. In this light, Clarendon was not replaced because he was moderately competent. On the one hand, the allies actually won the war but they had to pay for the costs of it, both political and material. The war eventually put enormous pressure on the Aberdeen government, which resigned in 1855. On the other hand, Clarendon was not an internal challenger; the challenger was Palmerston, who ended up succeeding Aberdeen and keeping Clarendon in the Foreign Office.

As I explained in Chapter 3, lack of competence is an even more effective political asset in autocracies. In the aftermath of the first Iraq War, former US secretary of state James A. Baker III recalls an encounter with Tariq Aziz, the Iraqi foreign minister who, along with Saddam Hussein, remained in power even after the victory of the allies:

> In occasionally reflecting on this perverse twist of history, I'm reminded of something Tariq Aziz said to me in Geneva: 'We will be here long after you're gone.' It was one of the few things he said that proved to be true.
> (Baker 1995: 442)

More recently, and as I write these lines, it has been announced that the US and Russia agreed in Munich to deliver humanitarian aid to Syria and follow up with a potential cessation of hostilities. The deal has been greeted with optimism but also with caution, particularly since Syrian president Bashar al-Assad had promised to 'retake the whole country' just a few hours before the announcement was made. Since pro-democracy protests started in Syria in 2011, more than 250,000 individuals have lost their lives, while 11 million have fled their homes, contributing to an immigration crisis in Turkey and the European Union.[10] Meanwhile, the conflict has facilitated the emergence of some brutal Islamic groups, such as the so-called Islamic State.

In spite of the international sanctions and the military defeats and political setbacks, the Assad government has managed to continue ruling the majority of the country and its capital. Assad's father controlled the country from 1971 to 2000, when the young Bashar al-Assad took over. He kept Farouk al-Sharaa as foreign minister, who had been in the Foreign Ministry since 1984. Walid al-Mualem succeeded al-Sharaa in 2006 and was then appointed vice president. It is quite striking that Mualem has kept his cabinet position in spite of his government's blunders in the area of foreign affairs. Although he has secured Russian and Iranian support, he has not been able to prevent the imposition of sanctions by the US, the UK, the EU, Canada, Turkey, and the Arab League, who have implemented travel bans, the freezing of assets, and import bans that have had negative consequences on the regime.

Foreign ministers like Mualem are almost a contradiction; it seems that the poorer the performance, the longer their hold on power. And yet this is a systematic feature of cabinet politics in autocratic governments. *The Economist* recently reported on a historical figure of Chinese diplomacy, Wanyan Chonghou, a nobleman of the late nineteenth century who managed to hold on to several high-ranking government positions in spite of his dismal performance in all of them. When the river he managed near Beijing was flooded, he was relocated to oversee trade with foreigners. When French clerics were massacred during his administration, he became imperial envoy to France. Then, "less than three years later he was promoted to the emperor's side in Beijing, as one of a team of advisers that botched an entanglement with Japan. How did this man keep getting work?"[11] China's worst diplomat, as labeled by *The Economist*, was a member of a team of advisers who failed to anticipate Japan's intentions to claim Taiwan and only after China paid a ransom to Japan did the latter abandon its stake over the island. In a clearer case of diplomatic incompetence, Chonghou was sent to Russia to establish a border in the aftermath of Russian-backed independence movements in northwestern China. The Qing government had the upper hand, as it had defeated the rebel movements. Then, in September 1879, Chonghou "agreed to a treaty that, instead of returning territory to Qing rule, awarded the tsar a number of important parts of Xinjiang and gave Russia valuable long-term trading privileges deep in Qing territory."[12]

In spite of having one of the oldest civil service exams in the world – and Chonghou's father and older brother had passed some of the most difficult imperial exams – the corrupt regime also needed, as I predicted, loyal bureaucrats. Wealthy loyalists could also join the government ranks by paying for a position; apparently, Chonghou's family paid for his first appointments and promotions. Chonghou had also distinguished himself by dealing with foreigners, which was not a top job in Imperial China. What is striking about this example is that in spite of Chonghou's numerous failures, he continued to be employed by the

Imperial government. Chonghou got his first high-ranking job in 1856 as manager of the Yongdin river; two years later he was dismissed and yet he was appointed superintendent of trade at Tianjin. His failure to extract concessions from Russia in 1879 earned him a place in prison – and China an international crisis – and he was sentenced to death. This was a twenty-two-year-long career marked by blunders that included flooding, the slaughter of foreigners, and the potential loss of territory, along with an international crisis. Chonghou was not executed by the Imperial government and rather was freed in 1880 after foreign dignitaries – including Queen Victoria – pleaded for his life. He retired to his mansion with over 100 rooms.

I believe that there is a strong selection bias in the observability of blunders by diplomats representing autocratic countries. In other words, we do not get to observe their mistakes because they do not have incentives to act in the first place. As I explained before, competent ministers are replaced in autocracies because they are potential challengers. However, an intelligent minister only needs to stay relatively quiet and show loyalty in order to keep a cabinet position; there is no need to show either competence or incompetence, unless it is strictly necessary. Nevertheless, as demonstrated by the examples of Mualem in Syrian, Chonghou in Imperial China, and even Iraq's Tariq Aziz, we get to see some of their blunders. Some of these diplomatic blunders were recently explored in a study of modern New York City, which happens to be a fantastic place to observe the behavior of diplomats.

In a recent study of corruption, Fisman and Miguel (2006) harnessed a natural experiment in New York City, where thousands of diplomats enjoying diplomatic immunity live. As argued by Fisman and Miguel (2006: 4): "Diplomatic immunity provides consular officials and their families with protection from prosecution or lawsuits in their host country." The authors believe that the behavior of diplomats reflects a propensity to break rules when they face little chance of prosecution; hence, the experiment allowed the researchers to explore social norms as causes of corruption. Using the number of parking tickets issued to diplomatic missions, Fisman and Miguel found that diplomats from high-corruption countries had significantly more parking violations. The top five countries according to the number of violations per diplomat – as some missions are quite large – were Kuwait, Egypt, Chad, Sudan, and Bulgaria, with 246.2, 139.6, 124.3, 119.1, and 117.5 violations, respectively. These are not very democratic countries. Some of the countries that did not have any violations are the UK, the Netherlands, the UAE, Canada, and Australia, among many others. Of course, these are relatively minor issues – although they have infuriated city officials in New York and London, where many diplomatic missions avoid paying congestion charges – and yet they provide a revealing picture of the type of diplomatic practices of autocratic countries. The question that I explore in the next chapter is whether the performance of diplomats, in this case ministers of foreign affairs, has an effect on their tenure in office. Rather than using case studies and anecdotes, I base my evidence on the systematic analysis of large quantities of data on ministers' tenure in office.

Before I do that, however, I would like to make a note: peace by itself is not a sign of ministerial competence. A peace that yields the same outcome as war but without incurring the costs of fighting is, however, the product of competence. Although it is not possible to observe what a country would obtain in the counterfactual, it is reasonable to believe that such a peace is self-enforcing and part of an equilibrium, which suggests that countries do not have incentives to deviate from it and try to obtain the same results by fighting. Hence, long periods of peace should resemble a settlement that produces similar results to those of war but without incurring its costs. In this sense, it is not the case that ministers who simply avoid war are more competent than others. More formally, if war takes place, say, at time t, we know that a minister at that same time did not avoid it; but we do not know if other ministers at time $t-1, t-2, \ldots, t-j$ facilitated the war such that it takes place at time t. In other words, it is possible that a minister is not responsible for a war that her predecessors facilitated.

This notwithstanding, I assume that the government responsible for war at time t is the government at time t. First, it is very difficult to know exactly who is responsible for a war that has taken time to develop, such as the Mexican-American War. In this case, tensions between Mexico and the United States started in 1835 when Texas began to move toward independence from Mexico. However, the war only started in 1846. By that time, Antonio Lopez de Santa Anna had declared himself president, while the prelude of the war had been experienced mainly by a previous administration. Second, it is often the case that negotiations practically start anew when there is a change in administrations or even a change in the cabinet. That is precisely why the British government was rushing to reach a settlement with Guatemala over Belize, as Guatemalan minister Arenales was dying and a new government would probably demand new negotiations. Hence, it is safe to argue that the minister responsible for the war is the minister who is in office when the war starts.

Conclusions

This chapter makes three very important points. First, diplomacy plays an important role in war and the avoidance of war. Second, foreign ministers rather than leaders carry out the majority of diplomatic efforts. Lastly, competence determines whether foreign ministers can secure a peace that provides the same goals of war but without incurring its costs. These three points are essential for the test of the predictions developed in Chapter 3, as they establish the significance of the role of foreign ministers, the scope for agency, and the role of competence in agency. As I mentioned before, I assume that generally speaking, foreign ministers and their leaders share the same preferences in foreign policy, and deviations from the leader's ideal point are caused by incompetence. It is not the case that ministers and leaders disagree on foreign policy; when this is the case, foreign ministers can simply resign, as Robin Cook did in 2003.

I have tried to provide strong foundations for my argument on ministerial competence. It fits into a theoretical framework of rational war and, perhaps more importantly, is quite intuitive. Indeed, it is safe to argue that foreign ministers are their country's highest-ranking diplomats and that they act as agents of leaders who do not have either the diplomatic credentials or the time to carry out lengthy international negotiations. It is also safe to argue that some ministers are better than others, although in this case I define this as their ability to secure the goals of war without actually fighting it. In this light, competent foreign ministers are efficient.

What is important to note at this point is that the tests that follow in the next sections are tests of the effect of competence on ministerial change. In this sense, I will explore whether time of peace as described above as a measure of competence leads to permanency in the cabinet in democratic presidential systems, and in some parliamentary systems. Likewise, it should be the case that diplomatic competence should cause cabinet change in autocracies, although I am inclined to believe that foreign ministers from autocratic countries might be risk averse and prefer to not act at all rather than show competence. At the end of the day, competence is important because it reflects whether a minister can depose a leader; if ministers in autocracies remain passive while convincing their leaders of their loyalty, then time of peace is likely to be insignificant in their tenure in office. The following empirical tests will explore these predictions.

Notes

1. www.state.gov/secretary/rm/2009a/01/115196.htm
2. George Packer, "The Last Mission." *The New Yorker*, Sept 28, 2009. www.newyorker.com/magazine/2009/09/28/the-last-mission
3. Robin Wright. "Letter from Iran. Tehran's promise." *The New Yorker*, July 27, 2015. www.newyorker.com/magazine/2015/07/28/tehrans-promise
4. www.state.gov/secretary/rm/2009a/01/115196.htm
5. www.theguardian.com/environment/2015/dec/07/paris-climate-summit-key-players
6. Robin Wright, *op. cit.*
7. George Packer, *op. cit.*
8. http://news.bbc.co.uk/2/hi/2859431.stm
9. It could be argued that sometimes war is inevitable, and therefore competence has absolutely nothing to do with it. Several references have been made to events that led to inevitable conflict, such as the Pearl Harbor attack in 1941 and the Vietnam War after the death of President Kennedy. In reality, this is rarely the case. It is now well known that the United States and Japan had been engaged in negotiations over the Pacific for over nine months before the Pearl Harbor attack, as indicated by a series of official communications that involved the president and secretary of state of the United States and the Japanese emperor and the Japanese ambassador to the United States. On Vietnam, research has disqualified the "inevitability" thesis of its escalation in 1965. According to Logevall (2004: 102): "At no point from his ascension to the White House in November 1963 through the winter of 1965 was [Johnson] confined to a certain course of action on Vietnam. He inherited a difficult Vietnam problem from John F. Kennedy, and his choices were few and difficult. But exist the choices did."
10. www.bbc.co.uk/news/world-middle-east-26116868
11. www.economist.com/node/21591796/print
12. www.economist.com/node/21591796/print

6 Evidence in autocracies

Introduction

This chapter presents the first set of empirical tests of the hypotheses developed in Chapter 3. The hypotheses on ministerial change are as follows:

1 In small-coalition countries, competent ministers are more likely to be dismissed from office than incompetent ones.
2 In large-coalition presidential systems, competent ministers are less likely to be dismissed from office than incompetent ones.
3 In large-coalition parliamentary systems where the party elite does not receive perks, moderately competent ministers are less likely to be deposed than highly incompetent or highly competent ministers. When the party elite receives perks, relatively more competent ministers are less likely to be deposed than highly incompetent or highly competent ministers.

Chapter 5 explains why foreign ministers provide us with an opportunity to test these hypotheses. More specifically, I argued that diplomacy plays an important role in war, that foreign ministers rather than leaders carry out the majority of diplomatic efforts, and that competence determines whether foreign ministers can secure a peace that provides the same goals of war but without incurring its costs.

With these building blocks in place, I expect to find that incompetent ministers in authoritarian countries last longer in office than competent ministers in the same conditions. Moreover, competent secretaries in presidential democracies will be cabinet members longer than mediocre secretaries. In parliamentary democracies I expect cabinet ministers with average skills to last longer in office than very talented or quite mediocre ministers.

Unfortunately, testing these propositions, even with rich data on ministerial tenure at hand, presents an econometric challenge. The challenge resides in the interdependent character of the tenure in office of ministers and their leaders. Indeed, whether a minister stays in office depends on the leader's likelihood of deposition, and the leader's probability of deposition also depends on whether the cabinet minister holds on to office. If these two processes were independent of each other, I could simply estimate an event history model of leaders' tenure like the models of Bueno de Mesquita et al. (2003, 2004) or Chiozza and Goemans (2003, 2004). Likewise, I could estimate another survival model of ministerial tenure similar to the studies of Kerby (2009), Quiroz Flores (2009), or Berlinski, Dewan, and Dowding (2010). However, a leader's time in office cannot simply be added as an explanatory variable of ministerial change because leader tenure is endogenous.

Recent advances in the econometrics literature have looked at this problem in a context of survival models (Gordon 2002; Boehmke, Morey, and Shannon 2006; Blake, Box-Steffensmeier, and Woo 2010; Chiba, Martin, and Stevenson 2015; Fukumoto 2015), and they show that the solution is neither trivial nor perfect. One of the problems is the complexity of probability distributions adequate for two non-normal, continuous random variables, such as time in office for two different subjects. Distributions such as the bivariate exponential or bivariate Weibull exist, but they place important restrictions on estimation, such as the ability to explore right- and left-censored observations and time-varying covariates. They also place restrictions on the degree of interdependence between the two time processes. In addition, these distributions make strict assumptions about time dependence, which is rather limiting. Unfortunately, there is a lack of distributions that are more flexible in terms of the form of time dependence; for instance, there is no bivariate equivalent to the Cox proportional hazards model.

Given the limitations of bivariate survival models, I rely on two solutions. First, I use an instrumental variable approach. An instrumental variable is correlated with the endogenous variable – leader's tenure – but not with the disturbance. This approach, technically a probit model with instrumental variables, is only used in the context of nondemocratic countries presented in this chapter. In the next chapter I overcome the lack of an instrumental variable applicable to all countries by estimating a bivariate discrete survival model that explores the joint probability of leader and minister deposition conditional on their time in office.

Before I present estimation results, I need to describe the organization of my data on foreign ministers, particularly since pairing minister and leader survival times is not a trivial task. I will also describe my independent variables for a model of ministerial tenure, as I need to make sure that I have controlled for other potential determinants of time in office at the Ministry of Foreign Affairs.

Data organization

I already introduced and described the largest database in the social sciences related to ministers of foreign affairs – it covers 7,300 ministers of foreign affairs in more than 180 countries spanning the years 1696–2004. The dataset is very detailed and reflects the realities of political life at the ministerial level in dozens of countries for hundreds of years. One aspect of political life captured by the dataset that needs to be noted at this point is that ministers of foreign affairs

Evidence in autocracies 97

may serve under different leaders. This is important because, as I argued above, the minister's and the leader's tenure in office are interdependent. Therefore, it is crucial that the datasets of ministers and leaders are carefully organized. Otherwise we may mask the effect of a leader's tenure in office and how it affects ministerial deposition.

I match my foreign minister data with the leader data from *Archigos*, a database of political leaders collected by Goemans, Gleditsch, and Chiozza (2009). These data provide the dates for the entry and exit of political leaders and their age. It covers 2,937 leaders with a median time in office of 1.99 years and a standard error of .094. Tenure in office can be easily represented with a graph that reflects the hazard of deposition of leaders. For instance, if median time in office is 2 years, we can interpret this as if 50 percent of all leaders have been deposed by the time they reach their second year in office. This may suggest that the hazard rate is increasing over time, that is, the rate at which leaders are deposed from office increases the longer they are in office.

Figure 6.1 presents the hazard rate for leaders across all political systems in the *Archigos* database and its 95 percent confidence interval. As I explained previously, a hazard rate presents the rate at which units – in this case, leaders – lose office at different periods in time. Increasing hazard rates suggest that leaders are replaced at higher rates over time. In other words, this means that as leaders accumulate time in office, they are more likely to be replaced. In contrast, decreasing hazard rates indicate that leaders are less likely to be deposed over time.

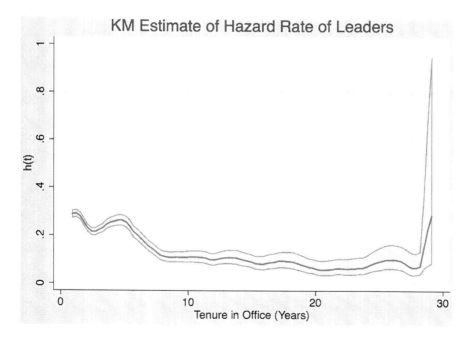

Figure 6.1 Hazard rate of leaders, 1840–2004

98 *Evidence in autocracies*

This graph indicates that leaders are deposed at different rates up to year 5, but once they have passed this five-year threshold, they are less and less likely to be removed from office. In other words, leaders are fragile at the beginning of their administrations, but once they have managed to hold on to office for about five years, they face a decreasing likelihood of deposition. As I explained in Chapter 4, loyalty is weak during a leader's early term in office because both the leader and her supporters have yet to confirm mutual support. It is precisely for this reason that coups and purges often take place at the beginning of leaders' administrations, which explains why leaders' hazard rates are very high at the beginning of their terms in office. However, once leaders and their coalition members are committed to an exchange of political support for private goods, leaders become more difficult to depose, particularly in autocracies.

Having said this, I organized the data for ministers and leaders as multiple record data: there is a line of data for each year a leader and a minister hold office. In other words, the unit of analysis is the leader-minister-year. A leader may have several ministers in one single year. In these cases, the year in question is broken down into several observations, one for each minister. Likewise, a minister may serve under different leaders during the same year. To account for this, the database includes multiple lines of data points for a single minister, for the same year, but with different leaders.

Figure 6.2 presents an example of how the data are organized. The figure illustrates the changes in the position of secretary of state during the transition from the first to the second Clinton presidency. President Clinton had worked

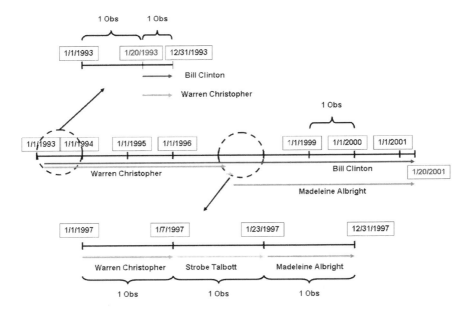

Figure 6.2 Data organization

Evidence in autocracies 99

with Warren Christopher during his first administration but once he was reelected, he asked Madeleine Albright to replace Christopher. During the transition, Strobe Talbott acted as secretary of state. For the purposes of data organization, this particular transition requires that the year 1997 be broken down into three data points: one for Warren Christopher, one for Strobe Talbott, and another one for Madeleine Albright. Each data point accounts for the duration of each president and secretary of state. This type of data organization had to be carried out for all cabinet ministers included in the database.

Variables

Having described the organization of the data, but before discussing the estimation framework, I would like to elaborate on the variables of interest. I am mainly interested in the deposition of ministers of foreign affairs (*Minister Fails*) and how this is related to the deposition of leaders (*Leader Fails*). I coded these variables as dummy variables – they are equal to zero as long as the respective politicians are in office, and equal to one at the year when they lose office. Evidently, the likelihoods of minister and leader deposition are related to their duration in office. In order to account for this, I will control for the variables (*ln(Leader's Tenure)*), which is the natural logarithm of the number of years a leader holds office plus one, and the variable (*ln(Minister's Tenure)*), which is the natural logarithm of the number of years a minister of foreign affairs holds office plus one. This type of functional form gives a larger weight to early time in office; as I explained before, early periods in office are crucial for long-term survival.

As I argued in Chapter 5, a minister's competence is measured by peacetime. I operationalize this variable with (*ln(Minister's Peace Time)*), which is the natural logarithm of the number of years of peace plus one that a minister has produced. The longer the peace produced by a minister, the more competent the minister is. As an illustration of how this variable works, consider US president Woodrow Wilson, who was in office from 1913 to 1921. As president of the United States he produced four years of peace before entering the First World War in 1917. Wilson had two secretaries of state: William Jennings and Robert Lansing. Jennings was in office from 1913 to 1915, whereas Lansing was in office from 1915 to 1921. Jennings produced three years of peace, whereas Lansing produced only two years of peace in spite of being more than five years in office. Similarly, President Roosevelt and Secretary Hull were in office for twelve years, but they produced less than nine years of peace.[1]

As I explained in Chapter 5, leaders who initiate war may want to back down, but the potential for domestic punishment in the case of defeat or a poor war settlement might force them to continue fighting (Croco 2011). In addition, I mentioned that the worst and most incompetent foreign ministers will lead their countries to a war that they will lose. Therefore, I use the variable (*Incompetent Minister*) as an additional indicator of ministerial ability. This variable is equal to one if a minister held office while her country initiated a war that was eventually lost, and equal to zero otherwise. War and its outcome are defined according to the Correlates of War (COW) project (Sarkees 2000). The COW project, founded in 1963 at the University of Michigan, is perhaps the largest and most reputable effort to systematically collect data on interstate conflict. At the time of writing, the project was hosted by Penn State.

The tenure of ministers in office is determined not only by their competence. Indeed, there are other variables that explain why some cabinet members stay in office longer than others; some of these control variables also contribute to the determination of leader tenure. A perfect example of such variable is the size of the winning coalition (W). The estimate of the winning coalition is an index that reflects the openness of a political system. More specifically, it is a composite index of Polity IV data that includes information on the competitiveness of executive recruitment, openness of executive recruitment, and competitiveness of participation regime. It also includes regime type as defined by Arthur Banks's cross-national time-series data. The size of the winning has a minimum normalized value of zero, and a maximum of one, and it is organized in intervals of .25 points (Bueno de Mesquita et al. 2003, 2004).

As I explained in the Introduction to this volume, leaders maximize their tenure in office by keeping the support of members of the winning coalition through the provision of goods. In small-coalition systems, leaders provide a larger mix of private goods, while in large-coalition systems, they provide a larger mix of public goods. Bueno de Mesquita et al. (2003, 2004), as well as others who have studied leader survival (e.g., McGillivray and Smith 2008; Smith 2008; Bueno de Mesquita and Smith 2009, 2010; Quiroz Flores and Smith 2011), operationalize public goods provision with the natural logarithm of gross domestic product (GDP) per capita ($ln(GDPpc)$). I expect the provision of public goods to have positive externalities on a minister's tenure and therefore I also include this variable in my specifications. This variable was obtained from the World Bank's World Development Indicators.

Lastly, I also control for the overall capabilities of a country. This variable is labeled (*Capabilities*) and it is the composite indicator of national capabilities produced by the COW project (Sarkees 2000). This is an important variable because national capabilities might have an impact on how difficult it is to be a foreign minister. It could be the case that powerful countries have interests across the globe and must reach out to a larger number of nations, while less powerful countries only interact with neighbors and international organizations. No other variable seems to better capture the difficulty of being a minister of foreign affairs.

As I mentioned before, I use an instrumental variable approach to identify the effect of a leader's tenure on a minister's likelihood of deposition. Recall that permanence in the cabinet depends on ministerial competence and ambition and a leader's incentives to stay in office. This suggests that the time in office of both leaders and ministers is interdependent. For this reason, I cannot simply add a leader's time in office as an explanatory variable in my analysis of ministerial change – leaders' tenure is endogenous in my model of cabinet change.

Evidence in autocracies 101

This is a problem because endogenous covariates are correlated with a disturbance, and such correlation causes biased estimates that invalidate inference in linear and nonlinear models. Instrumental variables are a popular method to solve the problem of endogenous covariates. As an example of how instrumental variables work, consider the work of Miguel, Satyanath, and Sergenti (2004), who explore the effects of economic conditions on the prospects of civil conflict. The endogeneity problem arises because lack of economic opportunities may lead people to fight, but the conflict itself further weakens the economy, which then forces people to fight. The authors solve this problem by using an instrumental variable for economic conditions – rainfall variation. The latter is evidently correlated with economic conditions but is not correlated with conflict (or at least the authors show that this is the case). Therefore, rather than using economic conditions in their specification, they use the economic conditions predicted by rainfall variation and other exogenous covariates to estimate the effect of economic opportunities on the likelihood of conflict.

The endogeneity problem in the estimation of minister and leader tenure is similar; both tenure processes are mutually determined. To solve this, I use a leader's age (*Leader Age*) as an instrument for a leader's tenure in office. This variable, also obtained from the *Archigos* dataset (Goemans, Gleditsch, and Chiozza 2009), is correlated with leaders' tenure but is not associated with ministerial permanency in office, particularly in countries with small-coalition systems. Leaders in small-coalition systems are advantaged over their rivals because they can better commit to provide private goods. Unfortunately, this stream of goods will come to an end when the leader dies. In this sense, a good indicator of actuarial risk is age.

Before I move on to discussing estimation techniques and results, I need to introduce a categorization of regimes. This categorization is crucial because several empirical tests restrict the estimation sample in order to investigate the effect of covariates in different political systems, such as autocracies, parliamentary democracies, and presidential democracies. For instance, the tests of this chapter are restricted to autocratic regimes because the instrumental variable I use here is applicable to only this type of political system.

Table 6.1 Summary statistics

Variable	Mean	Standard Deviation	N
Minister Fails	0.337	0.473	11,924
ln (Minister's Peace Time)	1.219	0.721	13,191
Winning Coalition Size	0.499	0.324	18,922
ln (Leader's Tenure)	1.625	0.791	11,924
Leader Age	54.412	12.337	17,380
ln (GDPpc)	7.485	1.546	7,719
Incompetent Minister	0.021	0.143	29,342
Capabilities	0.014	0.038	17,547

Table 6.2 Coalition size and system

W	Autocracy	Parliamentary Democracy	Mixed Democracy	Presidential Democracy	Total
0	739	0	0	1	740
0.25	1,485	0	0	33	1,518
0.5	2,155	7	19	78	2,259
0.75	593	682	188	724	2,187
1	51	1,397	219	380	2,047
Total	5,023	2,086	426	1,216	8,751

As mentioned before, the ease of leader and minister deposition varies according to political institutions such as the level democracy and the presidential or parliamentary character of countries. Przeworski et al. (2000) capture these differences across regimes in the variable (*INST*), which takes values from zero to three. The value zero corresponds to an autocracy, value one to a parliamentary democracy, value two to a mixed democracy, and value three to a presidential democracy. Since there is variation of *W* within each type of system according to Przeworski et al. (2000), Table 6.2 presents the relationship between these two variables.[2]

I combine the size of the winning coalition *W* and the variable *INST* to define a new variable called (*Regime Type*). This new variable defines three regime types: autocracies, large-coalition parliamentary systems, and large-coalition presidential systems. The country is an autocracy if Przeworski et al. (2000) define it as such and $W \leq .5$. The country is a large-coalition parliamentary system if Przeworski, Alvarez, Cheibub, and Limongi define it as such and $W \geq .75$. Lastly, a country is a large-coalition presidential system if Przeworski, Alvarez, Cheibub, and Limongi define it as such and $W \geq .75$. It is very important to note that neither the variable *INST* nor the size of the winning coalition *W* can be used on their own to classify regimes in terms of the difficulty and procedures to replace a leader and a minister. This is why the variable *Regime Type* is so important. It must also be noted that *Regime Type* is not included in the models' specifications but rather is used to separate different types of regimes and appropriately test the theory advanced in the previous chapter.

Instrumental variable estimation

If ministers' tenure in office was unrelated to their leaders' time in office, I could explore ministerial change with well-known survival models (e.g., Box-Steffensmeier and Zorn 2001; Box-Steffensmeier and Jones 2004). As mentioned before, the empirical challenge in this book resides in the interdependent character of the tenure in office of ministers and their leaders. Indeed, whether a minister stays in office depends on the leader's likelihood of deposition, and the leader's probability of deposition also depends on whether the cabinet minister holds on to office. Recent advances in the econometrics literature have tried to solve this problem in a context of survival models (Gordon 2002; Boehmke, Morey, and Shannon 2006; Blake, Box-Steffensmeier, and Woo 2010; Chiba, Martin, and Stevenson 2015; Fukumoto 2015), but the solutions are not perfect. They fail to explore right- and left-censored observations and time-varying covariates and make strict assumptions about time dependence, which is rather limiting. However, it is possible to make modifications to continuous survival processes in order to estimate other models based on instrumental variables or bivariate distributions. For instance, discrete survival models can be used to analyze the hazard rate of a subject by including the effect of time on the probability of a subject's failure (Beck, Katz, and Tucker 1998). These models are essentially probit or logit models where the dependent variable is the occurrence of an event as determined by time dependence and other covariates. It is precisely for this reason that I created the dummy variables *Minister Fails* and *Leader Fails*, which are equal to zero as long as the respective politicians are in office, and equal to one at the year when they lose office.

As I explained in the previous section, since the likelihoods of minister and leader deposition are related to their duration in office, I included the variables (*ln(Leader's Tenure)*) and (*ln(Minister's Tenure)*). These variables capture time dependence. There are other ways of estimating duration dependence in discrete survival models, which are discussed by both Beck, Katz, and Tucker (1998) and Carter and Signorino (2010), who argue that a cubic polynomial of time outperforms other methods. In this chapter, the empirical results with the natural logarithm and the cubic polynomial are equivalent. However, since the natural logarithm is easier to interpret, and because it gives a larger weight to early time in office, the tests use this functional form.

Perhaps the most important reason for using a discrete survival process is that it can use instrumental variables and bivariate distributions. Discrete survival models are nonlinear regression, which can be estimated via least squares, maximum likelihood, or generalized method of moments. These estimation methods allow for the use of instrumental variables (Greene 2003). Hence, the challenge does not reside in estimation but, as usual, in finding an appropriate instrumental variable. As I mentioned before, I solved this problem by using a leader's age as an instrument for her tenure in office.

Having said this, I use discrete duration processes in order to estimate the impact of covariates that change over time on the hazard rate of leaders and ministers. Specifically, I estimate the probability of leader or minister deposition (i.e., the probability of observing a value of one in the dependent variables *Leader Fails* and *Minister Fails*) conditional on their time in office (i.e., *ln(Leader's Tenure)* and *ln(Minister's Tenure)*) and other covariates. In this context, it is important to note that a minister's tenure and time of peace are equivalent for periods without war. I address this potential collinearity problem by replacing a minister's tenure with the natural logarithm of time of peace (*ln(Minister's Peace Time)*).

104 *Evidence in autocracies*

The probit model with instrumental variables used in this chapter was developed by Newey (1987) and is described by the following.

$$y_1^* = y_2 \beta + x_1 \gamma + u; \quad (1)$$

$$y_2 = x_1 \Pi_1 + x_2 \Pi_2 + v. \quad (2)$$

where y_2 is a vector of endogenous variables, x_1 is a vector of exogenous variables, and x_2 is a vector of additional instruments. We do not observe y_1^* but instead $y_1 = 1$ if $y_1^* \geq 0$, or $y_1 = 0$ otherwise. Estimation is done via maximum likelihood, where the joint density $f(y_1, y_2|x)$ is estimated by breaking it down to $f(y_1|y_2,x)f(y_2|x)$, where $x = (x_1, x_2)$.

In this chapter, y_1 is the dependent variable *Minister Fails*, which is equal to 0 if the minister is in office and equal to one when the minister loses office. The variable y_2 is given by the variable *ln(Leader's Tenure)*. The vector x_1 essentially consists of *ln(Minister's Peace Time)* and other controls, while the vector of instrumental variables x_2 consists of the variable *Leader Age* and its interaction with *W*. It is important to recall that the tests focus only on autocratic regimes because age is a good indicator of actuarial risk and the provision of private goods is valid only in countries with small coalitions.

Estimation results

Having said this, Table 6.3 presents estimation results for three instrumental variable probit models of minister deposition.[3] Standard errors clustered on the minister are presented below coefficients. As a reference, Model 1 pools all political systems. Model 2 restricts the sample to autocratic countries and places an emphasis on a minister's competence as measured by the number of years of peace she has produced. Model 3 also restricts the sample to autocratic countries but examines both the number of years of peace produced by ministers and whether they led their countries to initiate a war that was eventually lost. This case is captured by the variable *Incompetent Minister*. This third model also includes a country's capabilities. The instruments in all models pass a Wald test of exogeneity that is not reported here.[4]

Models 2 and 3 use the natural logarithm of peacetime as a measure of ministerial competence. As argued above, this is an appropriate specification for the effect of time. However, such specification assumes a monotonic effect of time on the probability of minister deposition. This means that the likelihood of deposition either increases or decreases over time. However, it could well be the case that time has a non-monotonic effect, that is, it may increase the probability of deposition up to a point and then it may decrease it, or vice versa. In order to explore this more nuanced effect of time and competence, Model 4 replaces the natural logarithm of peace years with a cubic polynomial of peace years. A cubic polynomial consists of three variables: *peacetime*, *peacetime²*, and *peacetime³*.

Table 6.3 Instrumental variable probit

Variable	Model 1	Model 2	Model 3	Model 4
ln (Minister's Peace Time)	0.0795 (0.134)	0.336* (0.176)	0.305* (0.177)	
Winning Coalition Size	−0.545 (0.496)	3.640*** (1.206)	3.788*** (1.174)	4.744*** (1.186)
(W) (ln (Minister's Peace Time))	0.213 (0.159)	−0.421 (0.373)	−0.385 (0.375)	
ln (Leader's Tenure)	−0.0905 (0.0977)	−0.221* (0.118)	−0.129 (0.110)	−0.134 (0.115)
Minister's Peace Time				0.480*** (0.124)
(Minister's Peace Time)^2				−0.0484*** (0.0163)
(Minister's Peace Time)^3				0.000694 (0.000474)
(W) (Minister's Peace Time)				−0.444 (0.345)
(W) (Minister's Peace Time)^2				0.0314 (0.0505)
(W) (Minister's Peace Time)^3				0.000833 (0.00174)
ln (GDPpc)	−0.0909* (0.0533)	0.0511 (0.0659)	0.0560 (0.0651)	0.143** (0.0621)
(W) (ln(GDPpc))	0.0505 (0.0593)	−0.539*** (0.166)	−0.575*** (0.161)	−0.675*** (0.163)
Capabilities			−7.420*** (2.511)	−7.570*** (2.476)
Incompetent Minister			−0.105 (0.287)	
Constant	0.0441 (0.413)	−0.854 (0.520)	−0.972* (0.507)	−1.946*** (0.452)
athrho	−0.0517 (0.0681)	0.0148 (0.0926)	−0.0556 (0.0849)	−0.0514 (0.0904)
lnsigma	−0.403*** (0.0186)	−0.346*** (0.0284)	−0.352*** (0.0288)	−0.351*** (0.0285)
Observations	4,394	1,739	1,731	1,731
Log-likelihood	−6997.3927	−2829.5168	−2805.0745	−2780.016

*** $p<0.01$, ** $p<0.05$, * $p<0.1$

106 *Evidence in autocracies*

The interpretation of the coefficients in instrumental variable probit models is not straightforward. However, the significance of the estimates as well as their sign provide evidence about the role of a minister's competence. For instance, positive significant coefficients indicate an increase in the likelihood of ministerial deposition. In turn, negative significant coefficients indicate a decrease in the likelihood of deposition. Having said this, recall that the variable *ln(Minister's Peace Time)* captures a foreign minister's competence – competent ministers produce long lasting peace. Estimation results indicate that in the model that pools all types of political regimes, competence is irrelevant. However, competence plays a very different role across political systems, as established by my game theory model of Chapter 3. In Model 2, the estimate of *ln(Minister's Peace Time)* is positive and significant when $W=0$. This indicates that competent ministers in very autocratic systems are more likely to be replaced. This is precisely what I expected to see because leaders in small-coalition systems are predicted to dismiss competent ministers in order to eliminate internal challengers. However, as the regime becomes more democratic, competence loses significance, as suggested by a test on the restriction for *ln(Minister's Peace Time)* + *(.5) ln(Minister's Peace Time)* for the 'less autocratic' autocracies. The point estimate of this restriction is .1256 with a standard error of .097, which is statistically insignificant.

The substantive results are very similar in Model 3: competence increases a minister's hazard in very autocratic systems but not in less autocratic systems where $W=.5$. Here, the point estimate of the restriction *ln(Minister's Peace Time)* + *(.5)ln(Minister's Peace Time)* is .1118 with a standard error of .104, which is also statistically insignificant. The same is true for Model 4, where the test for the linear restriction *peacetime + peacetime^2 + peacetime^3* is .4317 with a standard error of .1094, which is highly statistically significant. Interestingly, the estimate for the linear restriction of *peacetime + peacetime^2 + peacetime^3 + (.5)(peacetime + peacetime^2 + peacetime^3)* is .2256 with a standard error of .0786, which is also statistically significant. For this cubic polynomial, even in the less autocratic autocracies, competence increases the hazard of ministerial deposition

Perhaps more interestingly, the estimate for the variable *Incompetent Minister* in Model 3 shows that leading an autocratic country to initiate a war and losing it does not increase a minister's hazard. This also constitutes evidence in favor of the theory of cabinet change in autocratic systems whereby ministers are not fired due to their incompetence. Indeed, in an autocratic system such as Libya's, Egypt's, or Syria's, a minister who presides over the initiation of a war that is lost is not more likely to be deposed from office. If the minister leads a particularly powerful autocratic country, she is even less likely to be deposed from office, as indicated by the negative and significant coefficient for a country's capabilities.

To illustrate the effect of peacetime as a measure of ministerial competence on a cabinet member's likelihood of deposition, Figure 6.3 presents the hazard rate of a minister of foreign affairs as a function of the number of years of peace

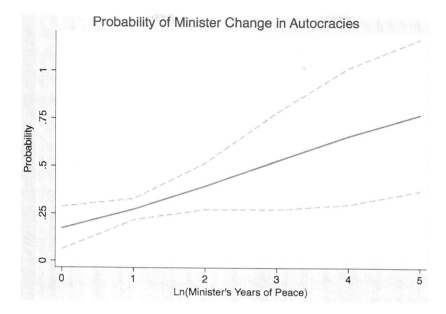

Figure 6.3 Model 2: probability of minister deposition in autocracies and $W = 0$

according to Model 2 in Table 6.3. The simulation of the probability of deposition holds all relevant variables at their mean, with the exception of W, which is assumed to be equal to 0. The dashed lines represent the lower and upper bounds of the 95 percent confidence interval.

The figure clearly shows that as foreign ministers secure more years of peace, they are more likely to be removed from the cabinet. This has important consequences because ministers in autocratic systems therefore have incentives to underperform. This allows them to remain in the cabinet and enjoy the benefits of belonging to the ruling class. Unfortunately, these ministerial incentives only reproduce the poor conditions of nondemocratic countries.

Types of autocracies

The previous analysis assumes that both a leader and a minister's incentives to stay in office are the same across autocratic governments. This may not be necessarily the case. In Chapter 3 I argued that the size of the pool of potential ministers, and consequently loyalty toward a leader, depends on the type of autocracy. The number of potential cabinet ministers in North Korea is very small and possibly limited to individuals with undisputed allegiance to Kim Jong-un. In contrast, the pool of cabinet ministers in autocracies that rely on rigged elections, such as Mexico, is much larger. In some cases, the number of cabinet positions for the same country changes over time, as in Pakistan, where

108 *Evidence in autocracies*

leaders can extend and shrink the cabinet according to different political circumstances (Mufti 2015). Thus, in order to explore the effect of heterogeneity across autocracies, I further rely on the classification developed by Przeworski et al. (2000). These authors classify autocracies as civilian dictatorships, military dictatorships, and monarchical dictatorships. Mexico in 1968 is an example of a civilian autocracy, while Burma in 2002 represents a military regime, and Nepal in 1970 is representative of a monarchical autocracy. Civilian dictatorships represent 49 percent of all autocracies, while military and monarchical dictatorships account for 36 and 15 percent, respectively.

The models in Table 6.4 reproduce Model 2 in Table 6.3 but restrict the sample to civilian dictatorships and military dictatorships in cases where $W \leq .5$. The first model is limited to the sample of civilian dictatorships, while the second model applies to military dictatorships. Unfortunately, the analysis applied to monarchical dictatorships presents convergence problems and could not be estimated.

The estimation results present two important features. First, in these small-coalition regimes where $W=0$, the duration of peace increases the likelihood of deposition, as demonstrated by the positive and significant coefficients of the variable *ln(Minister's Peace Time)*. Second, the magnitude of the effect of a minister's competence, as measured by the duration of peace, varies greatly across these two types of autocracies. In fact, the coefficients show that competent ministers are quickly dismissed in civilian autocracies relative to competent

Table 6.4 Instrumental variable probit

Variable	Model 1	Model 2
ln (Minister's Peace Time)	4.512***	0.747***
	(1.007)	(0.181)
Winning Coalition Size	17.69***	6.491***
	(5.289)	(1.808)
(W) (ln(Minister's Peace Time))	−8.390***	−1.235**
	(2.042)	(0.509)
ln (Leader's Tenure)	−0.207	−0.258
	(0.143)	(0.158)
ln (GDPpc)	0.606	0.225***
	(0.440)	(0.0592)
(W) (ln(GDPpc))	−1.405	−0.835***
	(0.893)	(0.247)
Constant	−8.962***	−2.410***
	(2.572)	(0.466)
athrho	0.0569	−0.0516
	(0.107)	(0.111)
lnsigma	−0.476***	−0.415***
	(0.0432)	(0.0400)
Observations	571	927
Log-likelihood	−834.9786	−1452.8719

*** $p<0.01$, ** $p<0.05$, * $p<0.1$

Evidence in autocracies 109

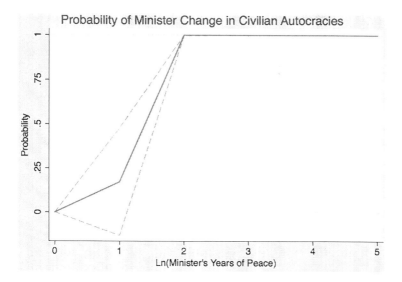

Figure 6.4 Model 1: probability of minister deposition in civilian autocracies and $W = 0$

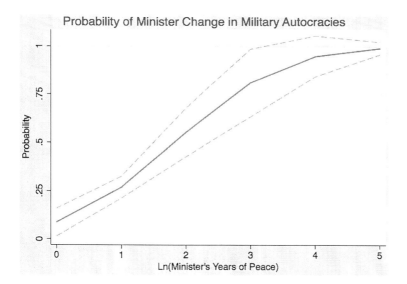

Figure 6.5 Model 2: probability of minister deposition in military autocracies and $W = 0$

ministers in military regimes. This difference is better illustrated by Figures 6.4 and 6.5, which present the hazard rate of ministers of foreign affairs as a function of the logarithm of the number of years of peace according to Models 1 and 2 in table 6.4. The simulation of the probability of deposition holds all

110 *Evidence in autocracies*

relevant variables at their mean, with the exception of W, which is assumed to be equal to 0. The dashed lines represent the lower and upper bounds of the 95 percent confidence interval.

In these two political systems, ministers of foreign affairs who produce many years of peace are dismissed from office. However, ministers in civilian autocracies are more rapidly dismissed from the cabinet relative to ministers in military autocracies. This is partly explained by the size of the pool across these two types of nondemocratic systems. In civilian regimes the pool of potential ministers is larger and therefore loyalty is not very strong, at least relative to military autocracies. This results in rapid minister turnover. Competent ministers are also replaced in military autocracies, but not at the same rate as in civilian ones. Ministers in military regimes such as those ruled by juntas – where the pool of ministers is quite small – are very loyal to the leader and therefore the latter has fewer incentives to replace them. In other words, leaders in military systems seem to be better off 'keeping the devil they know.'

Heterogeneity

The data originally collected for this book cover 7,311 foreign ministers in 181 countries, spanning the years 1696–2004. The fact that the book covers several historical periods does not present a problem, as predictions should hold regardless of time. The same is true for many theories of war, as well as for theories of political survival, which are arguably applicable to all time periods. For instance, neo-realist theories of war that emphasize the role of *realpolitik* variables (e.g., Waltz 1959, 1979; Fearon 1995; Powell 1999) focus on changes to the balance of power. This balance clearly changes over time – and this is what explains the occurrence of war – but the theory is applicable to all time periods.

Nevertheless, it is substantively interesting to explore potential variation in minister and leader survival across time periods. Indeed, both domestic and international politics have changed considerably over the last 300 years – some countries have become democratic and the number of nations in Europe has changed between the Napoleonic Wars and the end of the Second World War. Decolonization has also increased the number of countries in the international system. In this light, I explore the survival of ministers of foreign affairs across three different time periods: 1800 to 1918, 1919 to 1945, and the postwar years. Unfortunately, not all covariates are available for the long period starting in 1696 and therefore estimation results are limited to the years 1800 to 2004.

Testing for variation of coefficients across sections of the data is straightforward. Such test is known as a test of structural breaks (Chow 1960) and it is extensively used in linear models and time-series analysis (Greene 2003), where the 'structural break' takes place at some point in time. However, as originally developed by Chow, the method is applicable to any break in the data, including subsets of units. Intuitively, the test consists of comparing estimates from a restricted regression and an unrestricted regression. The former assumes that the coefficients are the same for all observations in the sample, while the latter assumes that they vary across sections of the data. The model can also be applied to several estimation methods, including maximum likelihood (Andrews and Fair 1988), and therefore to the instrumental variable probit model used in this chapter. In this setting, Chow's test of structural change is simply a test for nested models using a likelihood ratio test. Model 1 is the restricted model and it assumes that coefficients are the same across periods. The unrestricted model assumes that coefficients vary across the three time periods described above. Consequently, the unrestricted model consists of three regressions, one for 1800 to 1918, one for 1919 to 1945, and one for the postwar years: Models 2 to 4. Table 6.5 presents estimation results.[5]

A look at the table and a quick comparison of log-likelihoods suggests that coefficients vary across time periods. More formally, the Chow test produced a chi-squared statistic of 350.51 with 34 degrees of freedom, which is highly statistically significant. This indicates that the models are not nested and consequently that coefficients do vary across time periods. Substantively, the results indicate that ministerial competence, as measured by time of peace, did not have

Table 6.5 Instrumental variable probit

Variable	Model 1	Model 2	Model 3	Model 4
ln (Minister's Peace Time)	0.0704 (0.0739)	−0.109 (0.204)	−0.202 (0.189)	0.454*** (0.107)
Winning Coalition Size	2.666*** (0.631)	1.083 (1.325)	−3.242 (3.469)	5.568*** (0.921)
(W) (ln (Minister's Peace Time))	−0.488 (0.397)	−0.166 (0.718)	1.017 (1.749)	−1.477*** (0.516)
ln (Leader's Tenure)	−0.736*** (0.202)	−0.712 (0.471)	−0.725 (0.945)	−0.803*** (0.178)
ln (Energy Consumption)	0.0283* (0.0155)	0.00317 (0.0291)	−0.0515 (0.0584)	0.0574*** (0.0221)
(W) (ln(Energy Consumption))	−0.202*** (0.0660)	−0.0220 (0.114)	0.211 (0.264)	−0.410*** (0.101)
Constant	0.609** (0.306)	1.103* (0.609)	1.666 (1.859)	−0.0637 (0.308)
athrho	0.667** (0.262)	0.845 (0.873)	0.434 (0.824)	0.664*** (0.202)
lnsigma	−0.184*** (0.0124)	−0.0290 (0.0219)	−0.370*** (0.0282)	−0.302*** (0.0178)
Observations	3,250	1,041	629	1,580
Log-likelihood	−6098.5587	−2124.0941	−1085.8556	−2713.3545

*** $p<0.01$, ** $p<0.05$, * $p<0.1$

112 *Evidence in autocracies*

a significant effect in small-coalition systems before 1945. However, the model for the post-1945 period indicates that competence does in fact lead to the replacement of ministers of foreign affairs. This is consistent with previous evidence and with the theory developed in a previous chapter. Future research should explore why competence in other time periods does not seem to have an effect on ministerial turnover.

Conclusion

The previous chapters in this book presented the building blocks of the empirical tests of my theory of cabinet change. Chapter 3 developed specific hypotheses of ministerial survival. Chapter 4 presented my data on ministers of foreign affairs, while Chapter 5 explains why these ministers provide us with an opportunity to test these hypotheses. This chapter tests my theoretical propositions in autocratic governments. The tests focus on these political regimes because it uses a method that is only applicable to leaders in small-coalition systems.

Conventional wisdom suggests that leaders appoint competent ministers to the cabinet. Consequently, it is reasonable to expect that when ministers underperform, they are replaced. In Chapter 3, I show that, in fact, leaders in small-coalition countries replace competent ministers rather than incompetent ones in order to prevent internal challenges to their leadership. As I explained before, the masses can and do depose autocrats, often through revolutionary means, but the costs are high and probably marked by violence. In a context of a small coalition, internal threats are much more salient. Hence, leaders in these regimes tend to clear the political landscape of potential challengers by dismissing popular, able cabinet ministers.

The empirical evidence provides strong support in favor of the hypothesis of cabinet change in small-coalition systems, where leaders have incentives to depose competent ministers to prevent internal challenges to their leadership. The evidence shows that competent ministers in these systems are more likely to be deposed if they demonstrate competence and produce many years of peace.

Notes

1 I assume that during war, leaders and ministers produce zero years of peace. Furthermore, changes in administration are often accompanied by changes in policy (Bunce 1981; Brunk and Minehart 1984; Roeder 1985; Quiroz Flores 2012; Geddes, Wright, and Frantz 2014), and it is therefore important to account for the arrival of the new minister, whose competence is likely to differ from the competence of his predecessor. Thus, the peace counter is reset due to the initiation of peace after the end of a war, or due to the arrival of a new minister.
2 Mixed regimes are particularly problematic, so they are not analyzed here.
3 The model requires that the endogenous variable is continuous and with a disturbance that is normally distributed. A leader's tenure in this case is continuous, but its random component is not necessarily normally distributed. Unfortunately, there are no other methods available to get around endogenous regressors in duration models. The tests

presented here use the best and only available technology to estimate this type of relationship between a leader's tenure and the survival of her ministers. The next chapter, however, uses models that do not require these types of restrictions.

4 For the purposes of space, the estimation results from the first stage, as well as the Wald tests of exogeneity, are presented in an online appendix available at the author's website.

5 It is very important to note that in order to carry out this test, several modifications to the model had to be implemented. First, the standard errors cannot be clustered. Second, since data for GDP per capita is not available for all time periods, it was replaced with the natural logarithm of energy consumption. This variable is one of the composite indicators of national capabilities produced by the Correlates of War project (Sarkees 2000). Lastly, I used data for countries with very small winning coalitions where W is smaller than or equal to .25, as the data on the types of autocracies developed by Przeworski et al. (2000) are only available for the postwar years.

7 Global evidence

Introduction

In the previous chapter I argued that an empirical analysis of leader and minister tenure is challenging because both time processes are interdependent. However, I harnessed the fact that an autocrat's tenure in office is determined by her age – which is independent of a minister's time in office – to overcome this endogeneity problem and estimated an instrumental variable probit model with duration dependence. Unfortunately, the relationship between a leader's tenure and her age is only applicable to autocratic leaders. This effectively prevents me from exploring ministerial survival in democracies using the instrumental variable method. The results of the game theory model indicate that in presidential democracies, leaders dismiss incompetent ministers and keep competent ones in the cabinet. Skillful ministers contribute to the provision of public goods – which is electorally beneficial – and they do not present an internal threat to the leader. In contrast, democratic prime ministers face a complicated balancing act whereby competent ministers are electorally beneficial but represent a potential challenge for the party leadership. Hence, prime ministers dismiss very incompetent and very competent cabinet members, thus keeping only the moderately able cabinet ministers. Internal party rules make the decision to fire a minister even more complex.

This book argues that a leader's tenure determines whether a minister stays in office or not. In democracies, a leader's time in office cannot be replaced, at least econometrically speaking, by her age. For this reason, age as an instrument of leader tenure is only valid in autocracies. Therefore, I need a method to include a leader's time in office in a model of ministerial change that is applicable globally. Fortunately, the field of econometrics has made great advances in the analysis of this type of interdependent processes. For instance, it is possible to extend a simple probit model into a bivariate probit model that resembles a system of equations (Greene 2003). Rather than exploring the interdependent relationship between two continuous variables – a minister's and a leader's time in office – this model estimates a joint or bivariate probability of losing office. In a simplified version of the relationship between a minister's and a leader's time in office, we can define the probability of minister deposition – conditional on time in office – as p(MD) and the probability of leader replacement – also conditional on tenure in office – as p(LD). The argument in this book is that these two probabilities are interdependent. The technique used in this chapter will estimate the joint probability of minister and leader deposition, that is, p(MD and LD), conditional on their respective times in office and other covariates, in order to test the game theory model's hypotheses relevant to ministerial change in democracies.

A general framework and a bivariate probit model

First, consider two different survival times t_1 and t_2. Here t_2 can be interpreted as a foreign minister's tenure in office, while t_1 can be interpreted as the leader's time in office. In the game theory model of Chapter 3, I argued that leaders increase their tenure t_1 by manipulating the tenure of a minister t_2. Clearly, this manipulation is interpreted as dismissal from the cabinet. In very simple terms, in autocracies, t_1 increases if the tenure of a competent minister t_2 decreases, that is, if the minister is replaced. In presidential democracies, t_1 increases if the tenure of a competent minister t_2 increases, that is, if the competent cabinet secretary remains in office. In parliamentary democracies, t_1 increases if the tenure of a moderately competent minister t_2 increases. However, the prime minister should be careful to keep other types of ministers in the cabinet: the tenure of a minister t_1 increases if the tenure of a very competent or very incompetent minister t_2 decreases.

Each of the two time processes t_1 and t_2 depends on some covariates and a particular disturbance, such that $t_1 = f(t_2, X, \varepsilon_1)$ and $t_2 = f(t_1, Z, \varepsilon_2)$. For instance, these covariates X and Z could include political institutions, war occurrence, and GDP per capita, among others; I assume that both X and Z meet the exclusion restriction. These functions can be more elegantly organized in a system of equations:

$$t_1 = t_2 \gamma_2 + X \beta + \varepsilon_1; \tag{1}$$
$$t_2 = t_1 \gamma_1 + Z \Pi + \varepsilon_2. \tag{2}$$

In my study of ministerial change in autocracies in Chapter 6, I estimated a version of equation (2) using an instrument for t_1, a leader's age. In this chapter, I use a very different technique.

Keeping the above system of equations in mind, now think of a probability $p(T_1 = t_1)$ as the probability that a leader's time in office T_1 takes on a specific value t_1.[1] In other words, I am looking at the probability that the tenure of a leader is, say, ten years in office, or fifteen years, or ten months, or thirty-five years. Any number t_1 that is larger than zero is valid. The same applies to the probability $p(T_2 = t_2)$, which is the probability that a minister's time in office T_2 takes on a specific value t_2. It is very important to note that at least intuitively, asking 'what is the probability that a minister will stay in office for 7.2 years?'

116 *Global evidence*

is the same as asking 'what is the probability that a minister will lose office in year 7.2 conditional on her tenure?'

In a case where the tenure of leaders does not determine the tenure of ministers, or where the tenure of ministers does not determine the tenure of leaders, we could use some simple econometric models to estimate the effect variables on the probability of leader or minister deposition; these are the marginal distributions $p(T_1 = t_1)$ and $p(T_2 = t_2)$. Here, we can simply ask what is the probability that a minister will stay ten years in office if she has demonstrated competence. This is, of course, precisely not the case – the probabilities of losing office for ministers and leaders depend on their performance in office and most crucially on their interdependence and links, which are shaped by political institutions. In this context, I am interested in questions such as: 'what is the probability that ministers will be replaced early in their period in office, say, three months, given that she has demonstrated incompetence and that the leader, perhaps an autocrat, has been in office for ten years?' The trick for estimation thus resides in using a bivariate distribution that describes the probability that both events – leader and minister deposition – occur jointly (i.e., $p(T_1 = t_1, T_2 = t_2)$).

It is important to note that, as mentioned in the previous chapter, we can modify these continuous duration processes T_1 and T_2 and turn them into discrete ones. Hence, the final trick resides in estimating the joint probability of leader and minister deposition and the other three possible outcomes (i.e., leader deposition and minister continuation, leader continuation and minister deposition, and leader and minister deposition). In order to estimate these probabilities, I use the well-known bivariate probit model to estimate the joint probability of leader and ministerial change (Van de Ven and Van Pragg 1981; Maddala 1983; Petersen 1995; Greene 2003). The specific bivariate probit model estimated in this paper is the following (Greene 2003):

$$y_1^* = x_1 \beta_1 + \varepsilon_1, y_1 = 1 \text{ if } y_1^* > 0, 0 \text{ otherwise};$$
$$y_2^* = x_2 \beta_2 + \varepsilon_2, y_2 = 1 \text{ if } y_2^* > 0, 0 \text{ otherwise};$$
$$E[\varepsilon_1 | x_1, x_2] = E[\varepsilon_2 | x_1, x_2] = 0;$$
$$Var[\varepsilon_1 | x_1, x_2] = E[\varepsilon_2 | x_1, x_2] = 1;$$
$$Cov[\varepsilon_1, \varepsilon_2] = \rho.$$

In this setup, y_1 is the dependent variable *Leader Fails*, which is equal to 0 if the leader is in office and equal to 1 when the leader loses office. Likewise, y_2 is the dependent variable *Minister Fails*, which is equal to 0 if the minister is in office and equal to 1 when the minister loses office. The tenure in office of each individual is included in the covariates, which is what makes this model a discrete duration model. However, the key to this model resides in the interdependence between the two processes (i.e., leader and minister failure), which is determined by the association parameter ρ. This model is equivalent to the seemingly unrelated regressions in the linear model: if the covariance between the disturbances is equal to zero, then the processes are independent of each other – therefore they can be estimated separately. Standard econometric software produces the necessary tests for the null $\rho = 0$.

Intuitively, this model is the correct tool to explore ministerial change because it is based on the joint probability of leader and minister change. Mathematically, this is a very important point. In econometrics, we are often interested in the partial effect of an independent variable on a dependent one; in some contexts, this is known as a marginal effect. In a linear model that meets all the Gauss–Markov assumptions where the expected value of the dependent variable conditional on a set of independent variables X, that is, $E[Y|X]=X\beta$, the marginal effect of X on Y is β. Marginal effects in nonlinear models such as logit or probit are not so simple. In these models we choose a probability distribution for the expected value of Y, which in models of binary choice takes on values 0 or 1. To make sure that the predictions of the model fall within the correct interval, among other reasons, we establish $E[Y|X]=F(X,\beta)$, where $F(.)$ is a cumulative probability distribution. In probit models, we use the normal cumulative probability distribution. What is crucial for our discussion is that the marginal effect of X in such models is not β, but $f(X,\beta)\beta$, where the function $f(.)$ is the probability distribution function. In probit models, this is normal probability distribution function.

As applied to the bivariate probit model, assume that $x = x_1 \cup x_2$ and that $x_1 = x'\gamma_1$ where γ_1 contains all the non-zero elements of β_1 after estimation and zeros in the positions of the variables in the second equation (Greene 2003). The same is true for γ_2. Therefore, the joint probability of leader and minister failure is given by $p[y_1=1, y_2=1|x] = \Phi_2[x'\gamma_1, x'\gamma_2,\rho]$, where Φ_2 is the bivariate normal cumulative density function. The marginal effects are a complex derivative of Φ_2 in respect to x. Intuitively, this means that in our model of leader and minister change, the effect of *competence*, for instance, on the probability of ministerial replacement depends not only on the corresponding γ of the independent variable *competence*, but also on the full specification of the bivariate normal probability distribution Φ_2, which includes the covariance parameter ρ. This parameter measures the connection between the tenure of leaders and ministers. In other words, if there is a connection between leaders and their ministers – and the argument of this book is that there is a strong connection – then not modeling interdependence leads to inconsistent estimates and biased substantive effects. More simply, by not modeling interdependence, our estimates suffer or a type of omitted variable bias given by the parameters ρ and γ_2.

The bivariate probit model is a complicated model. However, it is in fact quite powerful and intuitive. Often, we estimate econometric models to directly determine marginal effects, as explained above. However, this might not be necessary, as we can indirectly estimate the effect of a variable using other tools, such as prediction. In the previous discussion, I have been referring to $p(T_1 = t_1, T_2 = t_2)$, the joint probability of leader and minister deposition. Useful as this is, I am not very interested in this joint probability per se, as I want to know, for instance, what the probability is that ministers will be replaced early in their periods in office, say, three months, given that she has demonstrated incompetence and that the leader, perhaps an autocrat, has been in office for ten years.

By the properties of probabilities, I can always transform this joint probability $p(T_1 = t_1, T_2 = t_2)$ into a conditional probability, such as $p(T_2 = t_2 | T_1 = t_1)$. This is simply the probability that T_2 takes on a specific value t_2, given that T_1 has taken on a specific value t_1. Evidently, this is key to test my hypotheses because I can ask and answer questions about the probability of ministerial change conditional on leader tenure, and other covariates such as competence and political institutions. I can even turn this probability upside down and explore the probability of leader change conditional on minister tenure. What is even better about this model is that it can be used across all political systems.

Estimation results

Before I elaborate on estimation results, let's revisit the hypotheses related to democracies derived in Chapter 3. Chapter 6 explores cabinet change in autocracies. Leaders across systems face internal and external challenges. Opportunities for external challenges are provided by elections, which leaders can lose. In order to be re-elected, leaders provide a large mix of public goods to their supporters, and cabinet ministers are instrumental in doing so. However, good cabinet ministers might be attractive to party supporters because they can also win elections; therefore, able ministers represent a source of internal challenge. In presidential democracies, however, the system does not provide ample opportunities for ministers to replace their leaders while they hold office. More often than not, they 'wait their turn' and take over once the leader has completed her period. Most presidents have fixed terms in office, and cabinet secretaries succeed their bosses often in an orderly manner, as in Mexico and the US.

In parliamentary democracies, prime ministers are subject to the confidence of parliament and their party colleagues, who may replace them with a competent minister who can keep the party in government, although with a different leader. As mentioned previously, this type of internal deposition of leaders in parliamentary democracies takes place at different rates, depending on party rules and other factors. As I explained previously, British prime ministers are exposed to internal party challenges, but not as exposed as Australian ones, who have been replaced by their colleagues numerous times. Given the potential internal threat, prime ministers face a tradeoff: competent ministers who deliver public goods but who can replace the leader, or incompetent ministers who are not realistic party leaders but cannot produce the private goods necessary to buy electoral support. In this context, prime ministers dismiss very incompetent and very competent cabinet members, thus keeping only the moderately able cabinet ministers. Internal party rules make the decision to fire a minister even more complex.

Moving on to estimation, and taking into consideration the bivariate probit model described above, I would like to describe the variables that belong to the minister equation and the variables in the leader equation. To begin with, I control for a minister's competence with the natural logarithm of the number of years of peace plus one that she has produced: (*ln(Minister's Peace Time)*).[2] The longer the peace produced by a minister, the more competent the minister is assumed to be. Ministerial tenure is also determined by other factors, such as the size of the winning coalition (*W*). The winning coalition is important because it determines not only the mix of public and private goods that should be provided to keep the leader and the minister in office, but also because it shapes the loyalty between leaders and their ministers. The estimate of the winning coalition is a composite index of Polity IV data that includes information on the competitiveness of executive recruitment, openness of executive recruitment, and competitiveness of participation regime, and includes regime type as defined by Arthur Banks's cross-national time-series data. It has a minimum normalized value of zero, and a maximum of one, and it is organized in intervals of .25 points (Bueno de Mesquita et al. 2003). Lastly, I also control for the overall (*Capabilities*) of a country, and it is the composite indicator of national capabilities produced by the Correlates of War project (Sarkees 2000). This is an important variable because national capabilities might have an impact on how difficult it is to be a foreign minister.

The bivariate probit model also requires a specification for the leader equation. This is necessary not only to identify the leader equation, but also to adequately estimate the parameter ρ, which measures covariance between the leader's and the minister's probability of losing office. To specify the leader equation, I use the variables originally determined by Bueno de Mesquita et al. (2003) and that continue to play an important role in application of the theory (e.g., Bueno de Mesquita et al. 2008; Bueno de Mesquita and Smith 2009, 2010; Quiroz Flores 2012; Quiroz Flores and Smith 2013). First of all, since this is a discrete duration model, I control for a leader's tenure in office (*ln(Leader's Tenure)*), which is the natural logarithm of the number of years a leader holds office plus one. Second, I also include the size of the winning coalition (*W*), which I just described above. Third, I use the variable (*ln(GDPpc)*) as a measure of public goods provision, which is essential for political survival, particularly in democracies. Lastly, I control for a leader's age, which is an excellent indicator of actuarial risk in autocracies.

It must be noted that both the leader and the minister equations contain variables that measure competence. In the case of the minister, ability is measured by peacetime, as I explained in Chapter 4. Leaders, on the other hand, show competence by providing goods, both public and private. The effect of competence for both types of politicians depends on political institutions. Ministerial competence only reduces the probability of minister change in presidential democracies, but it reduces it in autocracies and parliamentary democracies, at least at high levels of competence for the latter. Public goods provision has a larger effect on the tenure of leaders in large-coalition systems, while on less inclusive political regimes it does not have an effect and might even be counterproductive, as it might facilitate rebellion (Bueno de Mesquita and Smith 2009, 2010). I approach the mediating effect of political institutions by using an

120 *Global evidence*

interaction of the size of the winning coalition W with ministerial competence as measured by *ln(Minister's Peace Time)* and an interaction of the size of the winning coalition W with leaders provision of wealth as measured by *ln(GDPpc)*. Interaction terms are simple multiplications of variables and their interpretation is quite straightforward (Brambor, Clark, and Golder 2006).

Having said this, Table 7.1 presents estimation results for three models. Standard errors clustered on the leader are presented below coefficients. For reference

Table 7.1 Bivariate probit

Variable	Model 1	Model 2	Model 3
Minister Equation			
ln (Minister's Peace Time)	0.0571	0.615	2.764***
	(0.124)	(0.694)	(0.874)
Winning Coalition Size	−0.286	−0.771	3.225**
	(0.200)	(0.884)	(1.374)
(W)(ln(Minister's Peace Time))	0.180	−0.323	−2.659***
	(0.157)	(0.731)	(0.966)
Capabilities	1.374	6.783***	0.746
	(1.053)	(2.286)	(1.169)
Constant	−0.656***	−0.352	−3.800***
	(0.149)	(0.818)	(1.215)
Leader Equation			
Winning Coalition Size	−1.834***	−3.066	−16.92**
	(0.548)	(3.271)	(7.453)
ln (Leader's Tenure)	−0.337***	−0.597	5.013***
	(0.0794)	(0.622)	(1.015)
(W)(ln(Leader's Tenure))	0.234*	0.761	−5.406***
	(0.121)	(0.651)	(1.115)
Leader's Age	0.0276***	−0.00970	−0.151*
	(0.00569)	(0.0341)	(0.0850)
(W)(Leader's Age)	−0.0164**	0.0314	0.177*
	(0.00828)	(0.0370)	(0.106)
ln(GDPpc)	−0.138***	0.0743	−1.386**
	(0.0436)	(0.277)	(0.556)
(W)(ln(GDPpc))	0.304***	−0.0651	1.735***
	(0.0594)	(0.315)	(0.618)
Constant	−1.091***	0.573	12.18**
	(0.336)	(2.898)	(6.172)
athrho	0.196***	0.412***	0.136
	(0.0340)	(0.0597)	(0.0889)
Observations	4,189	1,238	555
Log-likelihood	−4079.1724	−1270.7618	−616.2294

*** $p<0.01$, ** $p<0.05$, * $p<0.1$

purposes, Model 1 pools all political systems. Model 2 explores democratic parliamentary regimes, while Model 3 concentrates on democratic presidential systems. As explained in Chapter 6, a country is a large-coalition presidential system if Przeworski et al. (2000) define it as such and $W \geq .75$, while a country is a large-coalition parliamentary system if Przeworski, Alvarez, Cheibub, and Limongi define it as such and $W \geq .75$. The tests for the joint failure of leaders and ministers place an emphasis on the role of ministers in war initiation.[3]

As I explained before, interpretation of estimation results of bivariate probit models are quite complex. What is crucial is that these models are estimated in order to control for the connection between leaders' and ministers' tenure in office. By estimating the parameter ρ, we can be sure that we are not omitting this key interdependence between political actors. Having done this in Table 7.1, I will concentrate on the effects of ministerial competence on a minister's probability of deposition. I do so by looking at the significance of the variable *ln(Minister's Peace Time)* and its sign, as well as its interaction with *W*. The sign of the estimate for *ln(Minister's Peace Time)*, which can be positive or negative, will tell me if peacetime has a positive effect on the probability of minister change or a negative one, thus reducing the likelihood of cabinet change. The degree of significance will tell me to what extent this result is given by a systematic relationship between ministerial tenure and performance, as opposed to a result produced by chance. Although this method will not tell me the magnitude of the effect of ministerial competence, which is in fact given by a complex derivative of Φ_2 in respect to peacetime, it tells me whether the evidence supports my hypothesis. I will obtain the magnitudes of the effects by producing predictions.

I follow the same approach to the mediating effect of political institutions. For instance, to test whether ministerial competence reduces the likelihood of ministerial deposition in presidential democracies, I need to test whether the interaction *ln(Minister's Peace Time) + (W)ln(Minister's Peace Time)* is different than zero in models for this type of political system. Such a test is straightforward. What is crucial is that in this chapter I explore democratic systems (i.e., *W* is greater than or equal to .75) and therefore a substantive interpretation requires tests of the linear restriction *ln(Minister's Peace Time) + (W)ln(Minister's Peace Time)* for relevant values of *W*.

Having said this, estimation results from Model 2 for democratic parliamentary systems do support my expectations about the survival of foreign ministers. Recall that in this analysis we cannot simply look at the isolated effect of *ln(Minister's Peace Time)* because it interacts with large values of the size of the winning coalition. Instead, we should look at the point estimates of the linear restriction *ln(Minister's Peace Time) + (W)ln(Minister's Peace Time)*. The point estimate for $W=.75$ is .3720, while the estimate when $W=1$ is .2912. Their standard errors are .1608 and .0865, respectively. Clearly, they are both positive and significant, which suggests that time of peace increases the probability of ministerial deposition. This is consistent with my hypothesis on cabinet change in parliamentary democracies: prime ministers have incentives to dismiss very competent ministers when parties do not provide perks for party members, as they are likely to become challengers and party peers are not particularly loyal. Even when parties provide

122 *Global evidence*

perks to party members, only very competent leaders can have very competent ministers in the cabinet. In this sense, competent ministers are more likely to face greater hazards in these parliamentary systems.[4] This is driven by the fact that there is a positive correlation between the failures of leaders and ministers in these parliamentary systems, as given by the positive and significant coefficient for ρ. This parameter captures the interdependent relationship between the tenure of ministers of foreign affairs and their leaders. This positive estimate indicates that the dismissal of a minister is correlated with the dismissal of a leader.

As I explained before, the approach that looks at the signs and significance of estimated parameters do not tell us much about the actual magnitude of the effect, given the complex specification of the bivariate problem model. However, I can use a simulation tool to explore predicted probabilities. For instance, I can fix the tenure of a leader at some particular value, say ten years or even the mean leader tenure, as well as the values of other variables, such as a country's capabilities, and predict the probability that a foreign minister will be deposed as she produces more years of peace. In the case of democratic parliamentary systems, I expect that this probability will increase as ministers show competence as measured by peacetime. Figure 7.1 presents the probability of minister deposition and leader continuation as a function of the number of years of peace in parliamentary regimes where $W = 1$ according to Model 2 in Table 7.1. In other words, this figure shows the probability that a minister will be replaced while

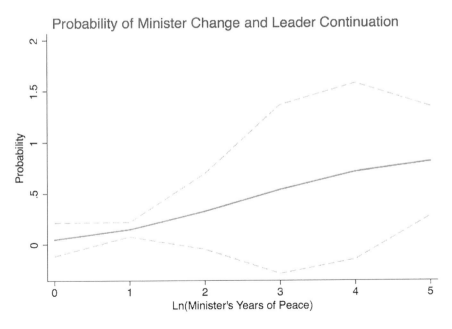

Figure 7.1 Model 2: probability of minister change and leader continuation in parliamentary systems and $W = 1$

the leader is not, which is precisely what I am interested in. All relevant covariates are held at their means.

Evidently, competence increases the hazard of ministers in parliamentary systems with large coalitions. Recall that Figure 3.2 in Chapter 3 shows that in cases where party members do not receive private goods, only moderately competent ministers are kept in the cabinet. Very competent or very incompetent ministers are dismissed from the cabinet. Figure 3.3 shows that in cases where party members receive private goods, only a very competent prime minister will surround herself with competent ministers. Even in these systems where leaders are relatively safe from internal challenges, less competent leaders never keep very capable ministers in their cabinet. Figure 7.1 shows that, indeed, ministers in large-coalition parliamentary systems that produce many years of peace are indeed more likely to be deposed.

Now let's look at the effect of competence in democratic presidential systems. Surprisingly, the results in for this type of system do not seem to support my predictions. The point estimates for the linear restrictions $ln(Minister's\ Peace\ Time) + (W)ln(Minister's\ Peace\ Time)$ for the $W=.75$ and $W=1$ are .7695 and .1046, respectively. Their standard errors are .1882 and .1602. The first estimate is positive and significant, while the second is indistinguishable from zero. In all, this suggests that in very democratic presidential systems, ministerial performance does not affect the probability that a minister of foreign affairs will be deposed. In less democratic presidential systems, performance increases the rate of ministerial deposition. Although this is not consistent with the theoretical expectations for countries with very large-coalition systems, presidential systems with $W=.75$ do seem to loosely fit the theory's prediction. Presidential systems with $W=.75$ are, for instance, the Dominican Republic in 1978, Nigeria in 1979, Uganda in 1980, and Indonesia in 1999. These are not the most democratic countries on the planet. Hence, it is very possible that coalition dynamics in these countries follow the dynamics of more autocratic systems where a minister's competence increases her hazard rate. Quite interestingly, the parameter ρ is statistically insignificant, which indicates that the replacement of a minister of foreign affairs does not have consequences for the survival of a president in a democratic country.

Polynomials and parliamentary politics

The purpose of empirical tests is to use evidence to confirm or reject our theoretical claims. In order to do so, we must be able to eliminate alternative explanations of the phenomena at hand, in this case, ministerial and leader change. It is for this reason that empirical exercises 'control' for other independent variables. For instance, although my theory focuses on the effect of ministerial competence on ministerial change, I must make sure that I take into consideration other causes of ministerial replacement. In this section of the chapter, I explore some additional variables that might determine the likelihood of the deposition of a minister of foreign affairs.

First, I analyze the non-monotonic effect of peacetime and a leader's time in office by replacing their natural logarithms with their cubic polynomials. In other

124 Global evidence

words, rather than using *ln(peace time)*, I use *peacetime*, *peacetime²*, and *peacetime³*. The same applies to a leader's time in office. As mentioned before, this functional form is relevant for discrete survival models (Carter and Signorino 2010). This is a method that I also used in Chapter 6. Table 7.2 presents estimation results for three models. Standard errors clustered on the leader are presented below coefficients. Model 1 pools all political systems. Model 2 explores democratic parliamentary regimes, while Model 3 concentrates on democratic presidential systems.

Table 7.2 Bivariate probit

Variable	Model 1	Model 3	Model 4
Minister Equation			
Minister's Peace Time	0.318***	2.206**	6.692***
	(0.0760)	(0.973)	(1.468)
(Minister's Peace Time)²	−0.0360***	−0.487**	−1.674***
	(0.00907)	(0.219)	(0.411)
(Minister's Peace Time)³	0.000714***	0.0263**	0.128***
	(0.000243)	(0.0123)	(0.0350)
Winning Coalition Size	0.0328	0.464	7.284***
	(0.191)	(1.180)	(1.781)
(W)(Minister's Peace Time)	−0.0789	−1.871*	−6.786***
	(0.113)	(1.004)	(1.535)
(W)(Minister's Peace Time)²	0.00654	0.448**	1.696***
	(0.0151)	(0.221)	(0.420)
(W)(Minister's Peace Time)³	0.000293	−0.0251**	−0.129***
	(0.000511)	(0.0124)	(0.0352)
Capabilities	1.371	6.669***	0.551
	(1.088)	(2.418)	(1.186)
Constant	−1.067***	−1.785	−7.675***
	(0.128)	(1.097)	(1.663)
Leader Equation			
Winning Coalition Size	−1.812***	−2.462	−9.128
	(0.574)	(3.354)	(7.921)
Leader's Tenure	−0.0880*	0.290	6.476***
	(0.0534)	(0.685)	(2.005)
(Leader's Tenure)²	0.00483	−0.0856	−1.294**
	(0.00515)	(0.111)	(0.512)
(Leader's Tenure)³	−0.000136	0.00396	0.0825**
	(0.000129)	(0.00416)	(0.0354)
(W)(Leader's Tenure)	0.138*	−0.112	−8.624***
	(0.0824)	(0.712)	(2.536)
(W)(Leader's Tenure)²	−0.0134	0.0661	1.778***
	(0.00906)	(0.113)	(0.664)

Variable	Model 1	Model 3	Model 4
(W)(Leader's Tenure)^3	0.000391	−0.00338	−0.112**
	(0.000246)	(0.00422)	(0.0467)
Leader's Age	0.0285***	−0.00519	−0.141
	(0.00585)	(0.0367)	(0.0863)
Wage	−0.0167**	0.0279	0.163
	(0.00841)	(0.0393)	(0.108)
(W)(Leader's Age)	−0.139***	0.0413	−1.160**
	(0.0438)	(0.289)	(0.558)
(W)(ln(GDPpc))	0.305***	−0.0337	1.373**
	(0.0597)	(0.327)	(0.623)
Constant	−1.330***	−0.178	7.542
	(0.363)	(2.970)	(6.473)
athrho	0.190***	0.426***	0.171*
	(0.0343)	(0.0599)	(0.0916)
Observations	4,189	1,238	555
Log-likelihood	−4039.5042	−1257.9856	−598.3334

The effect of ministerial competence on minister deposition and leader replacement is given by the test of the linear restriction *peace time + peace time^2 + peace time^3 + (W)(peace time + peace time^2 + peace time^3)*. I am mainly interested in Models 2 and 3 for parliamentary and presidential systems. The point estimates of these restrictions in these two samples and $W=1$ are .2972 and −.0735, respectively. They have standard errors of .0804 and .1437, respectively. Substantively, these estimates confirm previous evidence – competence as measured as peacetime in democratic parliamentary systems increases the probability of ministerial deposition, while the same variable does not determine the probability of minister change in democratic presidential systems.

Now I will control for the role of executive constraints. Most leaders face some form of institutional or political constraints when making decisions. According to the Polity IV project, chief executives might be constrained by legislatures in democracies but also by the armed forces or other political elites in autocracies. These 'accountability groups' might reduce a leader's ability to make decisions and consequently might reduce the likelihood of ministerial deposition. In this sense, I control for the variable (*Executive Constraints*), which is essentially Polity IV's well-known *XCONST* variable. This variable has a mean of 3.81 and a variance of 5.85, as well as minimum and maximum values of 1 and 7, respectively. The minimum value represents unlimited executive authority, that is, there are no regular limitations on actions – although there might be some irregular ones, such as potential coups. If the variable takes on value 3, executives face moderate limitation on their authority; for instance, legislatures or an independent judiciary might block executive acts or decrees. For a value of 5, executives face substantial limitations, which are best represented by refusing funds or the imposition of administrative posts. Lastly, for the maximum value of 7, leaders are simply subordinates of the accountability groups, which might actually be choosing the executive.

126 *Global evidence*

I also control for the number of veto players in a political system. In one of the most influential works in political science, George Tsebelis (2002: 2) argued: "In order to change policies – or, as we will say henceforth, to change the (legislative) status quo – a certain number of individual or collective actors have to agree to the proposed change. I call such actors veto players." Although Tsebelis focuses on institutional change and not necessarily on the ability of leaders to, for instance, replace their ministers – which does not always require changes to formal institutions such as a constitution – the concept of veto players is important because they might impose constraints on an executive. For this reason I control for the (*Number of Veto Players*), as developed by Tsebelis. This variable has a mean of 2.33 and a variance of 1.7, as well as a minimum value of 1 and a maximum of 7.53. This variable was obtained from George Tsebelis' Veto Player Data.[5]

Lastly, I also control for minority coalition governments, and specifically for whether a government is formed by a single party or by a (*Minimum Winning Coalition*) of multiple parties. As I explained before, this is a key feature of political systems that affects both the selection and deselection of cabinet ministers. For instance, coalition governments might force agents to respond to multiple principals (Dowding and Dumont 2009). Coalition governments also reduce the size of the pool of cabinet ministers (Berlinski, Dewan, and Dowing 2010). Moreover, leaders of coalition governments face great restrictions on their ability to replace ministers because doing so might bring the government to an end (King et al. 1990; Warwick 1994; Laver and Shepsle 1994, 1996; Diermeier and Stevenson 1999). This does not mean that single-party governments are free of the effect of fractionalization. As suggested by Dowding and Lewis (2015), faction leaders tend to have an enormous influence on cabinet selection in Australia, partly because Australian prime ministers can be replaced by the simple majority vote of the party in parliament. Having said this, I control for single party or multiple party governments. This variable was also obtained from George Tsebelis' Veto Player Data and is equal to 1 if the government is composed of a single party and equal to 0 otherwise. The variable has a mean of .509 and a variance of .22.[6]

Table 7.3 presents estimation results for three models. Standard errors clustered on the leader are presented below coefficients. Model 1 explores the effect of executive constraints on ministerial tenure. Models 2 and 3 explore the effect of the number of veto players and multiparty governments, respectively.

Before I discuss substantive results, it is very important to recall that this chapter focuses on large-coalition systems. Therefore, the size of the winning coalition only takes on values .5, .75, and 1. This is particularly relevant for Model 1 because ministerial competence interacts with the winning coalition. Hence, the appropriate tests had to be calculated for *ln(Minister's Peace Time)* + *(W)ln(Minister's Peace Time)* when $W=.5$, $W=.75$, and $W=1$. It is also important to note that the winning coalition is not included in Models 2 and 3 because these models focus on democratic parliamentary systems that present very little variation in winning coalition size.[7]

Table 7.3 Bivariate probit

Variable	Model 1	Model 2	Model 3
Minister Equation			
Executive Constraints	0.0352 (0.0238)		
Number of Veto Players		−0.0709* (0.0403)	
Minimum Winning Coalition			−.0100 (0.107)
ln(Minister's Peace Time)	0.140 (0.196)	0.260*** (0.0958)	0.243*** (0.0988)
(W)(ln(Minister's Peace Time))	0.102 (0.240)		
Winning Coalition Size	−0.231 (0.398)		
Capabilities	1.382 (1.021)	10.33*** (2.848)	11.13*** (2.797)
Constant	−0.920*** (0.271)	−0.976*** (0.178)	−1.109*** (0.161)
Leader Equation			
Winning Coalition Size	1.648 (1.458)		
ln(Leader's Tenure)	−0.171 (0.194)	0.106 (0.0830)	0.110 (0.0864)
(W)(ln(Leader's Tenure))	0.0918 (0.241)		
Leader's Age	0.00267 (0.0135)	0.0275*** (0.00726)	0.0269*** (0.00751)
(W)(Leader's Age)	0.0128 (0.0166)		
ln(GDPpc)	0.272** (0.116)	−0.217 (0.141)	−.2156 (0.1424)
(W)(ln(GDPpc))	−0.236* (0.137)		
Constant	−3.607*** (1.172)	−0.556 (1.361)	−.5399 (1.382)
athrho	0.249*** (0.0400)	0.611*** (0.0863)	0.570*** (0.0860)
Observations	3,152	670	645
Log-likelihood	−3054.4185	−651.1858	−629.2843

*** $p<0.01$, ** $p<0.05$, * $p<0.1$

128 *Global evidence*

Estimation results are quite illuminating. First, out of this broad class of 'executive limitations,' only the number of veto players seems to have an effect – in fact, they reduce the probability of minister change, probably because they reduce the ability of a leader to depose of a minister in the first place. In addition, the substantive results for ministerial competence confirm previous evidence for democratic parliamentary systems – years of peace increase the likelihood of ministerial replacement. In Model 1, the point estimates for the familiar restriction *ln(Minister's Peace Time) + (W)ln(Minister's Peace Time)* are positive and significant for $W=.5$, $W=.75$, and $W=1$. As I mentioned earlier, Models 2 and 3 do not have interactions with W and therefore the estimate for *ln(Minister's Peace Time)* is sufficient to explore the role of ministerial competence. The estimates for this variable are also positive and significant, which confirm my expectations for democratic parliamentary systems.

Heterogeneity

In the previous chapter I explored heterogeneity across autocracies. In this chapter I also explored the survival of ministers across different types of democracies, presidential and parliamentary. It remains to be tested whether there is coefficient variation across time periods, as I did in Chapter 6. In this light, I will also use the Chow test of structural breaks (1960) to explore coefficient variation across three different time periods: 1800 to 1918, 1919 to 1945, and the postwar years. Recall that the Chow test explores coefficient variation across subsets of the data. Although the test mostly applies to time series where the break takes places at some point in the series, the procedure can actually be applied to any subset of the data, for instance, historical periods in my analysis of ministerial tenure. Informally, the test consists of comparing estimates from a restricted regression and an unrestricted regression. The former assumes that the coefficients are the same for all observations in the sample, that is, for all historical periods, while the latter assumes that they vary across sections of the data: 1800 to 1918, 1919 to 1945, and the postwar years. Hence, the restricted model consists of one regression for all units in the sample, while the unrestricted model consists of several regressions, one for each subset of units. In maximum likelihood, Chow's test of structural change is simply a test for nested models using a likelihood ratio test whose statistic is a distributed chi square and is available in most statistics software.

Table 7.4 presents estimation results for a restricted model and an unrestricted model. Model 1 is the restricted model and assumes that coefficients are the same across periods. The unrestricted model assumes that coefficients vary across the three time periods described above. Consequently, the unrestricted model consists of three regressions, one for 1800 to 1918, one for 1919 to 1945, and one for the postwar years. These are Models 2 to 4. Table 7.2 presents estimation results with standard errors below coefficients.

Table 7.4 Bivariate probit

Variable	Model 1	Model 2	Model 3	Model 4
Minister Equation				
ln(Minister's Peace Time)	−0.247*** (0.0427)	−0.415*** (0.0873)	−0.150 (0.0998)	−0.0901 (0.0613)
Winning Coalition Size	−0.476*** (0.0861)	−0.288 (0.204)	−0.351** (0.178)	−0.374*** (0.123)
(W)(ln(Minister's Peace Time))	0.264*** (0.0664)	0.579*** (0.186)	0.0515 (0.148)	0.209** (0.0897)
Capabilities	−1.208*** (0.364)	−3.999*** (0.594)	−1.563** (0.704)	−0.145 (0.691)
Constant	−0.0360 (0.0542)	0.177* (0.101)	0.0699 (0.114)	−0.386*** (0.0835)
Leader Equation				
Winning Coalition Size	0.293 (0.271)	0.570 (0.741)	0.390 (0.642)	−0.264 (0.345)
ln(Leader's Tenure)	−0.341*** (0.0446)	−0.195** (0.0792)	−0.585*** (0.119)	−0.302*** (0.0642)
(W)(ln(Leader's Tenure))	0.0828 (0.0706)	−0.210 (0.153)	0.482*** (0.185)	0.0979 (0.0964)
Leader's Age	0.0248*** (0.00295)	0.0248*** (0.00637)	0.0320*** (0.00663)	0.0203*** (0.00414)
(W)(Leader's Age)	−0.0137*** (0.00463)	−0.00450 (0.0123)	−0.0300*** (0.0102)	−0.00756 (0.00614)
ln(Energy Consumption)	−0.0291*** (0.0105)	−0.00320 (0.0206)	−0.0408* (0.0238)	−0.0563*** (0.0155)
(W)(ln(Energy Consumption))	0.0672*** (0.0157)	0.0438 (0.0358)	0.119*** (0.0358)	0.0906*** (0.0221)
Constant	−1.776*** (0.163)	−2.217*** (0.367)	−1.662*** (0.402)	−1.443*** (0.214)
athrho	0.158*** (0.0199)	0.201*** (0.0443)	0.117*** (0.0414)	0.145*** (0.0267)
Observations	10,562	2,186	2,102	6,274
Log-likelihood	−10962.441	−2260.4203	−2389.5066	−6173.4768

*** $p<0.01$, ** $p<0.05$, * $p<0.1$

Again, a look at the table and a quick comparison of log-likelihoods suggests that coefficients vary across time periods. More formally, the Chow test produced a chi-squared statistic of 278.07 with 28 degrees of freedom, which is highly statistically significant. This indicates that the models are not nested and consequently that coefficients do vary across time periods.

Conclusion

This chapter explores the relationship between ministerial competence and ministerial deposition across democratic countries, both presidential and parliamentary. In contrast to autocratic leaders, democratic presidents and prime ministers have different incentives to replace their ministers of foreign affairs. Specifically, democratic presidents replace incompetent ministers, while prime ministers depose both highly incompetent and highly competent ministers. At the heart of these predictions is a tradeoff of internal and external threats to the leader. Presidents do not fear their ministers, as presidential change is driven by elections. Prime ministers fear elections and extremely competent ministers. Here lies a very complex balancing act for leaders in parliamentary systems. On the one hand, they need competent ministers who can deliver public goods to their supporters. On the other hand, competent ministers can become internal political challengers. I illustrated this type of problem with a reference to Australian politics. There, labor governments between 2007 and 2013 were subject to constant leadership challenges: Kevin Rudd was replaced by his deputy Julia Gillard in 2010. Gillard was in turn replaced in 2013 by Rudd, who had been appointed minister of foreign affairs and was regarded as a better electoral prospect (Dowding and Lewis 2015). For this reason, I expect prime ministers to replace very incompetent and very competent ministers. In this sense, I predict that mediocre ministers are the most able survivors in parliamentary systems.

The evidence does confirm my expectations about ministerial deposition in democratic parliamentary systems. In all models, peacetime consistently increases a minister's hazard rate, even when other crucial factors of parliamentary politics are taken into consideration, such as multiparty governments, executive constraints, and veto players. Unfortunately, results for presidential systems are more mixed. This is surprising but also encouraging, as the results provide ample space to explore new hypotheses and control for additional factors relevant to presidential politics. In the conclusion to this book, presented next, I elaborate on these potential avenues of research.

Notes

1 Technically, this probability is zero because time is assumed to be continuous. It is better to think of the realization of the variable T_1 as a realization over a very small interval around t_1. The same applies to T_2.
2 In Chapter 4, I discussed the relationship between this variable and a minister's tenure in office.
3 It is worth noting that the specification for the probability of leader deposition does not include the number of years of peace. First, in cases where a country does not fight a war, a leader's tenure and the peacetime she has produced are exactly the same. Hence, the specification avoids collinearity problems. Second, the specification assumes that the responsibility for war lies primarily – yet not exclusively – on the minister of foreign affairs. Extensive research focuses on the role of leaders in war (Downs and Rocke 1994; McGillivray and Smith 2000, 2008; Byman and Pollack 2001; Bueno de

Mesquita et al. 2003, 2004; Chiozza and Choi 2003; Quiroz Flores 2009; Croco 2011). These investigations assume that leaders are solely responsible for war initiation and duration. However, as I argued extensively before, ministers contribute to the initiation and duration of war.
4 Unfortunately, there are no data for party institutions for all parliamentary systems for all the years covered in this dissertation.
5 https://sites.lsa.umich.edu/tsebelis/data/veto-players-data/
6 Specifically, 41.4 percent of the observations are coded as 0, while 42.5 percent are coded as 1. The rest take on continuous values between 0 and 1. I use this variable as presented by Tsebelis (2002).
7 In fact, for the data made available by Tsebelis, there is not much variation in the size of W – of 1,184 observations, 1,171 have a $W=1$ while 13 have $W=.75$. Moreover, 947 correspond to parliamentary democracies, while the rest are assigned to presidential or mixed democracies.

8 Conclusions

This book is the result of research at the intersection of two research agendas: political survival and ministerial careers. My approach to ministerial careers presented in this book is based on Bruce Bueno de Mesquita et al.'s *The Logic of Political Survival* (2003), which explains why leaders who produce 'good policy' stay in office for short periods of time, while those who produce 'bad policy' endure in office. My approach to cabinet politics has been greatly enriched by a large body of work on ministerial careers that covers countries, regions, and time periods, as well as substantive topics such as accountability and government stability, as well as coalition and party politics, among others. Both strands of research are strictly necessary to understand my argument and evidence on cabinet change.

To start with political survival, Bueno de Mesquita et al. (2003, 2004) often refer to leaders as the main unit of analysis. The fact is that a careful reading of their argument indicates that the term 'leaders' actually refers to one or several persons. The number of 'leaders' in nations ruled by military juntas, as in Argentina in 1976, is different than the number of 'leaders' in a country like North Korea, which is effectively led by a single person, Kim Jong-un. However, in more democratic countries, it is more difficult to separate a leader from a ruling coalition. Hence, my analytical challenge resided in how to disaggregate a country's leadership into two groups: a single leader and 'special' members of the winning coalition. Should we explore, say, Burma as a country with one leader – General Thein Sein – and other generals as 'special' members of the winning coalition, or as a nation with one small group of leaders that behave as a single unit?

This disaggregation has important consequences for an argument on survival. If it is assumed that a country such as Burma is ruled by a small number of leaders who behave as a unit, then the problem of loyalty, and consequently the potential for coups and purges, is effectively eliminated. If the leadership of a country is disaggregated into a leader and 'special' members of the winning coalition, then the explanatory power of *The Logic of Political Survival* (Bueno de Mesquita et al. 2003) greatly increases because it can be extended to cabinet change. In this context, ministers are important because they are agents of the leader. Indeed, leaders need ministers to help them rule. At the same time, it was rather clear that some ministers had a propensity to replace their own leaders, sometimes peacefully and according to established rules, and sometimes illegally and violently. In this light, ministerial careers provide a lens to explore stability and political change.

The connection between political survival and cabinet change is relatively simple. In this story of survival, leaders aim at holding office for as long as they can. In order to do so, leaders need supporters; they are the leader's winning coalition. The members of the winning coalition are drawn from a larger group of people, the selectorate. Leaders keep the support of members of the winning coalition by providing goods. Notice that all leaders, regardless of how autocratic they are, need supporters. The difference between political regimes resides in the number of supporters in the leader's winning coalition relative to the size of the selectorate. All else equal, some coalitions are large, as in Canada or Norway, while others are small, as in Burma or North Korea. This is important because, depending on the size of the coalition, leaders exchange political support for public or private goods. In inclusive political systems with large coalitions, it is more efficient to provide public goods. In small-coalition nations, it is more efficient to provide private goods.

This logic translates into leader change as follows. Political supporters can always replace an incumbent leader with a challenger. Loyalty and support for a leader thus depends on access to goods. Incumbent leaders have a set of well-known supporters who receive a stream of public and private goods. In contrast, challengers can only promise goods to potential supporters. This means that under new leadership, access to goods is probabilistic. The consequences of this probability in large-coalition systems are not particularly dire because winning coalitions are large and because leaders provide public goods. In other words, citizens in large-coalition systems are relatively well-off regardless of leadership, which does not make them loyal. In contrast, the consequences of probabilistic access to goods in small-coalition systems might be a matter of life and death because coalitions are small and because leaders provide private goods. This means that the wealth of political supporters in small-coalition nations is closely connected to the leader, which makes supporters incredibly loyal. Clearly, loyalty leads to long leader tenure in office, while the lack of loyalty is associated with increased leader turnover.

In *The Logic of Political Survival*, Bueno de Mesquita et al. (2003) explore the effect of the provision of public and private goods on leader tenure. In this sense, goods provision is a tool for survival. In this book, I explore cabinet change as a new instrument that leaders use to maximize their tenure in office. In this light, this book is also part of a research agenda that explores alternative methods of survival in office, including interstate war (Bueno de Mesquita et al. 2003, 2004), international sanctions (McGillivray and Smith 2008), foreign aid (Smith 2008; Bueno de Mesquita and Smith 2009), revolutions and institutional change (Bueno de Mesquita and Smith 2010), war termination (Quiroz Flores 2012), and natural disasters (Quiroz Flores and Smith 2013; Quiroz Flores 2016), among many others.

In this book, I assume that cabinet ministers also maximize their time in office. In order to do so, they rely on the fact that leaders cannot rule alone and therefore need to delegate their authority. Delegation thus gives ministers an opportunity to demonstrate competence and loyalty, although in some cases ministers will display only one or the other based on the leader's incentives to stay in office and on how these incentives are shaped by political institutions. This already seems at odds with the conventional wisdom indicating that leaders choose the most competent ministers to act on their behalf. Indeed, I show that in some circumstances, a minister can find herself replaced if she is actually good at her job, particularly in an autocratic country like Zimbabwe or Saddam Hussein's Iraq.

The explanation for the apparent lack of competence in nondemocratic nations resides in the fact that delegation creates a space for potential internal political competition. In autocratic countries, most threats to a leader come from within the ruling coalition – the 'special' members of the winning coalition are the agents who often precipitate leader change in these systems. Leaders might anticipate such problems by observing the competence of a minister, as an able cabinet member might have the necessary skills to replace a leader. This is unlikely to happen with ministers who lack ability. For this reason, autocratic governments are led by paranoid leaders and their incompetent but loyal ministers.

Leaders in democratic systems lose office by term limits or elections, and by the efforts of their colleagues. Democratic presidents do not face significant internal deposition. In these regimes, cabinet secretaries do not have or desire elected political positions, and even if they did, they do not ordinarily threaten the president. Instead, leaders face external pressures in the form of elections. To win these elections, presidents recruit ministers who will contribute to the distribution of public goods. Life is not so easy in democratic parliamentary systems, as a prime minister's term in office is subject to legislative confidence and party support but is also subject to the electoral preferences of voters. In other words, leaders in democratic parliamentary systems can be deposed by a popular vote but also by their party members, often led by senior cabinet ministers. This presents a complex problem because leaders need competent ministers to provide goods and win elections, but competent ministers are also potential internal challengers to leadership. In this light, prime ministers must trade off internal and external political threats.

This logic helps us understand ministerial tenure in office because ministerial competence in small-coalition systems should lead to increased cabinet turnover, while competence in presidential democracies should reduce the likelihood of cabinet change. In parliamentary democracies, I expect incompetent ministers to be dismissed from the cabinet. I expect very talented ministers to be sacked as well in a prime minister's effort to eliminate internal challenges. This strategic dismissal of ministers should also have an effect on the quality of cabinets and their policies. It also helps us understand leader turnover, as the strategic dismissal of ministers is executed with the sole purpose of extending a leader's time in office.

Cabinet change is important not only because it is an instrument for leader survival, but also because it reflects larger issues of democracy and politics in general. Indeed, the cabinet plays an essential role in the functioning of government, while cabinet change is central to accountability mechanisms and representative democracy (Dowding and Dumont 2009; Fischer, Dowding, and Dumont 2012). It also provides advice to leaders and serves as intermediary between leaders and industry. In parliamentary democracies, cabinets use their collective character to implement policy in single-party governments and help to maintain multiparty coalitions through the distribution of portfolios. I also find cabinet change important because cabinet members tend to succeed their leaders. Of course, this is partly why autocrats and some prime ministers replace talented cabinet members. Indeed, cabinet ministers are in a unique position to succeed their bosses. Golda Meir, Kevin Rudd, Angela Merkel, Martin Van Buren, Michelle Bachelet, Thomas Jefferson, Taro Aso, James Madison, Thabo Mbeki, James Monroe, John Q. Adams, and Julia Gillard, among many other heads of governments, were first cabinet ministers.

Given the potential for internal replacement, it is not surprising to observe leaders dismissing cabinet ministers. However, cabinet change takes place for a number of other reasons. More recently, cabinet change has been explored as a method to eliminate, or at least reduce, agency problems. Agency problems can take a number of shapes, from lack of effort and divergence in preference, to risky behavior and heterogeneity. These problems have different labels across literatures, but they all point to problems caused by delegation. What is important to note here is that cabinet change as a solution to agency problems is executed only once the contract between a leader and a minister is active. In other words, cabinet turnover is a tool implemented after cabinet formation. This is relevant because cabinet selection and appointment can be carefully orchestrated to avoid potential agency problems. In other words, once the cabinet is appointed, leaders might eliminate ministers who 'slipped through the cracks' of the selection process. The extent to which cabinet selection and change can minimize agency depends on political institutions and party politics. They determine the size of the pool of potential ministers, the quality and heterogeneity of the candidates, the need to distribute portfolios for coalition purposes, the approval of the legislature, and the support of party factions. In some cases, institutions can even prevent leaders from actually dismissing ministers!

This discussion indicates that cabinet change is important for our understanding of political survival, as well as other aspects of politics. My theory of cabinet change presented in this book, as any other theory, must be falsifiable, which in part means that we should be able to test it. Here I have been mainly interested in how ministerial competence, as well as a leader's ambitions for office – represented by her tenure in office – determine a minister's time in the cabinet. Under simple circumstances where leader's tenure is exogenous, I could simply add this variable into my specification for a minister's hazard rate and estimate a survival model (e.g., Box-Steffensmeier and Zorn 2001; Box-Steffensmeier and Jones 2004). I have argued that this approach is incorrect because of the interdependence between the tenure in office of ministers and the tenure of their leaders. Indeed, whether a minister stays in office depends on the leader's likelihood of deposition, and the leader's probability of deposition also depends on whether the cabinet minister holds on to office. In other words, leader tenure is endogenous, which causes a serious problem of inference.

To get around this problem, I rely on two solutions. First, I use an instrumental variable approach. Instrumental variables are a popular method to replace endogenous covariates. I like to explain how instrumental variables work using the study by Miguel, Satyanath, and Sergenti (2004), who explore the effects of economic conditions on the prospects of civil conflict. In their article, the endogeneity problem arises because lack of economic opportunities may lead people to fight, but the conflict itself further weakens the economy, which then forces people to participate in the conflict. They solve this problem by using an instrumental variable for economic conditions – rainfall variation. The latter is evidently correlated with economic conditions, but is not correlated with conflict (or at least the authors show that this is the case). I use a similar approach and use leader's age as an instrument for leader tenure in office. Leader's age is an indicator of actuarial risk and is correlated with the provision of private goods in small-coalition systems. This explains why a dictator like Zimbabwe's Robert Mugabe – who is ninety-two years old – celebrates his birthday quite publicly, as it shows that he is still active and in control. For the same reason, Cuba's Fidel Castro used to make public appearances after medical procedures. However, this relationship between age and risk in office is only applicable to nondemocratic countries.

To overcome the lack of an instrumental variable in countries with large-coalition systems, I use bivariate discrete survival models to explore the probability of leader and minister deposition conditional on their time in office. More specifically, I estimate a bivariate probit model of the joint probability of leader and minister change. Specifically, I estimate a bivariate probability of losing office rather than exploring the interdependent relationship between a minister's and a leader's time in office. I define the probability of minister deposition – conditional on time in office – as p(MD) and the probability of leader replacement – also conditional on tenure in office – as p(LD). Since these two probabilities are interdependent, I explore the joint probability of minister and leader deposition, that is, p(MD and LD), conditional on their respective times in office and other covariates.

Ever since I started working on this project, it was rather clear that there were econometric models adequate to test the hypotheses derived from my theoretical model. A more formidable challenge resided in getting data on ministerial tenure and ministerial competence. Leader tenure has been explored very thoroughly elsewhere (e.g., Bueno de Mesquita and Siverson 1995; Goemans 2000a, 2000b, 2008; Bueno de Mesquita et al. 2003, 2004; Chiozza and Goemans 2003, 2004; Smith 2008; Bueno de Mesquita and Smith 2009; Quiroz Flores and Smith 2013). In this sense, access to leader data did not present a challenge. Unfortunately, this was not the case for cabinet ministers. Ideally, I would have liked to develop a dataset of ministerial tenure similar to the data that Jean Blondel (1985) uses in his book *Government Ministers in the Contemporary World*, perhaps the largest completed empirical work on cabinet politics – it examines the careers of thousands of individuals across 2,000 cabinet positions in 154 countries from 1945 to 1980. Unfortunately, this was clearly out of the scope of this project and therefore I took a different route.

Other researchers of cabinets opted for obtaining ministerial data for geographical regions or countries over long periods of time. Earlier work focused on democracies and parliamentary systems, mostly in Europe and former British colonies. Since these countries have been wealthy democracies for a significant period of time, they have detailed records of their governments that have provided us with rich and reliable data on cabinet careers, particularly in the UK, Australia, and Canada. As researchers continue to collect data, we now have access to information that ten years ago was quite inaccessible, especially in countries like Chile, Mexico, Russia, South Korea, and Pakistan. In theory, I could have merged these datasets, but as they were originally collected, they are not ready for comparative analysis. Members of the Selection and Deselection of Political Elites (SEDEPE) research network are getting closer to providing a comparable dataset of ministerial careers. In the meantime, without consistent data for a large number of countries and cabinet positions, it is difficult to draw conclusions from an analysis of ministries that are not necessarily comparable.

Since I did not have access to a comparable dataset of ministerial tenure that covered countries with different political institutions and levels of wealth, and because I was strongly interested in the occurrence of war, I decided to focus on a single cabinet ministry: Foreign Affairs. By limiting data collection to a single cabinet position, which also happened to be one of the most recognizable and essential roles in national government, I could trace ministerial tenure for large numbers of countries over extended periods of time. At the end, I compiled a database for the tenure of 7,311 foreign ministers in 181 countries, spanning the years 1696–2004. It includes the specific day, month, and year in which 4,911 foreign ministers took and left office. This is the most comprehensive dataset of foreign affairs ministers available now. This is the dataset that I used for the empirical tests of my theoretical propositions.

The empirical tests presented throughout the book rest on three foundations. First, diplomacy plays an important role in war initiation and termination. Second, foreign ministers rather than leaders carry out the majority of diplomatic efforts. Lastly, competence determines whether foreign ministers can secure a peace that provides the same goals of war but without incurring its costs. The first point is based on the logic that diplomacy and war are part of the same bargaining process (Wittman 1979; Werner 1998; Wagner 2000; Goemans 2000b; Filson and Werner 2002, 2004, 2007; Slantchev 2003; Mattes and Morgan 2004). In this light, as countries fight, they also try to find a negotiated settlement. Also, as countries take part in negotiations before hostilities start, they engage in power politics practices represented by alliance formation and military buildups in a form of 'tough diplomacy.' The second point is based on the simple fact of delegation.

Since most national leaders do not have credentials as diplomats, and since diplomacy is often lengthy, it is safe to argue that diplomacy is mostly practiced by ministers of foreign affairs rather than their leaders.

The first two foundations of the tests are not necessarily controversial, as they are based on rigorous theory, intuition, and common sense. The last foundation might be slightly more provocative. Essentially, I use a well-known result in international relations that shows that governments can reach prewar bargains that leave them as well off as if they had fought a war while avoiding the costs of fighting, hence effectively preventing armed conflict (Fearon 1995). Based on this, and having established that ministers of foreign affairs have the space to implement foreign policy with some degree of agency, but that this agency is not caused by ideological differences but competence, I argued that a highly competent foreign minister can solve the puzzle of war by securing a peace that yields the same goals of the war but without incurring the costs of fighting. My favorite example of such an exemplary foreign minister is Jose Maria da Silva Paranhos, the Baron of Rio Branco and Brazil's minister of foreign affairs from 1902 to 1912. As I explain in Chapter 5, Rio Branco used diplomacy, international law, and arbitration to secure vast amounts of territory for Brazil in a context of uncertainty and revisionist neighbors. If Rio Branco's work represents excellence and showcases outstanding diplomatic abilities, incompetent ministers at the other end might produce two undesirable situations: a peace that does not yield the same goals of the war – and therefore a peace that is not an equilibrium – or interstate war. The worst and most incompetent of ministers will lead their countries to a war that they will lose.

I acknowledge that this is not a perfect measure of competence. However, to the best of my knowledge, there is no widely agreed measure of the competence of a minister of foreign affairs. Unlike secretaries of the treasury or chancellors of the exchequer, whose performance may have clearer links to the economy of a country – although there is no guarantee that macroeconomic indicators are a valid measure of their ability – the role of ministers of foreign affairs is not as evident; take, for example, secret negotiations. In this light, I will argue that a minister's competence in foreign affairs is best measured by his ability to provide peace.

Based on these three foundations, my estimation results of Chapters 6 and 7 are quite positive. To begin with, the instrumental variable approach applied to autocratic countries worked very well. Conventional wisdom suggests that leaders appoint competent ministers to the cabinet. Consequently, it is reasonable to expect that when ministers underperform, they are replaced. I argued that leaders in small-coalition countries replace competent ministers rather than incompetent ones in order to prevent internal challenges to their leadership. As I explained before, the masses can and do depose autocrats, often through revolutionary means, but the costs are high and probably marked by violence. In a context of a small coalition, internal threats are much more salient. Hence, leaders in these regimes tend to clear the political landscape of potential challengers by dismissing popular, able cabinet ministers. Using a probit model with instrumental

Conclusions 139

variables developed by Newey (1987) as applied to a setting of discrete survival time (e.g., Beck, Katz, and Tucker 1998; Carter and Signorino 2010), the empirical evidence of Chapter 6 provides strong support in favor of this hypothesis. In fact, the evidence shows that competent ministers in these systems are more likely to be deposed if they demonstrate competence and produce many years of peace.

These results hold even when different types of autocracies and historical periods are considered. In military and civilian autocracies, ministers of foreign affairs that produce many years of peace are dismissed from office. However, ministers in civilian autocracies are more rapidly dismissed from the cabinet relative to ministers in military autocracies. This is partly explained by the size of the pool across these two types of nondemocratic systems. In civilian regimes the pool of potential ministers is larger, and therefore loyalty is not very strong, at least relative to military autocracies. This results in rapid minister turnover. Competent ministers are also replaced in military autocracies, but not at the same rate as in civilian ones.

My approach to interdependent duration time for leaders and ministers in Chapter 7 also works quite well. Using a bivariate probit model to estimate the joint probability of leader and ministerial change (Van de Ven and Van Pragg 1981; Maddala 1983; Petersen 1995; Greene 2003), also in a setting of discrete survival time, I find that time of peace increases the probability of ministerial deposition in parliamentary systems. This is consistent with expectations about the survival of foreign ministers in these political systems. Prime ministers have incentives to dismiss very competent ministers when parties do not provide perks for party members, as they are likely to become challengers and party peers are not particularly loyal. Even when parties provide perks to party members, only very competent leaders can have very competent ministers in the cabinet. In this sense, competent ministers are more likely to face greater hazards in these parliamentary systems.

Surprisingly, the results for democratic, presidential systems are more mixed. This suggests that future research could improve on this work in a number of ways. For instance, the evidence indicates that in very democratic presidential systems, ministerial performance does not affect the probability that a minister of foreign affairs will be deposed. It could be the case that the deposition of a secretary of state may be related to other factors, such as a president's popularity, which tends to rise during times of war and decrease over time in general. Although there is rich data on presidential approval ratings in the US, there is much to be learnt about it in other democratic, presidential systems. I hope that future research addresses this missing variable.

Nevertheless, the results for parliamentary systems are in fact quite robust to different specifications and additional theories of cabinet change. I estimated additional models that include the non-monotonic effect of peacetime and a leader's time in office by replacing their natural logarithms with their cubic polynomials, as well as the role of executive constraints, the number of veto players in a political system, and the presence of minority coalition governments.

Of these, multiple-party coalition governments are quite important because they force agents to respond to multiple principals (Dowding and Dumont 2009), reduce the size of the pool of cabinet ministers (Berlinski, Dewan, and Dowing 2010), and impose restrictions on cabinet dismissal because leaders need their coalition partners to keep the government functioning (King et al. 1990; Warwick 1994; Laver and Shepsle 1994, 1996; Diermeier and Stevenson 1999). The effects of competence under these additional specifications remain the same for parliamentary democracies – years of peace increase the likelihood of ministerial replacement.

As I mentioned before, this book is the result of research at the intersection of studies of political survival and ministerial careers. I have presented an argument that explains cabinet change as an instrument that leaders use to extend their tenure in office. My empirical evidence is quite positive and in general supports my argument. Moving things forward, I can think of a number of ways in which future research can extend the work presented in this book. First, researchers can use the data, which will be available to the public, to explore the effect of cabinet change on leader tenure. Although this might be more difficult in the context of instrumental variables in autocracies, the bivariate setup that I used in Chapter 7 is ideal. This requires the estimation of new models with an emphasis on leader tenure and the calculation of marginal effects and first differences as determined by the replacement of foreign ministers. Second, perhaps new research can improve on my measure of competence. I would be particularly interested in how cabinet change determines the duration of war. I recently explored the interdependent relationship between war termination and leader change (Quiroz Flores 2012), and this method could be easily applied to foreign ministers.

I am even more interested in a different kind of extension to this work. This involves the collection of more databases on ministerial careers and performance for more countries over long periods of time. In this context, it will be fascinating to explore cabinet change and performance more closely in autocratic countries, particularly in the areas of economic development. As I mentioned before, the SEDEPE network is already coordinating data collection efforts and thus I look forward to exploring databases that facilitate the comparative analysis of ministerial careers. They will help us understand cabinet change and its connections to accountability and democracy, as well as more specific issues of leader survival as a powerful force of economic and political change and stability.

Altogether, I hope that this book, in spite of its weaknesses, will provide a theoretical basis and an empirical strategy to explore new data on political elites.

References

Adler, J. (1960) 'Water rights and cabinet shuffles: How Claus Spreckels' Hawaiian career began', *Business History Review*, 34: 50–63.
Alderman, R. K. and Cross, J. A. (1987) 'The timing of cabinet reshuffles', *Parliamentary Affairs*, 40: 1–19.
Andrews, D.W.K. and Fair, R. C. (1988) 'Inference in nonlinear econometric models with structural change', *Review of Economic Studies*, 55: 615–639.
Anene, J. N. (1997) 'Military administrative behavior and democratization: Civilian cabinet appointments in military regimes in sub-Saharan Africa', *Journal of Public Policy*, 17: 63–80.
Arendt, H. (1963) *Eichmann in Jerusalem: A Report on the Banality of Evil*, New York: Viking Press.
Baker, C. (2001) *Revolt of the Ministers: The Malawi Cabinet Crisis, 1964–1965*, New York: I.B. Tauris.
Baker III, J. A. (1995) *The Politics of Diplomacy: Revolution, War, and Peace, 1989–1992*, New York: G.P. Putnam.
Bausch, A. W. (2014) 'An experimental test of selectorate theory', *International Interactions*, 40: 533–553.
Beck, N., Katz, J. N. and Tucker, R. (1998) 'Taking time seriously: Time-series cross-section analysis with a binary dependent variable', *American Journal of Political Science*, 42: 1260–1288.
Berlinski, S., Dewan, T. and Dowding, K. (2007) 'The length of ministerial tenure in the United Kingdom, 1945–97', *British Journal of Political Science*, 37: 245–262.
Berlinski, S., Dewan, T. and Dowding, K. (2010) 'The impact of individual and collective performance on ministerial tenure', *Journal of Politics*, 72: 559–571.
Berlinski, S., Dewan, T., and Dowding, K. (2012) *Accounting for Ministers: Scandal and Survival in British Government, 1945-2007*, New York: Cambridge University Press.
Bertelli, A. M. and Grose, C. R. (2007) 'Agreeable administrators? Analyzing the public positions of cabinet secretaries and presidents', *Presidential Studies Quarterly*, 37: 228–247.
Besley, T. and Reynal-Querol, M. (2011) 'Do democracies select more educated leaders?', *American Political Science Review*, 105: 552–566.
Blake, D. J., Box-Steffensmeier, J. M., and Woo, B. (2010) 'Structural interdependence and unobserved heterogeneity in event history analysis', in K. Van Montfort, J.H.L. Oud, and A. Satorra (eds.) *Longitudinal Research with Latent Variables*, Berlin: Springer.
Blondel, J. (1985) *Government Ministers in the Contemporary World*, London: Sage.

Boehmke, F. J., Morey, D. S. and Shannon, M. (2006) 'Selection bias and continuous-time duration models: Consequences and a proposed solution', *American Journal of Political Science*, 50: 192–207.

Borrelli, M. (2002) *The President's Cabinet: Gender, Power, and Representation*, Boulder, CO: Lynne Rienner.

Borrelli, M. (2010) 'The contemporary presidency: Gender desegregation and gender integration in the president's cabinet, 1933–2010', *Presidential Studies Quarterly*, 40: 734–749.

Box-Steffensmeier, J. M. and Jones, B. S. (2004) *Event History Modelling: A Guide for Social Scientists*, New York: Cambridge University Press.

Box-Steffensmeier, J. M. and Zorn, C.J.W. (2001) 'Duration models and proportional hazards in political science', *American Journal of Political Science*, 45: 972–988.

Brambor, T., Clark, W. R. and Golder, M. (2006) 'Understanding interactions models: Improving empirical analyses', *Political Analysis*, 14: 63–82.

Brunk, G. G. and Minehart, T. G. (1984) 'How important is elite turnover to policy change?', *American Journal of Political Science*, 28: 559–569.

Bueno de Mesquita, B. and Lalman, D. (1992) *War and Reason: Domestic and International Imperatives*, New Haven, CT: Yale University Press.

Bueno de Mesquita, B. and Siverson, R. M. (1995) 'War and the survival of political leaders: A comparative study of regime types and political accountability', *American Political Science Review*, 89: 841–855.

Bueno de Mesquita, B., Siverson, R. M., and Woller, G. (1992) 'War and the fate of regimes: A comparative analysis', *American Political Science Review*, 86: 638–646.

Bueno de Mesquita, B. and Smith, A. (2009) 'A political economy of aid', *International Organization*, 63: 309–340.

Bueno de Mesquita, B. and Smith, A. (2010) 'Leader survival, revolutions, and the nature of government finance', *American Journal of Political Science*, 54: 936–950.

Bueno de Mesquita, B., Smith, A., Siverson, R. M., and Morrow, J. D. (2003) *The Logic of Political Survival*, Cambridge, MA: MIT Press.

Bueno de Mesquita, B., Smith, A., Siverson, R. M., and Morrow, J. D. (2004) 'Testing novel implications from the selectorate theory of war', *World Politics*, 56: 363–388.

Bunce, V. (1981) *Do New Leaders Make a Difference? Executive Succession and Public Policy under Capitalism and Socialism*, Princeton, NJ: Princeton University Press.

Byman, D. L. and Pollack, K. M. (2001) 'Let us now praise great men: Bringing the statesman back in', *International Security*, 25: 107–146.

Camerlo, M. (2015) 'Argentina: The ministers of the president, 1983–2013', in K. Dowding and P. Dumont (eds.) *The Selection of Ministers around the World*, London: Routledge.

Camerlo, M. and Perez-Linan, A. (2015) 'Minister turnover, critical events, and the electoral calendar in presidential democracies', *Journal of Politics*, 77: 608–619.

Carey, J. M. (2008) 'Presidential versus parliamentary government', in C. Menard and M. M. Shirley (eds.) *Handbook of New Institutional Economics*, Berlin: Springer.

Carter, D. and Signorino, S. (2010) 'Back to the future: Modeling time dependence in binary data', *Political Analysis*, 18: 271–292.

Chiba, D., Martin, L. W. and Stevenson, R. T. (2015) 'A copula approach to the problem of selection bias in models of government survival', *Political Analysis*, 23: 42–58.

Chiozza, G. and Choi, A. (2003) 'Guess who did what: Political leaders and the management of territorial disputes', *Journal of Conflict Resolution*, 47: 251–278.

Chiozza, G. and Goemans, H. E. (2003) 'Peace through insecurity: Tenure and international conflict', *Journal of Conflict Resolution*, 47: 443–467.
Chiozza, G. and Goemans, H. E. (2004) 'International conflict and the tenure of leaders: Is war still ex post inefficient?', *American Journal of Political Science*, 48: 604–619.
Chow, G. C. (1960) 'Tests of equality between sets of coefficients in two linear regressions', *Econometrica*, 28: 591–605.
Clarke, K. A. and Stone, R. (2008) 'Democracy and the logic of political survival', *American Political Science Review*, 102: 387–392.
Cohen, J. E. (1986) 'On the tenure of appointive political executives: The American cabinet, 1952–1984', *American Journal of Political Science*, 30: 507–516.
Cohen, J. E. (1988) *The Politics of the U.S. Cabinet: Representation in the Executive Branch, 1789–1984*, Pittsburgh, PA: University of Pittsburgh Press.
Croco, S. (2011) 'The decider's dilemma: Leader culpability, domestic politics and war termination', *American Political Science Review*, 105: 457–477.
Debs, A. and Goemans, H. E. (2010) 'Regime type, the fate of leaders, and war', *American Political Science Review*, 104: 430–445.
Dewan, T. and Dowding, K. (2005) 'The corrective effect of ministerial resignations', *American Journal of Political Science*, 49: 46–56.
Dewan, T. and Hortala-Vallve, R. (2011) 'The three A's of government formation: Appointment, allocation, and assignment', *American Journal of Political Science*, 55: 610–627.
Dewan, T. and Myatt, D. P. (2007) 'Scandal, protection and recovery in the cabinet', *American Political Science Review*, 101: 63–77.
Dewan, T. and Myatt, D. P. (2010) 'The declining talent pool of government', *American Political Science Review*, 54: 267–286.
Diermeier, D. and Stevenson, R. T. (1999) 'Cabinet survival and competing risks', *American Journal of Political Science*, 43: 1051–1068.
Dogan, M. (1979) 'How to become a cabinet minister in France: Career pathways, 1870–1978', *Comparative Politics*, 12: 1–25.
Dowding, K. and Dumont, P. (2009) 'Structural and strategic factors affecting the hiring and firing of ministers', in K. Dowding and P. Dumont (eds.) *The Selection of Ministers in Europe: Hiring and Firing*, London: Routledge.
Dowding, K. and Dumont, P. (2015) 'Introduction', in K. Dowding and P. Dumont (eds.) *The Selection of Ministers around the World*, London: Routledge.
Dowding, K. and Kang, W. (1998) 'Ministerial resignations 1945–97', *Public Administration*, 76: 411–429.
Dowding, K. and Lewis, C. (2012) 'Culture, newspaper reporting and changing perceptions of ministerial accountability in Australia', *Australian Journal of Politics and History*, 58: 226–250.
Dowding, K. and Lewis, C. (2015) 'Australia: Ministerial characteristics in the Australian federal government', in K. Dowding and P. Dumont (eds.) *The Selection of Ministers around the World*, London: Routledge.
Dowding, K., Lewis, C. and Packer, A. (2012) 'The pattern of forced exits from the ministry', in K. Dowding and C. Lewis (eds.) *Ministerial Careers and Accountability in the Australian Commonwealth Government*, Canberra: ANU E Press.
Downs, G. W. and Rocke, D. M. (1994) 'Conflict, agency and gambling for resurrection: The principal-agent problem goes to war', *American Journal of Political Science*, 38: 362–380.

References

Dreher, A., Sturm, J. and Vreeland, J. R. (2009) 'Development aid and international politics: Does membership on the UN security council influence World Bank decisions', *Journal of Development Economics*, 88: 1–18.

Escobar-Lemmon, M. and Taylor-Robinson, M. M. (2009) 'Getting to the top: Career paths of women in Latin American cabinets', *Political Research Quarterly*, 62: 685–699.

Fairlie, J. (1913) 'The president's cabinet', *American Political Science Review*, 7: 28–44.

Farrar, M. M. (1980) 'Politics versus patriotism: Alexandre Millerand as French minister of war', *French Historical Studies*, 11: 577–609.

Fearon, J. D. (1995) 'Rationalist explanations for war', *International Organization*, 49: 379–414.

Fenno, R. F. (1958) 'President-cabinet relations: A pattern and a case study', *American Political Science Review*, 52: 388–405.

Fenno, R. F. (1959) *The President's Cabinet: An Analysis in the Period from Wilson to Eisenhower*, Cambridge, MA: Harvard University Press.

Filson, D. and Werner, S. (2002) 'A bargaining model of war and peace: Anticipating the onset, duration, and outcome of war', *American Journal of Political Science*, 46: 819–838.

Filson, D. and Werner, S. (2004) 'Bargaining and fighting: The impact of regime type on war onset, duration, and outcomes', *American Journal of Political Science*, 48: 296–313.

Filson, D. and Werner, S. (2007) 'Sensitivity to costs of fighting versus sensitivity to losing the conflict', *Journal of Conflict Resolution*, 51: 691–714.

Fischer, J., Dowding, K., and Dumont, P. (2012) 'The duration and durability of cabinet ministers', *International Political Science Review*, 33: 505–519.

Fisman, R. and Miguel, E. (2006) 'Cultures of corruption: Evidence from diplomatic parking tickets', *NBER Working Paper 12312*.

Fukumoto, K. (2015) 'What happens depends on when it happens: Copula-based ordered event history analysis of civil war duration and outcome', *Journal of the American Statistical Association*, 110: 83–92.

Gallagher, M. E. and Hanson, J. K. (2015) 'Power tool or dull blade? Selectorate theory for autocracies', *Annual Review of Political Science*, 18: 367–385.

Ganzert, F. W. (1934) 'The boundary controversy in the upper Amazon between Brazil, Bolivia, and Peru, 1903–1909', *Hispanic American Historical Review*, 14: 427–449.

Geddes, B., Wright, J. and Frantz, E. (2014) 'Autocratic breakdown and regime transitions: A new data set', *Perspectives on Politics*, 12: 313–331.

Goemans, H. E. (2000a) 'Fighting for survival: The fate of leaders and the duration of war', *Journal of Conflict Resolution*, 44: 555–579.

Goemans, H. E. (2000b) *War and Punishment*, Princeton, NJ: Princeton University Press.

Goemans, H. E. (2008) 'Which way out? The manner and consequences of losing office', *Journal of Conflict Resolution*, 53: 771–794.

Goemans, H. E. and Fey, M. (2009) 'Risky but rational: War as an institutionally induced gamble', *Journal of Politics*, 71: 35–54.

Goemans, H. E., Gleditsch, K. S. and Chiozza, G. (2009) 'Introducing Archigos: A dataset of political leaders', *Journal of Peace Research*, 46: 269–283.

Gordon, S. C. (2002) 'Stochastic dependence in competing risks', *American Journal of Political Science*, 46: 200–217.

Greene, W. (2003) *Econometric Analysis*, Upper Saddle River, NJ: Prentice Hall.

Halberstam, D. (1972) *The Best and the Brightest*, New York: Random House.

Heppell, T. (2008) *Choosing the Tory Leader: Conservative Party Leadership Elections from Heath to Cameron*, London and New York: Tauris Academic Studies.

Herkless, J. L. (1975) 'Stratford, the cabinet and the outbreak of the Crimean War', *The Historical Journal*, 18: 497–523.

Holbrooke, R. (1998) *To End a War*, New York: Random House.

Huber, J. D. (1998) 'How does cabinet instability affect political performance? Portfolio volatility and health care cost containment in parliamentary democracies', *American Political Science Review*, 92 (3): 577–591.

Huber, J. D. and Martinez Gallardo, C. (2008) 'Replacing cabinet ministers: Patterns of ministerial stability in parliamentary democracies', *American Political Science Review*, 102: 169–180.

Hwang, I. (2003) *Personalized Politics: The Malaysian State under Mahathir*, Singapore: Institute of Southeast Asian Studies.

Indridason, I. H. and Kam, C. (2008) 'Cabinet reshuffles and ministerial drift', *British Journal of Political Science*, 38: 621–656.

Jones, L. E. (1992) 'The greatest stupidity of my life: Alfred Hugenberg and the formation of the Hitler cabinet, January 1933', *Journal of Contemporary History*, 27: 63–87.

Kam, C., Bianco, W. T., Sened, I., and Smyth, R. (2010) 'Ministerial selection and intra-party organization in the contemporary British parliament', *American Political Science Review*, 104: 289–306.

Kam, C. and Indridason, I. H. (2005) 'The timing of cabinet reshuffles in five Westminster parliamentary systems', *Legislative Studies Quarterly*, 30: 327–363.

Kang, W. (2015) 'South Korea: Selection and de-selection of ministers in a presidential system', in K. Dowding and P. Dumont (eds.) *The Selection of Ministers around the World*, London: Routledge.

Kapuscinski, R. (1989) *The Emperor: Downfall of an Autocrat*, 1st international edn. New York: Vintage International.

Kenig, O. and Barnea, S. (2015) 'Israel: The choosing of the chosen', in K. Dowding and P. Dumont (eds.) *The Selection of Ministers around the World*, London: Routledge.

Kennedy, R. (2009) 'An analysis of the empirical support for "selectorate theory"', *International Studies Quarterly*, 53: 695–714.

Kerby, M. (2009) 'Worth the wait: Determinants of ministerial appointments in Canada, 1935–2008', *Canadian Journal of Political Science*, 42: 593–611.

Kerby, M. (2011) 'Combining the hazards of ministerial appointment and ministerial exit in the Canadian federal cabinet', *Canadian Journal of Political Science*, 44: 1–18.

King, G., Alt, J. E., Burns, N. E. and Laver, M. (1990) 'A unified model of cabinet dissolution in parliamentary democracies', *American Journal of Political Science*, 34: 846–871.

Kissinger, H. A. (1994) *Diplomacy*, New York: Simon & Schuster.

Kifordu, H. A. (2015) 'Nigeria: Cabinet dynamics amid structural changes in a post-colonial state', in K. Dowding and P. Dumont (eds.) *The Selection of Ministers around the World*, London: Routledge.

Krasno, J. E. and Sutterlin, J. S. (2003) *The United Nations and Iraq: Defanging the Viper*, Westport, CT: Praeger Publishers.

Krook, M. and O'Brien, D. Z. (2012) 'All the president's men? The appointment of female cabinet ministers worldwide', *Journal of Politics*, 34: 840–855.

Lafeber, W. (1977) 'Kissinger and Acheson: The secretary of state and the Cold War', *Political Science Quarterly*, 92: 189–197.

References

Lafer, C. (2000) 'Brazilian international identity and foreign policy: Past, present, and future', *Daedalus*, 129: 207–238.

Lambert, A. (1990) *The Crimean War: British Grand Strategy Against Russia, 1853–56*, Manchester: Manchester University Press.

Laver, M. and Hunt, B. H. (1992) *Policy and Party Competition*, New York: Routledge.

Laver, M. and Shepsle, K. A. (1994) 'Cabinet ministers and government formation in parliamentary democracies', in M. Laver and K. A. Shepsle (eds.) *Cabinet Ministers and Parliamentary Government*, New York: Cambridge University Press.

Laver, M. and Shepsle, K. A. (1996) *Making and Breaking Governments: Cabinets and Legislatures in Parliamentary Democracies*, New York: Cambridge University Press.

Lemke, D. (2002) *Regions of War and Peace*, New York: Cambridge University Press.

Logevall, F. (2004) 'Lyndon Johnson and Vietnam', *Presidential Studies Quarterly*, 34: 100–112.

Loss, R. (1974) 'Secretary of State Dean Acheson as political executive: Administrator of personnel security', *Public Administration Review*, 34: 352–358.

Lynn, L. E. and Smith, R. I. (1982) 'Can the secretary of defense make a difference?', *International Security*, 7: 45–69.

Maddala, G. S. (1983) *Limited Dependent Variables and Qualitative Variables in Econometrics*, New York, NY: Cambridge University Press.

Mann, D. E. and Smith, Z. A. (1981) 'The selection of U.S. cabinet officers and other political executives', *International Political Science Review*, 2: 211–234.

Mares, D. R. (2001) *Violent Peace: Militarized Interstate Bargaining in Latin America*, New York: Columbia University Press.

Martin, L. W. and Vanberg, G. (2004) 'Policing the bargain: Coalition government and parliamentary scrutiny', *American Journal of Political Science*, 48: 13–27.

Masuyama, M. and Nyblade, B. (2015) 'Japan: Ministerial selection and de-selection', in K. Dowding and P. Dumont (eds.) *The Selection of Ministers around the World*, London: Routledge.

Mattes, M. and Morgan, T. C. (2004) 'When do they stop? Modeling the termination of war', *Conflict Management and Peace Science*, 21: 179–193.

McGillivray, F. and Smith, A. (2000) 'Trust and cooperation through agent-specific punishments', *International Organization*, 54: 809–824.

McGillivray, F. and Smith, A. (2008) *Punishing the Prince: A Theory of Interstate Relations, Political Institutions, and Leader Change*, Princeton, NJ: Princeton University Press.

Miguel, E., Satyanath, S. and Sergenti, E. (2004) 'Economic shocks and civil conflict: An instrumental variable approach', *Journal of Political Economy*, 112: 725–752.

Miller, G. J. (2005) 'The political evolution of principal-agent models', *Annual Review of Political Science*, 8: 203–225.

Mitchell, M. and Buerkle, T. (May 13, 1999) 'Rubin resigns as treasury chief', *International Herald Tribune*.

Modelski, G. (1970) 'The world's foreign ministers: A political elite', *Journal of Conflict Resolution*, 14: 135–175.

Morrow, J. D., Bueno de Mesquita, B., Smith, A. and Siverson, R. M. (2008) 'Retesting selectorate theory: Separating the effects of W from other elements of democracy', *American Political Science Review*, 102: 393–400.

Mufti, M. (2015) 'Pakistan: Ministerial turnover in the federal cabinet', in K. Dowding and P. Dumont (eds.) *The Selection of Ministers around the World*, London: Routledge.

Mutlu-Eren, H. (2015) 'Turkey: Cabinet dynamics and ministerial careers', in K. Dowding and P. Dumont (eds.) *The Selection of Ministers around the World*, London: Routledge.

References

Newey, W. K. (1987) 'Efficient estimation of limited dependent variable models with endogenous explanatory variables', *Journal of Econometrics*, 36 (3): 231–250.

Niou, E.M.S. and Ordeshook, P. K. (1986) 'A theory of the balance of power in international systems', *Journal of Conflict Resolution*, 30: 685–715.

Norwich, J. J. (1997) *A Short History of Byzantium*, New York: Vintage Books.

Patterson, B. H. and Pfiffner, J. P. (2001) 'The White House Office of Presidential Personnel', *Presidential Studies Quarterly*, 31: 415–438.

Petersen, T. (1995) 'Models for interdependent event history data: Specification and estimation', *Sociological Methodology*, 25: 317–375.

Powell, R. (1999) *In the Shadow of Power: States and Strategies in International Politics*, Princeton, NJ: Princeton University Press.

Preston, J. and Dillon, S. (2004) *Opening Mexico: The Making of a Democracy*, New York: Farrar, Straus, and Giroux.

Przeworski, A., Alvarez, M., Cheibub, J. A., and Limongi, F. (2000) *Democracy and Development: Political Institutions and Material Well-Being in the World, 1950–1990*, Cambridge, UK: Cambridge University Press.

Quinn, T. (2012) *Electing and Ejecting Party Leaders in Britain*, Basingstoke, UK: Palgrave Macmillan.

Quiroz Flores, A. (2003) 'Territorial disputes and international crises between asymmetric powers: The dispute over Belize and the first Anglo-Guatemalan crisis of the 1970s', Unpublished M.Phil thesis, University of Oxford.

Quiroz Flores, A. (2009) 'The political survival of foreign ministers', *Foreign Policy Analysis*, 5: 117–133.

Quiroz Flores, A. (2012) 'A competing risks model of war termination an leader change', *International Studies Quarterly*, 56: 809–819.

Quiroz Flores, A. (2015) 'United States of America: The cabinet', in K. Dowding and P. Dumont (eds.) *The Selection of Ministers around the World*, London: Routledge.

Quiroz Flores, A. (2016) 'Protecting people from natural disasters: Political institutions and ocean-originated hazards', *Political Science Research and Methods*, forthcoming.

Quiroz Flores, A. and Smith, A. (2011) 'Leader survival and cabinet change', *Economics and Politics*, 23: 345–366.

Quiroz Flores, A., and Smith, A. (2013) 'Leader survival and natural disasters', *British Journal of Political Science*, 43: 821–843.

Reich, R. B. (1997) *Locked in the Cabinet*, New York: Alfred A. Knopf.

Reiter, D. and Stam, A. C. (2002) *Democracies at War*. Princeton, NJ: Princeton University Press.

Riggs, F. W. (1981) 'Cabinet ministers and coup groups: The case of Thailand', *International Political Science Review*, 2: 159–188.

Roeder, P. G. (1985) 'Do new soviet leaders really make a difference? Rethinking the "succession connection"', *American Political Science Review*, 79: 958–976.

Sarkees, M. R. (2000) 'The correlates of war data on war: An update to 1997', *Conflict Management and Peace Science*, 18: 123–144.

Schleiter, P. and Morgan-Jones, E. (2009) 'Constitutional power and competing risks: Monarchs, presidents, prime ministers, and the termination of east and west European cabinets', *American Political Science Review*, 103: 496–512.

Semenova, E. (2015) 'Russia: Cabinet formation and careers in a super-presidential system', in K. Dowding and P. Dumont (eds.) *The Selection of Ministers around the World*, London: Routledge.

References

Shotts, K. W. and Wiseman, A. E. (2010) 'The politics of regulatory enforcement by independent agents and cabinet appointees', *Journal of Politics*, 72: 209–226.

Siavelis, P. M. and Baruch Galvan, H. (2015) 'Chile: Ministerial selection and de-selection', in K. Dowding and P. Dumont (eds.) *The Selection of Ministers around the World*, London: Routledge.

Sisson, R. (1981) 'Ministerial power and the selection of ministers in India: Three decades of change', *International Political Science Review*, 2: 137–157.

Slantchev, B. L. (2003) 'The principle of convergence in wartime negotiations', *American Political Science Review*, 47: 621–632.

Slantchev, B. L. and Tarar, A. (2011) 'Mutual optimism as a rationalist explanation of war', *American Journal of Political Science*, 55: 135–148.

Smith, A. (2008) 'The perils of unearned income', *Journal of Politics*, 70: 780–793.

Spruyt, H. (1996) *The Sovereign State and Its Competitors: An Analysis of Systems Change*, Princeton, NJ: Princeton University Press.

Spuler, B., Allen, C. G. and Saunders, N. (1977) *Rulers and Governments of the World, Vols. 2–3*, London: Bowker.

Thomas, G. P. (1998) *Prime Minister and Cabinet Today*, Manchester: Manchester University Press.

Tomita, N., Baerwald, H. and Nakamura, A. (1981) 'Prerequisites to ministerial careers in Japan', *International Political Science Review*, 2: 235–256.

Truhart, P. (1989) *International Directory of Foreign Ministers, 1589–1989*, New York: K.G. Saur.

Tsebelis, G. (2002) *Veto Players: How Political Institutions Work*, Princeton, NJ: Princeton University Press.

Urquhart, B. (1998) *Ralph Bunche: An American Odyssey*, New York: W.W. Norton & Co.

Valeriano, B. and Vasquez, J. A. (2010) 'Identifying and classifying complex interstate wars', *International Studies Quarterly*, 54: 561–582.

Van de Ven, W.P.M. and Van Pragg, B.M.S. (1981) 'The demand for deductibles in private health insurance: A probit model with sample selection', *Journal of Econometrics*, 17: 229–252.

Vasquez, J. A. and Valeriano, B. (2010) 'Classification of interstate wars', *Journal of Politics*, 72: 292–309.

Vreeland, J. R. (2007) *The International Monetary Fund: Politics of Conditional Lending*, New York: Routledge.

Wagner, R. H. (2000) 'Bargaining and war', *American Journal of Political Science*, 44: 469–484.

Walt, S. M. (1987) *The Origins of Alliances*, Ithaca, NY: Cornell University Press.

Waltz, K. N. (1959) *Man, the State, and War: A Theoretical Analysis*, New York: Columbia University Press.

Waltz, K. N. (1979) *Theory of International Politics*, New York: McGraw-Hill.

Warwick, P. V. (1994) *Government Survival in Parliamentary Democracies*, Cambridge, UK: Cambridge University Press.

Weller, P. (1994) 'Party rules and the dismissal of prime ministers: Comparative perspectives from Britain, Canada and Australia', *Parliamentary Affairs*, 47 (1): 133–143.

Werner, S. (1998) 'Negotiating the terms of settlement: War aims and bargaining leverage', *Journal of Conflict Resolution*, 42: 321–343.

Wittman, D. (1979) 'How a war ends: A rational model', *Journal of Conflict Resolution*, 23: 743–763.

Index

Abbot, Tony 13, 23
Adams, John Q. 2, 22
Al Ahmad, Sheikh Sabah 3
Albright, Madeleine 99
Arenales, Emilio 87–9
Aso, Taro 2, 22
Australia 13, 14, 23, 32, 130; Data 66; Labor Party 32; Liberal Party 13
Authoritarian *see* Autocracy
Autocracy 11, 20, 38, 41, 42, 54, 74, 78, 95, 101, 102, 107, 125, 134, 139
Aziz, Tariq 44, 90, 92

Bachelet, Michelle 2, 3, 22
Banda, Hastings Kamuzu 14, 53
Belize 69, 87, 88
Bhatti, Shahbaz 1, 3
Bin Mohamad, Mahathir 53
Bivariate Probit 115–18, 136
Blondel, Jean 14, 17, 23, 137; Data 15, 60, 64, 67
Boivin, Jean 2
Boutros, Boutros-Ghali 2
Brazil 83, 88, 89
Brown, Gordon 13, 23
Bunche, Ralph 82
Burma 6, 108, 132
Bush, George H. W. 39
Bush, George W. 15

Cabinet: Change 20, 24, 25, 29, 31, 33–5, 75, 80, 118, 133, 135; Data 64, 65; Gender 67; Importance 20, 25; Pool 25, 29, 31–3, 36, 52, 107, 110, 126, 135, 139, 140; Positions 60, 61; Reshuffle (*see* Cabinet, Change); Restrictions 32, 35; Scandal 24, 25, 34, 39, 40, 66; Selection 31, 33, 34, 38
Cameron, David 21
Canada 2, 5, 6, 14, 34; Data 66
Chile 1, 3, 33, 63
Clegg, Nick 21
Clinton, Hilary 2, 19, 22, 77, 84
Clinton, William 20, 21, 39, 65, 98
Coalition Government 21, 30, 32, 33, 126, 140
Cohen, William 20
Council of Foreign Ministers 83
Coup 1, 13, 41, 75, 78, 98, 132

Delegation 10, 26, 36, 134, 135, 137
Democracy 11, 38, 41, 74, 134; Parliamentary 13, 42, 46–52, 55, 64, 78, 95, 101, 118, 121, 122, 134, 139; Presidential 12, 35, 42, 44–5, 55, 66, 78, 95, 101, 118, 123, 134, 139
Dern, George 39
Diplomacy 15, 16, 77, 78, 81–3, 95, 137; Blunders 91, 92; Negotiations 26, 138

Ethiopia 11, 43
Executive Constraints 125

Fabius, Laurent 84
Foreign Affairs Ministers 15, 73, 77, 79, 81, 85, 93, 99; Data 68, 69, 96, 98, 137
France 31, 32, 69, 70, 84, 85, 88, 89, 91
Fursenko, Andrey 11

Gates, Robert 15, 19, 21
Geithner, Timothy 2, 3
Germany 1, 50, 83, 85

Index

Ghandi, Indira 52
Gillard, Julia 13, 23, 130
Goods: Private 5, 6, 7, 9, 17, 48, 49, 50, 51, 52, 74, 78, 98, 100, 101, 104, 118, 119, 123, 133, 136; Public 6, 8, 9, 12, 37, 38, 39, 55, 60, 74, 78, 100, 114, 118, 119, 130, 133, 134
Gordeev, Alexey 11
Green, Arnold 3
Gromyko, Andrei 3
Guatemala 87

Heterogeneity 31, 110, 128
Holbrooke, Richard 19, 81, 85
Hussein, Saddam 11, 17, 44, 90

Ibrahim, Anwar 14, 53
Instrumental Variable 16, 101, 102, 104, 136
International Monetary Fund 28
Iran 6, 10, 83, 85
Iraq 11, 17, 43, 70
Israel 25, 33, 35

Japan 31, 62, 66, 70, 91
Jefferson, Thomas 2, 22

Kadirgamar, Lakshman 1, 3
Kennedy, John F. 10, 46
Kerry, John 85
Kim, Jung-il 1, 6
Kim, Jung-un 1, 5, 132
Ki-moon, Ban 2
Kissinger, Henry 19

Leader 26, 38, 56, 97, 98, 132; Age 17, 101, 104; Change 7, 8, 22, 41, 80; Competence 39; Data 15, 97, 101; Tenure 96, 114, 135
Letelier, Orlando 1
Lie, Trygve Halvdan 2

McMahon, William 14, 23
McNamara, Robert S. 2, 3, 46
Madero, Francisco 11, 22
Madison, James 2, 22
Malawi 14, 53
Malaysia 14, 53
Mbeki, Thabo 2, 22
Meir, Golda 2, 22

Merkel, Angela 2, 3, 22
Mexico 2, 11, 22, 45, 62, 63, 70, 87, 108
Minister 26, 38, 75; Competence 10, 15, 34, 38, 39, 43, 45, 78, 79, 84, 87–91, 95, 99, 106, 135, 138; Performance *see* Minister, Competence
Moniz, Egas 1, 3
Monroe, James 2, 22
Mugabe, Robert 11, 43
Multiparty Government *see* Coalition Government

New York City 92
Nigeria 43
Nobel Prize 1, 3, 82
North Korea 1, 6, 11, 132

Obama, Barack 2, 6, 15, 19, 21, 65, 84, 85

Pakistan 1, 62, 63, 77, 107; Data 66
Party Elite 22, 40, 41, 42, 43, 44, 49, 52, 56, 95
Peace 4, 16, 77, 81, 83, 86, 93, 94, 123; Democratic 1, 78, 80
Policy Discord 40, 41
Political Survival *see* Selectorate Theory
Principal-Agent Problems 26, 28, 33, 81, 86; Adverse selection 25, 26, 28, 29, 35; Agency Rent 25, 26, 28, 30; Incentive Compatible 27, 30, 31; Moral Hazard 25, 26, 28, 29, 35; Participation Constraint 27, 30, 31

Rathenau, Walter 1, 3
Reich, Robert 39
Rio Branco, Baron 88, 89, 138
Rubin, Robert 1, 3, 46
Rudd, Kevin 13, 23, 130
Russia 11, 62, 66, 71, 85, 89, 90, 91

SEDEPE 67, 137, 140
Selectorate Theory 4, 5, 9, 10, 80, 132; Loyalty 2, 7, 8, 133; Selectorate 5, 7, 9, 41, 133; Winning Coalition 5, 7, 9, 100, 119, 133
Sheil, Glenister 14
South Korea 12, 24, 32
Soviet Union 3, 71, 72
Sri Lanka 1

Summers, Lawrence H. 3
Survival Analysis 102, 103, 115, 135
Syria 9, 17, 90, 91

Thatcher, Margaret 13, 23, 31, 49
Trudeau, Justin 5, 6

United Kingdom 5, 13, 64, 69, 83; Belize 87; Cabinet 64, 65; Conservative Party 21, 22, 49–50, 52; Crimean War 89; Labor Party 23, 52; Liberal Democrats 21; Prime Minister 40, 89
United States 5, 12, 19, 25, 32, 45, 69; Cabinet 20, 25, 63, 66, 67; Department of Defense 21, 63; Department of State 63, 86; Senate 32, 35, 40; Treasury Department 3, 40, 63

Van Buren, Martin 2, 22
Veto Players 126
Voters 7, 12, 13, 20, 30, 39, 40, 41, 42, 46, 47, 50, 56, 80, 81, 134

War 4, 16, 17, 68, 69, 77, 110, 138; Alliances 83; Causes 79, 80; Crimean 89; Data 100; Diversionary 81; Initiation 81; Iraq 44, 86, 90; Mexican-American 93
Wolfowitz, Paul 2

Zarif, Mohammad Javad 85
Zedillo, Ernesto 65
Zimbabwe 11, 43
Zoellick, Robert 2
Zurabov, Mikhail 11